Happy Endings in Hollywood Cinema

Cliché, Convention and the Final Couple

James MacDowell

EDINBURGH
University Press

© James MacDowell, 2013, 2014

First published in hardback by Edinburgh University Press 2013

Edinburgh University Press Ltd
The Tun - Holyrood Road
12(2f) Jackson's Entry
Edinburgh EH8 8PJ
www.euppublishing.com

Typeset in 11/13 Ehrhardt by
Servis Filmsetting Ltd, Stockport, Cheshire,
and printed and bound in Great Britain by
CPI Group (UK) Ltd, Croydon CR0 4YY

A CIP record for this book is available from the British Library

ISBN 978 0 7486 8017 7 (hardback)
ISBN 978 0 7486 9977 3 (paperback)
ISBN 978 0 7486 8018 4 (webready PDF)
ISBN 978 0 7486 8020 7 (epub)

Contents

Acknowledgements

Firstly, I must thank the staff at Edinburgh University Press, particularly Gillian Leslie and Michelle Houston, for their kind help at various stages in writing, editing and publication. I would like to extend my gratitude to the Arts and Humanities Research Council, who funded the research that paved the way for this book. I also wish to thank the organisers of the various conferences at which I have presented nascent aspects of my work: Armelle Parey, Isabelle Roblin and Dominique Sipière ('Happy Endings in Literature and Film', Université de Caen Basse Normandie); Emre Caglayan, Frances Kamm and Pete Sillett ('The End Of . . .?', University of Kent); Ian Hunter and Melanie Williams ('Romcom Actually', De Montfort University, Leicester); and Lucy Fife Donaldson and Reina-Marie Loader ('Journeys Across Media: Authenticity', University of Reading).

The University of Warwick's Film and Television Studies Department provided my intellectual home for eight years, and I have its staff – as well as the greatly stimulating research climate the department fostered – to thank for my development as a student, teacher, and scholar. I must pay special tribute to Ed Gallafent, my doctoral supervisor, with whom I discussed happy endings for around five years; he was integral to the evolution of my thinking on this subject, and thus to this book, and I am deeply indebted to him for a great many reasons. I would also like to thank all the Warwick staff for their expertise, advice and assistance at various points in my education and career, and especially José Arroyo, Jon Burrows, Stella Bruzzi, Catherine Constable, Victor Perkins, Alastair Phillips, and Martin Pumphrey for the parts they played in helping this book to become what it is.

I have been surrounded over the years by many inspiring peers who deserve thanks for their friendship, ceaseless conversation, and intimidating smarts; particularly crucial to the growth of my thinking on subjects relevant to this study have been Paul Cuff, Stuart Henderson, Tom Hughes, Michael

Pigott, Nick Pillai, Tom Steward, Anna C. Sloan, Lauren Jade Thompson, Tim Vermeulen, Rick Wallace, and James Whitfield. Meanwhile, for constant intellectual inspiration and generosity of all kinds over the best part of a decade, especial thanks must go to Pete Falconer, James Zborowski, and Louise Zborowski. Amongst other colleagues, educators and friends, I wish to extend my gratitude to Tom Brown, Richard Dyer, Ian Garwood, John Gibbs, Doug Pye, and Michael Walker. Finally, thank you to my parents, Robert and Sylvia MacDowell, for the many ways in which they have contributed towards my education, in all senses of the word; this book, in the completion of which they have played a vital role, is dedicated to them, with love.

Introduction:
The 'happy ending':
the making of a reputation

Take something as obvious as Hollywood's happy endings . . .
                                         (Maltby 2003: 16)

The Hollywood 'happy ending' is among the most over-utilised and
under-analysed concepts in discussions of popular cinema.[1] Though it
has seldom been addressed in any detail, the term is nonetheless ceaselessly
employed by audiences, filmmakers, critics and scholars, and is one that evokes
a whole host of assumptions about mainstream American filmmaking.[2] This
book is the first to interrogate some of the most significant and tenacious of
those assumptions, and it does so by delving more deeply than is usual into one
especially famous feature associated with the 'happy ending': concluding a film
with the union of a romantic couple.

One way of describing the status of the Hollywood 'happy ending' would
be to say that it is burdened with a considerable reputation.[3] Indeed, as we will
see, for few phenomena of popular filmmaking does the matter of reputation
seem more relevant than for the 'happy ending'. A central aim of this book
is to question that reputation. As such, let us begin by outlining some of its
contours.

UBIQUITY AND HOMOGENEITY

As in the popular imagination so in academic discussion – the most fundamental assumption about the 'happy ending' is that it is a ubiquitous feature
of Hollywood cinema. It has thus become virtually traditional for scholars to
precede mentions of the term 'happy ending' with words like 'standard' (Dolar
1991: 38), 'standardised' (Mulvey 1978: 54), 'predetermined' (Maltby 2003:
16), 'predictable' (Schatz 1991: 152), 'typical' (Booker 2007: 42), 'necessary'

(Mayne 1990: 363), 'inevitable' (Kracauer 1960: 65), 'required' (Sharrett 2007: 60), 'requisite' (Tally 2007: 129), 'statutory' (Brownlow 1987: 122), 'mandatory' (Kapsis 1990: 39), 'expected' (Rowe/Wells 2003: 59), 'customary' (Sterrit 1993: 10), 'usual' (Žižek 2001: 7), 'formulaic' (Umphlett 2006: 38), or – most frequently – 'clichéd' (Orr 1991: 380). The same impulse can provoke claims such as 'few conventions of the Hollywood cinema are as noticeable to its producers, to its audiences, and to its critics as that of the happy ending' (Bordwell 1982: 2), and even that this is the 'most striking and persistent of all classical Hollywood phenomena' (Wood 1989: 52). Indeed, it is not uncommon to imply that virtually *all* Hollywood films have the 'happy ending' in common: Redman refers to 'the happy ending, which is present in almost every Hollywood film' (2003), Strinati to 'the "happy ending" associated with the typical Hollywood film' (2000: 34), Bratu-Hansen to 'the Hollywood convention of the always-happy ending' (1997: 101), and so on.[4]

These are very bold pronouncements. Given their assuredness and prevalence within an academic discipline, we might assume that they have been arrived at based on considerable evidence. Yet it is surprising to realise, in the light of the pervasiveness of these claims, that the 'happy ending' has received barely any in-depth attention, or even a satisfactory definition, from film studies. Perhaps the closest we have to a substantiated claim about the ubiquity of the 'happy ending' is David Bordwell's assertion that, 'of one hundred randomly sampled Hollywood films, over sixty ended with a display of the united romantic couple – the cliché happy ending, often with a "clinch" – and many more could be said to end happily' (1986: 159). This, at least, is certainly the most frequently cited scholarly proclamation on the subject. Neale and Krutnik, for instance, assert that 'as David Bordwell has pointed out, [. . .] the convention of the happy ending was almost universal in Hollywood during its classical period' (1990: 29).[5] There are several problems here. I will return later to the issue of defining a 'united romantic couple' as 'the cliché happy ending'. Regarding the rest of the statement, though: by never revealing the definition by which these many (unnamed) endings 'could be said to end happily', Bordwell exhibits two common impulses governing critical responses to the 'happy ending': (1) an assumption of its obvious intelligibility as something we all immediately recognise and understand, and (2) a use of this assumption to bolster an argument that the device is near-omnipresent in Hollywood cinema. When combined, these twin claims have an unfortunate potential for circular logic: we know what it looks like *because* we see it repeatedly, and we know we are seeing it *because* we know what it looks like.

One reason the 'happy ending' is an important subject is that it is common for scholars to use such unquestioned assumptions about it to mount broader generalisations about Hollywood filmmaking. Rather than attempting to demonstrate the prevalence and homogeneity of something called the 'happy ending', Rick Altman, for instance, moves directly from a citation of Bordwell's proffered statistics towards the proposal that classical Hollywood narrative 'reasons backward', is 'retro-fitted', in order to ensure that all films arrive at 'the same basic ending' (1992: 32). Similarly, in his book *Hollywood Cinema*, Richard Maltby says of the relationship between Hollywood and its audiences that,

> the hidden reason Hollywood movies have happy endings [is that the] re-establishment of order renders the viewer's experimentation with expressive behavior a matter of no consequence, contained within the safe, unexplored, unconsidered and trivialized space of entertainment. (2003: 36)

It is worth noting that both the claim about most Hollywood films sharing the 'same basic ending', and the statement 'Hollywood movies have happy endings', are treated here as agreed matters of common sense. We might imagine how persuasive Altman's and Maltby's arguments would appear if there did not exist an unquestioned assumption between critic and reader that Hollywood films do indeed regularly – even *usually* – offer something called the 'happy ending'. Even when quite possibly exaggerated beyond reason-ableness (here it is not simply that even *most* Hollywood films have virtually interchangeable 'happy endings', but that *all* do), so easily-mobilised are assumptions about the convention's reputation that they can be relied upon as key components in arguments that might otherwise have little chance of convincing.

Given the types of claims we have already encountered, it is perhaps unsurprising to discover that the 'happy ending' has not been viewed kindly by film studies. Indeed, it has regularly been seen as representative of Hollywood's worst tendencies.

IDEOLOGICAL CONSERVATISM

Probably the second most common scholarly assumption about the 'happy ending' is that it is inherently ideologically conservative. Mentions of the convention are often accompanied by suggestions that it constitutes an 'ideo-logical straightjacket' (Wood 1998: 37) designed to 'reaffirm the status quo of American society' (Benshoff/Griffin 2004: 28), and 'maintain the culture of which [Hollywood films] are a part' (Maltby 2003: 16).[6] It is extremely surprising that there should be a paucity of research into a convention that is routinely considered not only an 'extrinsic norm' (Bordwell 1986: 159) but *also* inherently ideologically pernicious. As it stands, however, even the only

English-language monograph on cinematic endings, Richard Neupert's *The End: Narration and Closure in the Cinema*, though it usefully addresses numerous aspects of closure (as will be discussed in Chapter 2), says little more on the matter of the 'happy ending' than that it 'has become a cliché of the classical Hollywood cinema' (1995: 71).[7] A recurrent underlying critical assumption should thus be becoming clear: we need not think too deeply about 'something as obvious as Hollywood's happy endings' (Maltby 2003: 16).

Yet, while film studies has tended to avoid addressing the 'happy ending' in detail, assumptions about it have helped greatly in the construction of many highly influential theoretical paradigms – even if often tacitly. For instance: models of 'classical narrative' stressing 'a process whereby problems are solved so that order may be restored to the world of the fiction' (Cook 1999: 40); theories of Hollywood genres focused on their purported 'methods of problem-solving based on tradition' (Hess 1995: 55); delineations of the 'Oedipal trajectory' – once treated by many as the key to understanding American popular narrative – which emphasise 'the resolution of a crisis and a movement towards social stability' (Hayward 2006: 286). Such models have been vital to the growth of some of film studies' most fundamental attitudes towards Hollywood movies. We might again consider how influential they would have proved if they were not undergirded by implicit assumptions about the homogeneity and prevalence of the 'happy ending'; note, for example, the ease with which Raymond Bellour enlists the term in the service of his argument that the American cinema as a whole 'finds itself enacting [. . .] the most classic paradigms elaborated for the subject of Western culture by Freudian psychoanalysis' – that is: 'the movement from the adventurer, lawless and faithless [. . .], to the husband, the future father and good citizen. In this case we have a film with a "happy ending"' (Bellour 1979: 93).

Lying behind many such theoretical tendencies is the further presupposition that narrative 'closure' is in itself ideologically suspect – a view rehearsed many times in both literary and film scholarship since at least the 1960s. In literature we might point to Eco (1962), Miller (1981), MacArthur (1990), Booth (1993) or Reising (1996) for extended critiques of 'closed' narrative form, while in film studies we could cite Oudart (1971: 5), Wollen (1998: 111/12), Mulvey (1989: 159) or Kuhn (1994: 16) for more localised objections to the narrative device. While less overt today than it once was, the suspicion of closure on ideological grounds has had a significant legacy – one that means that, as Don Fowler balefully puts it, 'given a simple choice of being open or closed, it is difficult for a twentieth [or twenty-first] century person to choose to be closed' (1997: 6). It is against this intellectual backdrop that one of the only extensive studies of cinematic closure, Russell (1995), concerns itself exclusively with championing various New Wave films for 'condemning "closure"' (1995: 3) –

a negative process framed as 'a practice of resistance, with aspirations toward a radical politics' (ibid.: 2). I will address explicitly closure's own unenviable critical reputation in Chapter 4, but for now it is enough to register that this theoretical context further ensured that the Hollywood 'happy ending' should fall into critical disrepute. Perhaps more surprising is that this climate did not prompt more thorough investigation into the convention, or even into film endings more broadly.[8]

Before we can conclude that the vast majority of Hollywood films conclude with the 'happy ending' – and *well* before we can use this assumption as a linchpin for ambitious arguments about Hollywood film as a whole – we need to know whether there is something called the 'happy ending' in the first place. This is one question I shall be addressing in this book.

THE IMPLAUSIBLE 'HAPPY ENDING'

Tellingly, the negative reputation of the Hollywood 'happy ending' has also been fundamental to the only widespread critical tendency ever to have made *positive* claims for the convention.

In 1948 Fritz Lang wrote an article called 'Happily Ever After'. In it, he condemns certain 'happy endings', yet argues that they are acceptable under certain circumstances, including in the case of one of his own films, *Woman in the Window* (1944). Lang here argues, specifically (and usefully), for what he calls 'the *affirmative* ending, in which virtue triumphs through struggle' (ibid.: 29). Meanwhile, by far the most famous dedicated scholarly work on the cinematic 'happy ending', David Bordwell's 'Happily Ever After, Part Two', is a riposte of sorts to Lang. Bordwell suggests that it is ironic that the director cites *Woman in the Window*, since this film's conclusion – by suddenly revealing the majority of the preceding narrative to have been a dream – is an example of what Bordwell calls the 'unmotivated happy ending' (1982: 6). By apparently reneging at the last minute on Hollywood cinema's conventional reliance upon cause-and-effect plotting, generic consistency, and coherent narrative point of view, Bordwell argues 'the unmotivated happy ending is of importance both aesthetically and ideologically' (ibid.: 6), since it 'puts on display the demands of social institutions (censorship, studios) which claim to act as delegates of audience desires' (ibid.: 7). By analysing only conclusions which supposedly 'pose problems for the happy ending' (ibid.: 2), Bordwell implicitly suggests that its 'motivated' instances are, by contrast, self-explanatory. This suggestion – that this convention requires our attention primarily when it is being undermined – is extremely common in film scholarship, and may take a number of forms.

It is sometimes argued that 'happy endings' become acceptable if they fail fully to resolve earlier narrative issues, meaning we should instead focus on 'the amount of dust the story raises along the road, [. . .] which [puts] up a resistance to being neatly settled in the last five minutes' (Mulvey 1978: 54). Equally, it may be claimed that a 'happy ending' includes dissonant elements which succeed in 'undercutting, even spoiling' the convention (Orr 1991: 384), or becoming in some other way unconvincing. This has become a ubiquitous and resilient critical category: the 'happy ending in which the mechanics of cinema are exposed' (Geraghty 2009: 106), the 'pseudo-happy ending' (Affron 1980: 51), the 'happy ending that seems to "wink" at its viewers' (Leonard 2007: 122), and thus 'ironically undermines the codes of the happy ending' (Straumann 2008: 186) – one which appears to be 'virtual self-parody' (Armes 1994: 75), or a 'deus ex machina' (Stern 1979: 95), apparently 'tacked-on' (Smith 1977: 1), 'ironic' (Grant 2007: 79) 'unconvincing' (Camper 1971: 61), 'forced' (Pollock 1977: 109), or 'self-consciously artificial' (Shingler/Mercer 2004: 60). As I will explore later, this critical category of 'false happy endings' (Harvey 2002: 186) that guarantee 'we cannot rest secure' (Modleski 1988: 54), or leave a 'subterranean bitter taste' (Žižek 1991: 9) took root early in the history of film studies, and clearly stems again from the familiar assumption that what might be considered the more *typical* 'happy ending' is both homogeneous and exceedingly prevalent. For convenience's sake, I will be calling this model the implausible 'happy ending'.

Claims about implausible 'happy endings' can serve different critical purposes. Since the 'happy ending' is often seen as a commercial and industrial demand, critics desiring to praise a filmmaker's artistic integrity may invoke the implausible 'happy ending' to recoup what might at first seem to be an uninspiringly traditional conclusion. Robin Wood provides a stark example of this tendency when he says that 'directors like Sirk, Ophüls and von Sternberg used various strategies of style and emphasis to produce irony: finding the happy ending a prison for the artist, they manage to suggest that it is also a prison for the characters' (Wood 1998: 37). The model of the implausible 'happy ending' has since been used to defend 'happy endings' in the movies of many auteurs, from Preston Sturges (Durgnat 1969: 169), through Alfred Hitchcock (Sterrit 1993: 24), to Kathryn Bigelow (Schneider 2003: 87). For other critics, the implausible 'happy ending' has served ideological purposes. As Barbara Klinger has noted, the concept was highly useful for the development of 1970s '*Screen* theory' as a whole (1984: 22), playing a key role in the establishment of the category of 'the formally subversive "progressive" text"' (ibid.: 17) – an ideologically acceptable permutation of Hollywood's 'classic realist text' (MacCabe 1974: 7).[9]

That the most common approach to the 'happy ending' should be to point to instances in which it somehow *fails* is indicative of the fact that critics have preferred to construct the convention as a 'bad object' rather than analyse it in depth. I do not wish to argue that there are not films in relation to which the implausible 'happy ending' might be a useful concept – indeed, we will encounter such films throughout this book. The category is significant, apart from anything, because it allows us to see the extent to which the negative reputation of the 'happy ending' controls the discourses surrounding it. However, we have not yet currently grasped the nature of the 'happy ending' *itself* anywhere near well enough to hold it as an assumed monolith that is only critically accessible when being undermined. This approach is only viable if we know there to be an existing standardised norm that it is desirable to 'subvert' – a claim virtually no one has yet attempted to prove. While an important topic for discussion, then, the implausible 'happy ending' model should not be the only critical game in town.

Despite the continual desire to refer to the concept, film studies has thus for too long been equipped with merely one or two vague, yet tenacious, assumptions to structure its dealings with the convention. Not only are these assumptions persistent but, as the preceding survey suggests, they are also pervasive. In whatever other ways theoretical approaches to Hollywood cinema differ, the 'happy ending' as 'bad object' seems one matter that virtually all can agree upon: from MacCabe's '*Screen* theory' to Robin Wood's close criticism, from Tania Modleski's psychoanalytic feminism to Kevin Brownlow's film historicism, from Bordwell's neo-formalism to Žižek's neo-Lacanianism. It may be that this convention's reputation turns out to be quite justified. My point is, however, that currently we simply cannot say, since that reputation has tended to be built upon assumption rather than demonstrated to be deserved. A major aim of this book is thus to begin a discussion about how merited the reputation of the 'happy ending' might be.

CLICHÉ OR CONVENTION?

Before we can begin interrogating the 'happy ending' and its reputation, it is necessary to do some preliminary thinking about what in fact it *is*. In his aforementioned article, Fritz Lang offers the following definition:

> The traditional happy-ending story is a story of problems solved by an invincible hero, who achieved with miraculous ease all that his heart desired. It is the story of good against evil, with no possible doubt as to the outcome. Boy will get girl, the villain will get his just deserts, dreams will come true as though at the touch of a wand. (ibid.: 26/27)

I think we can see something like this description as charting a basic discursive field regularly surrounding the 'happy ending'. A few points need to be made about this characterisation. Clearly, the account is exaggerated: certainly not all actual 'happy endings' feel as effortless ('with miraculous ease') or inevitable ('no possible doubt as to the outcome') as suggested here. Relatedly, what Lang presents is a hyperbolic compression of the possible endings of many different *kinds* of films into one imagined ending. A conclusion in which 'boy will get girl' will usually occur in a romantic comedy or musical (as well as certainly cropping up, with varying degrees of reliability, in films of other genres), while the references to 'good against evil', and a 'villain [who] will get his just deserts' are far more suggestive of genres such as Westerns, thrillers, science fiction, horror, or adventure movies.

It might be objected that Lang is not in fact attempting an image of an actual 'happy ending', but rather a general impression of what the 'happy ending' *represents*; we might say that we know, in short, what he means. This, however, is exactly the point: that Lang should allow himself to become so hyperbolic on this subject – and that we know roughly what he *means* – suggests how simple, exaggerated, and pervasive the convention is routinely viewed as being. The 'happy ending' he sketches is not 'traditional', it is *prototypical*. Yet the assumption (which the reader is encouraged to share) seems to be that to describe the 'happy ending' using such overstatement and generalisation is merely to choose the appropriate rhetoric for so overstated and generalisable a convention. What is being offered here, then, is in fact the *idea* – or, rather, an abstracted *ideal* – of the 'happy ending', and it is this that makes the account telling.

It seems to me that a prototypical description like Lang's is more representative of what *the* Hollywood 'happy ending' is than the conclusion of any real film could hope to be. That is to say: the 'happy ending' is less an actual, observable type of ending repeated again and again across Hollywood cinema than a discursive imaginary amalgam of the kinds of exaggerated images conjured up here. Rather like the way in which genres are sometimes treated, it is essentially a Platonic ideal, existing in the minds of critics, filmmakers, studios and audiences, and often exerting its influence most forcefully by what it represents *as an ideal*. Just as Hollywood cinema has plainly produced a great many of what we call Westerns, but never *the* prototypical Western, so has it produced a great many of what we call 'happy endings', but never *the* 'happy ending'. Yet this oversimplified conception of the 'happy ending' is unfortunately seldom acknowledged as such, but is rather understood to be referring to an actual, existing 'type' of ending. This is what permits the surprisingly common critical practice of implying that almost all Hollywood films have this ending in common – references to 'the "happy ending" of most Hollywood films' (Hallam/Marshment 2000: 63), or simply 'the Hollywood happy-ending convention' (Buckland 2006: 219). Unlike the critical discourses around genre, which have often been concerned to question just such Platonic understandings of the concept, film studies has demonstrated little interest in disabusing itself of the notion that the prototypical 'happy ending' not only exists, but may be virtually ubiquitous. In other words, viewed in this proto-typical, Platonic form – and tied to the definite article – *the* Hollywood 'happy ending' has come to be treated absolutely as a cliché. How appropriate is this characterisation?

Stemming from the French word for a particular mechanical printing process (Haberer 2005: 1), the term 'cliché' has gone on to mean, for language, 'set word-combinations which are reproduced in a form fixed once and for all' (Permakyov 1979: 12), and for literature, 'a hackneyed [. . .] expression whose origins and freshness of appeal have been lost through overuse' (Myers/Wukasch 1985: 65). This overuse, however, needs to be of a particular kind; as Ruth Amossy and Terese Lyons put it, 'clichés are clichés by virtue of a phenomenon of repetition [. . .]. Moreover, this repetition must be perceived as something purely mechanical, as parroting' (1982: 34–5). It is important to stress the fixed and mechanistic quality of cliché, for without it the word is easily confused with other useful terms. Shira Wolosky, for instance, distinguishes between cliché and topos – a particular recurring subject or conceptual scheme: 'a cliché [. . .] repeats something the same way. A topos repeats in different ways. It is always used distinctively. It is a building block, but one that is put to different uses from text to text' (2001: 69–70). Another helpful term whose relation to cliché might be said to be somewhat similar to that of topos is convention. Whereas cliché serves the function of a standardised code, 'a convention in art is not just an established rule,' but 'an agreement to be secured' (Perez 2000: 21, 23). Furthermore, the nature and development of that agreement – though still predicated on repetition – can in practice be a dynamic process that produces extremely varied results; indeed, as Andrew Britton puts it, 'artistic conventions are at the furthest possible remove from those of mathematics, and they are useful not because of their invariance, but because they conduce to the most complex particularized modifications and inflections' (1993: 214).

As we have seen, film studies has tended to treat the 'happy ending' as if it almost always functioned the same ways, and meant the same things – that is: as a cliché. By contrast, I will be concerned to suggest that the 'happy ending' is better conceptualised, not as an unvarying cliché, but rather as an artistic convention, and that it is thus – unsurprisingly – as conducive to variation as is any other convention. At the same time, however, I will be suggesting that the seeming flaws in the Platonic model of the clichéd, unchanging 'happy ending' do not mean that we shouldn't engage with this model. In fact, I believe it is necessary that we *do*, since that model (however misleading it may be) also exerts an extremely significant influence – over audiences and critics, but also over Hollywood films themselves (see, in particular, Chapter 3).

As common in public as in critical discourse, the characterisation of the Hollywood 'happy ending' as a standardised cliché has undoubtedly been helped by the fact that the history of the American cinema seems to be filled with well-rehearsed production stories about altered endings: *Baby Face* (1933), *Suspicion* (1941), *The Magnificent Ambersons* (1942), *Breakfast at Tiffany's* (1961), *The Vanishing* (1993) – tales of directors, writers or source texts betrayed by additions of 'upbeat' conclusions.[10] Such familiar tales help to present the process of creating cinematic conclusions as a battle between binary alternatives: 'happy' vs. 'unhappy', 'commercial' vs. 'artistic'. In doing so, they have the power to make the kind of hyperbole employed by Lang appear reasonable. It sometimes seems that, given a choice between two entirely demarcated options, Hollywood will always settle upon one rather than the other. It is absolutely true that many endings will have been affected by choices of this kind, and that there will have been screenwriters, directors and producers who conceptualised the issue along precisely such lines. Yet the truth is, of course, that – whatever may go on behind the scenes – what ends up on screen never merely reflects one simple choice. One aim of this book is to draw attention to the many choices that may affect film endings beyond the bald logic of merely 'happy' or 'unhappy'.

MY FOCUS AND APPROACH

Barbara Creed brings together several strands of the scholarly view of our subject when she refers to the 'happy ending' 'in which all loose ends are usually neatly tied up and the values of the status quo confirmed – the couple, family, society and the law' (1995: 155). Rather like Lang's list, and those scholars who imply that virtually every Hollywood film shares the 'happy ending' in common, Creed's words demonstrate that the convention is often taken to refer to something simultaneously very specific and very broad. This is in part facilitated, here and elsewhere, by ensuring that the clichéd Platonic image of the 'happy ending' evoked by the critic collapses distinctions between possible differences between different kinds of films and kinds of endings: how many Hollywood conclusions that we might wish to call 'happy' can be equally concerned to neatly tie up and 'confirm' values associated with the couple *and* the family *and* society *and* the law? A few, no doubt, but very far from all. A main point to note here, however, is that there are a great many features that are regularly linked to the 'happy ending' – all of which deserve careful scholarly attention.

While it would be theoretically possible to try to discuss all the many sub-features so often associated with this convention, to attempt this within the space of one book would risk sacrificing the penetration of depth for the illusion of breadth. As may already be clear, something like this mistake is far from uncommon, finding its most extreme expression in indiscriminate lists of all that this Platonic cliché called *the* 'happy ending' is imagined to contain. At this early stage in the development of critical work on this topic, a more productive approach, I argue, will be to restrict oneself to an aspect of the convention about which one can hope to be somewhat more detailed and specific. While I therefore look forward to future research on, for example, the convention of a hero defeating a villain, or the upholding of the law, this book will concern itself with one particularly famous element of what is commonly assumed to make up the 'happy ending': in Creed's terms 'the couple', in Lang's 'boy will get girl'.

The assumption that the 'happy ending' requires a 'united romantic couple' (Bordwell 1986: 159), can be seen again and again throughout film studies: Benshoff and Griffin define the 'Happy Ending' as a 'type of narrative closure usually found in Hollywood cinema as the protagonist [. . .] "gets the girl"' (2004: 325); Mellencamp economically twins the concepts via a hyphen: 'the couple – the happy ending' (1995: 56); Strinati refers to 'the coming together of the male and female leads in a romantic happy ending.' (2000: 217); Lapsley and Westlake refer to 'the standard happy ending in which the lovers come together all set to live happily ever after' (1992: 43). In large part because it is routinely considered so 'standard' a feature of 'the cliché "happy ending"' (Bordwell 1986: 159),[11] the presence of the romantic couple in a film's final moments will be my predominant focus in this book. For brevity's sake, I will henceforth be calling this convention the 'final couple'.[12]

Narrowing my main focus further, I will for the most part be restricting myself to films whose narratives concern themselves to a significant extent with romantic love. One reason for this is simply that – as will become clear – the scholarship surrounding romance genres (and particularly romantic comedy) has produced noticeably more thoughtful work on the subject of 'happy endings' than most other strands of film studies. It thus seems fitting, apart from anything, that the first extended study of the 'happy ending' should collect together some of this disparate writing and draw upon its most worthwhile findings – something that focusing on depictions of romantic love allows. However, a few more words regarding my corpus and approach are required.

I will be excluding from my account films that clearly grant their romantic storyline an auxiliary function, and whose endings thus render the final couple of only secondary concern. Equally though, so as not to narrow the focus *too* far, in order to be suitable for analysis a film does not necessarily need to be straightforwardly a 'romance' per se – be it a romantic comedy, romantic melodrama, or otherwise. This allows us to consider the function of the final couple beyond narrowly genre-specific parameters (a necessary measure, given the common association of the convention with Hollywood films of all kinds), whilst simultaneously not broadening our focus beyond all manageability. Whether or not a film is applicable for analysis, then, depends on how central matters of romance are to its resolution. The moment virtually any Hollywood movie introduces a potential romantic couple, narrative and ideological expectations surrounding fictional depictions of romance all but guarantee that one question in particular is likely to be raised: will these characters become and remain united by the film's end? However, this question will assume more significance in some cases than in others. For most romantic comedies it will almost certainly be the primary or sole focus. In other movies the development of a romantic relationship will exist alongside other concerns, but still be of significant importance. *The Best Years of Our Lives* (1946), for instance, although concerned with the 'social problem' of returning veterans, relates that issue intimately to its characters' romantic relationships. Equally, *The Graduate* (1967), for example, focuses on youthful alienation and ennui, but also establishes that the romance between Ben (Dustin Hoffman) and Elaine (Katharine Ross) may be importantly linked with that ennui being overcome. On the other hand, a film such as, say, *Shadow of a Doubt* (1943) does contain a potential, and finally united, romantic couple, but treats it as far more peripheral to the narrative and its ending than (in this case) the film's serial killer plotline. The function of the final couple for films as comparatively unconcerned with romance as Hitchcock's is an interesting topic in itself, but not one with which I will concern myself here.

My study will draw on many periods, with the earliest movie discussed in detail having been made in 1923, the latest in 2006. This is not, however, a history of the final couple 'happy ending', nor a survey of permutations it may have gone through over time. I will necessarily be taking into account the historical moments in which particular films were made and, where appropriate, will make reference to the significance of this context. Indeed, part of the reason for not confining myself to a finite period is in order to test the assumption that the final couple 'happy ending' is an unchanging monolith, or in other words that Hollywood narrative has 'since its codification', ended thus: 'the heterosexual couple is united romantically, [. . .] signaling a traditional "happy ending"' (Benshoff/Griffin 2004b: 61).[13] While not attempting a coherent history, it is nonetheless important for my study to remain cognisant of the role historical context can play in a convention's shifting meanings. This is partly why, as my thinking has progressed, I have become increasingly interested in the ways in which more recent films have navigated the concept, since they shoulder the greatest burden regarding the convention's foregoing history (see, in particular, Chapter 3). However, although historical specificity will always affect the development of any convention, when it comes to the final couple it is necessary to add a few qualifications.

The act of concluding a narrative with a final couple has just as material a historical genesis as any other artistic convention, even if its origins may be difficult to define with certainty (while Germaine Greer has suggested that Samuel Richardson's 1740 novel *Clarissa* is 'the real source of the marrying-and-living-happily-ever-after myth' [1971: 213], we can certainly trace the outline of the convention at least back to the Ancient Greek 'New Comedy' [Frye 1969: 1]). This is due to nothing so much as the plainly historical nature of conventions *tout court*. Yet, although not ahistorical, it is certainly true to say that the final couple 'happy ending' is most undeniably *old* – a fact that, for our purposes, is as important to the convention as its formation under specific historical conditions. Consider the film *Shakespeare in Love* (1998), in which one of Shakespeare's (Joseph Fiennes) benefactors demands of him, 'Let us have pirates, clowns and a happy ending' – the joke being that the convention's supposed stranglehold on the entertainment industry stretches back to the sixteenth century. Interestingly, though, looking at Shakespeare's plays themselves in fact confirms quite how old are precisely such assumptions about the convention's antiquity. The final scene of *Love's Labour's Lost* (first published 1598), for example, sees Berowne comment on the unceremonious interruption of the play's various courtship plots by observing that 'our wooing doth not end like an old play; Jack hath not Jill'.[14] Although made four hundred years apart, both these references to the 'happy ending' rely upon the assumption that it is equally '*old*'.

This, it seems to me, is because what is generally being referred to in invocations of the final couple 'happy ending' tends to be less a historically-specific phenomenon than a cross-medium version of the imagined, clichéd Platonic ideal mentioned previously. It is important to distinguish between the convention in this abstract sense and its embodiment in any particular instance – a distinction that will become key to this book. Quite evidently, to end a narrative with a final couple on an Elizabethan stage could only ever hope to mean something very different than to end a 90s Hollywood film in a superficially similar manner. Yet despite this, the references in both *Shakespeare in Love* and *Love's Labour's Lost* can be fairly unproblematically assumed to be referring to broadly the same (idealised) narrative convention. While its particular execution and meaning will always be historically specific, then, it seems likely that virtually any popular Western fiction engaging extensively with romance – especially if we are focused on the last one hundred years or so, as in the case of film – also necessarily finds itself in dialogue with a largely unchanged paradigm of the final couple as a narrative event. This book will be dedicated in part to exploring tensions arising from this relationship between the ideal and its navigation in actual, realised cases.

One immediately obvious potential problem for this study is the quite possibly subjective nature of the term 'happy ending'. The issue of opinion is never far from the surface of virtually any critical discussion, but the matter becomes even more relevant when speaking of a term made up of two words, one of which is an adjectival description of an emotion. We must of course face the fact that, for instance, although *I* may be made 'happy' by an ending, someone else may easily not be. Could this mean, then, that the task of addressing the 'happy ending' would in fact be best served by, say, research into audiences? I am keen not to engage in detail, at this early stage, with the hugely complex matter of whether meaning is better conceptualised as being dictated by text, context, viewer, etc. – something which must wait until Chapter 4 to be addressed somewhat more explicitly. Research into groups of viewers' responses to, or definitions of, 'happy endings' would undoubtedly produce interesting findings, but it will have to be carried out in a different book than this one. I do not at all wish to imply a hostility towards reception studies, ethnographic research, and so on; on the contrary, I will be drawing on useful findings of such work later on. However, I also agree with Judith Mayne that analysing spectatorship involves, at least in part, 'an analysis of one's *own* fascination and passion' (2002: 84). Furthermore, I am equally of the opinion that, as Carl Plantinga argues, a 'film's *intended* affective focus can be reasonably well determined in many cases' (2009: 11; emphasis added).

Given these twinned assumptions, throughout the book I will be making use of a similar process to that described by V. F. Perkins in 'Must We Say What They Mean: Film Criticism and Interpretation', wherein he explains his reason for analysing a particularly striking moment of the film *Caught* (1945): 'the starting point for an inspection of the *Caught* fragment was a desire to figure out what it was in the moment that made me smile' (Perkins 1990: 6). As Perkins goes on to say: 'the evidence of feeling demands an acknowledged place in the process of interpretation' (ibid.: 6). Yet this kind of evidence must also, as Perkins acknowledges, serve only as a 'starting point', a guide to judgment, which becomes valuable if practised in the context of the corresponding recommendation that 'film criticism becomes rational, if not "objective", when it displays and inspects the nature of its evidence and the bases of its arguments' (Perkins 1993: 7). It is primarily with these two complementary forms of 'evidence' that I shall be engaging in this book.

Tackling issues raised by 'the happy ending' from a variety of perspectives, and divided into four chapters, my discussion is focused around four key aspects of our subject's critical reputation: homogeneity, closure, 'unrealism', and ideology. Since this book is the first in-depth study of the cinematic 'happy ending', I believe it necessary for it to offer such a wide-ranging interrogation of these exceedingly widespread assumptions regarding the convention. The hope is that approaching the subject from multiple angles will both permit a better view of what the 'happy ending' can be and mean, as well as provide some alternative theoretical groundwork that may serve either to supplement, qualify or revise existing scholarly commonplaces.

Chapter 1 necessarily confronts the most basic assumption, touched on above: that there exists in Hollywood cinema something homogeneous that we can justifiably call *the* 'happy ending'. My discussion here tries to construct a definition for the 'happy ending' – and finds the task a challenging one. To avoid possible accusations of unfairly comparing chalk with cheese, this chapter confines itself to one demarcated period and one sub-genre: the romantic melodrama between 1939 and 1950. A central aim of this discussion is to allow me subsequently to begin analysing individual 'happy endings' relatively free from suspicions about the convention's innate uniformity; yet, almost as important as the many variations uncovered in this chapter are the traits that many 'happy endings' *do* seem to share, which will help guide our investigations in following chapters.

In Chapter 2 I interrogate the assumption that the 'happy ending' and the final couple necessarily create definitive narrative closure. Partly via a detailed discussion of *Sleepless in Seattle* (1993), I explore the process and implications of *ending* a film with a romantic *beginning*, arguing that while this film succeeds in making such an ending feel emphatically 'closed', other films (I look in detail at *The Best Years of Our Lives* and *The Graduate*) use different strategies to render the same convention comparatively 'open'.

Chapter 3 examines the familiar assertion that the 'happy ending' is in some sense 'unrealistic'. Firstly, I consider the traditionally close conceptual relationship between the final couple 'happy ending' and fictional narratives *tout court*, suggesting that this association has frequently motivated films (such as *Pretty Woman* [1990]) to cast doubt upon the plausibility of their own 'happy endings'. Secondly, in part through a discussion of *Eternal Sunshine of the Spotless Mind* (2004), I probe the relationship of the disordered, 'open' nature of life to the necessarily finite and 'closed' nature of narrative – particularly as this matter relates to the convention of the final couple.

Chapter 4 approaches the issue of ideology and the final couple from three main angles. Firstly addressing the broad question of popular film's potential for ideological influence, I discuss (with particular reference to *Before Sunrise* [1995]) the possibility that the cultural concept of the final couple might help structure viewers' attitudes towards real-life romantic relationships. Secondly, I take up the question of the ideological implications of closure, particularly as they relate to the model of the implausible 'happy ending', made especially famous by critical work on the films of Douglas Sirk. The chapter concludes by addressing conclusions taken from different periods within romantic comedy, a genre that is often taken to be innately 'conservative' precisely because of its 'happy endings'.

The films I will be analysing in detail have not usually been selected because I consider them typical, nor, for the most part, because they are somehow exceptional. Rather, they have been chosen because they dramatise certain key features associated with the 'happy ending' in a particularly potent fashion, and in ways which allow us either to deepen or challenge traditional critical understandings of the convention. As such, rather than attempt an overview of what percentage of Hollywood endings seem to do certain things and what percentage do not, this book aims primarily to open up new theoretical terrain by testing the flexibility of the convention against the relative inflexibility of its reputation. I might say I wish to broaden our conception of what 'happy endings' clearly have the *potential* to do, and to explore some of the implications of that potential. While I do not in the least intend to imply that 'happy endings' *never* function in the ways they have so frequently been assumed to function, I am nevertheless keen to convince the reader that, at the very least, there is little in the convention that ensures they must *always* do so. Demonstrating this is the necessary first step towards a much-needed reconsideration of this most famous and maligned of conventions.

NOTES

1. The term 'happy ending' seems to have been present in discussions of American cinema since some of its earliest years; see, for instance, Woods' (1910) citation of the concept in the course of making the point that critics should be concerned with 'not what the public most unmistakably wants but what it ought to want' (ibid.: 16); taking a contrasting view, an early screenwriting guide counsels, 'Happy Endings Preferred' (Sargent 1911: 613); see Bratu-Hansen (1991: 67).

2. I engage with scholarly assumptions about the 'happy ending' throughout this introduction and elsewhere. As for statements about the convention made by reviewers and filmmakers, we are spoilt for choice, since throughout Hollywood's history it has been, and remains, extremely common to decry the Hollywood 'happy ending' on a variety of grounds. *New York Times* critic Mordaunt Hall, for instance, claimed in 1931 that 'no muddle is beyond the motion picture producer when he desires to give the audiences a happy ending' (1931: 1); reviewer Parker Tyler described the 'happy ending' as 'purely conventional, formal, and often, like the charade, of an infantile logic' (1970: 177); Fritz Lang lamented that 'it has always been stated authoritatively by "authorities" that the motion-picture audience's preference is for "happy endings"' (1948: 23); the director Neil Labute more recently expressed his distaste for 'the pat Hollywood happy ending [. . .] that big lie that they tell us over and over and that has no correlation in reality' (O'Hagan 2001: 1), and so on. It will become clear throughout this book that there is considerable overlap between scholarly understandings of the convention and those employed outside the academy.

3. Of course, the reputation of the 'happy ending' is by no means confined to the cinema, and the convention's existing critical status in other art forms doubtless laid the groundwork for the standing it would come to enjoy in film. In relation to drama, as early as 1818 Charles Lamb was using the term to criticise Nahum Tate's notorious revision of *King Lear* (1818: 26), long before Bertolt Brecht and Kurt Weil notably mocked the convention in *Happy End* (1929). In fiction, we find Anthony Trollope in 1879 writing that the admiring reader of Hawthorne's *The Scarlet Letter* momentarily 'fears that he is again about to enjoy the satisfaction of a happy ending' (1879: 212); meanwhile, in 1912 George Bernard Shaw famously lamented that 'romance keeps its stock of "happy endings" to misfit all stories' (1958: 140).

4. I think we may at least admit that, given kinds of endings regularly found in *film noirs*, melodramas, and 'social problem films' alone, the hypothesis that *all* classical Hollywood films share the 'happy ending' cannot be reasonably entertained – no matter *what* definition one uses.

5. Other unhesitating citations of Bordwell's claim include Wexman (1993: 19), Cooper (2003: 226), Maltby (2003: 16), and Altman (1992: 32).

6. See also: Oudart (1971: 5), Aumont (1980: 53), Bordwell (1982: 6), Elsaesser (1987: 46), Creed (1995: 155), etc.

7. Neupert's approach to the Hollywood 'happy ending' seldom moves beyond the widespread assumptions that this book is dedicated to interrogating: that the convention is homogeneous ('overly codified' [ibid.: 35]), prevalent ('a cliché' [ibid.: 71]), and innately ideologically problematic ('satisfies individual and social desires for moral authority' [ibid.: 35]), yet potentially subversive if appearing 'unmotivated' ('unmotivated happy ends [. . .] do not just make the real world more palatable by unwarranted cathartic endings, rather they foreground the artifice of narrative films' [ibid.: 72–3]).

8. There are a few exceptions, including the aforementioned Neupert (1995) – to be addressed in Chapter 2 – though his book seldom engages the 'happy ending' itself (see previous note). Brylla (2004) largely concerns itself with confirming Neupert's approach (though expands it through reference to socio-historical and reception contexts), and likewise does not address the 'happy ending'. Russell's *Narrative Mortality* (1995) establishes a self-professedly 'idiosyncratic' (ibid.: vii) approach to closure within various European 'art' cinemas, and as such does not address the concept of the 'happy ending' in any detail. In Italian there exists Veronesi (2005), though this study too operates generally according to very familiar assumptions about the 'happy ending'. The recent edited collection *Happy Endings and Films* (2010), meanwhile, focuses exclusively on the 'happy ending', yet a number of its chapters still adopt the usual critical attitudes towards the convention's homogeneity and need for subversion

(e.g. Tuhkunen [2010: 125], Ludot-Vlazak [2010: 70], Wells-Lassagne [2010: 92]). Nevertheless, the collection does contain innovative work, some of which I shall be touching on later (see Azcona [2010], Deleyto [2010], Ruiz Pardos [2010], Chauvin [2010], and Sipière [2010], plus my chapter, Does the Hollywood Happy Ending Exist?). Other individual articles on cinematic endings will be acknowledged in the course of the book, including Colwell (1981), Preis (1990), and Meyer (2008).

9. In its generalising and prescriptive nature, the conception of the 'happy ending' as an unchanging trope that requires subversion is indeed a perfect fit for the now near-universally abandoned category of the 'classic realist text' (see Wilson [1986: 192–200] for one convincing repudiation of the model in relation to film, Lodge [1990: 45–57] in relation to literature, and Britton [2009: 314–34] in relation to both). Yet, while film studies may have largely left the illusions of that model firmly behind, those surrounding the 'happy ending' continue unabated (see Chapter 4).

10. For academic references to these changes, see: Jacobs (1991: 80) for *Baby Face*, Bordwell (1982: 6) for *Suspicion*, Perkins (1999: 72) for *The Magnificent Ambersons*, Gibson (2006: 1) for *Breakfast at Tiffany's*, and Leitch (2002: 57) for *The Vanishing*.

11. See also: Altman (1981: 197), Cowie (1984: 79), Orr (1991: 380), Polan (1991: 137), Wood (1998: 80), etc.

12. Acknowledgment must be given here to Carol Clover, who coined the term 'Final Girl' to refer to the heroine of the slasher film: a female character who survives the killer's rampage, often dispatching him. While stemming from very different generic traditions, there are ways in which the conventions of the Final Girl and the final couple are suggestively related. (1) Referring to endings in its wording, the Final Girl also implies, in its own way, a type of 'happy ending': the killer's threat eliminated or temporarily overcome, an indomitable character may go on living her life. (2) Just as we will usually be able to predict with certainty the putative outcome of a slasher film by quickly recognising who will likely become its Final Girl (1992: 39), so in most cases will we know in advance which characters will make up a final couple. This fact can have a similar significance for the hermeneutic drive of narratives in each genre; I will explore this in relation to closure in romantic comedy in Chapter 2.

13. For similar pronouncements about the convention's uniformity across history, see also Burch (1990: 196), Gianos (1998: 4); Dowd/Pallotta (2000: 568), etc.

14. A reference to what Shakespeare describes in *A Midsummer Nights Dream* as an 'old proverb': 'Jack shall have Jill / Naught shall go ill' (Act III, Scene II) – another suggestion of the longevity of cultural depictions of the final couple in public discourse.

CHAPTER I

The 'happy ending' and homogeneity

In an ideal world the central argument advanced by this chapter would not require making. Yet, such is the weight of reputation that it seems the necessary place to begin. This chapter is, first and foremost, concerned to question the existence of *the* 'happy ending', that is: a homogeneous, clichéd ending, which recurs consistently across the majority of Hollywood movies. This is a separate issue from the existence of 'happy ending*s*' – a broad category of conclusions that (according to criteria yet to be defined) 'could be said to end happily' (Bordwell 1986: 159) rather than 'unhappily'. Thus, while this chapter interrogates the usefulness of the category *the* 'happy ending', it will also suggest some productive means by which we might identify *a* 'happy ending'. The distinction between the two might seem pedantic, but for an academic discipline it should not be insignificant. Conjuring up images of a ruthlessly repetitive, production-line approach to filmmaking, to use the term '*the* happy ending' is to lend immediate credence to the kinds of critical generalisations we encountered in the introduction. This rhetorical strategy is exceedingly common in film studies, and is even repeatedly employed in Neupert's *The End: Narration and Closure in the Cinema* (1995: 40, 71, 72). If the term the 'happy ending' and the concept to which it refers have critical validity, then the 'happy ending' should be able to be defined – and, we might imagine, rather easily so. This is a task attempted by this chapter.

One outcome of the lack of detailed attention paid to the subject of the 'happy ending', however, is that few satisfactory definitions of the term have ever in fact been advanced. How, then, even to identify likely candidates for the 'happy ending'? Clearly, this is a driving question of what follows, and as such cannot be adequately answered at this early stage. We are thus immediately presented with a problem: if we do not know what the 'happy ending' might be, how are we to know which endings are even applicable for analysis?

Given this, it is worth briefly entertaining the possibility of constructing a provisional definition.

IN ADVANCE OF A DEFINITION

Carl Plantinga suggests that in Hollywood films 'the convention of the happy ending makes it probable that empathy will bring the rewards of a favourable outcome for the protagonists; thus our emotional investment will likely yield psychologically pleasing results' (1994: 12). I have no quarrel with the basic precepts of Plantinga's observation. Neither this chapter nor this book will challenge the proposal that very many Hollywood films provide broadly likable characters with broadly beneficial outcomes, nor that this provides a broadly pleasurable experience for viewers. Even if these claims themselves have not been subjected to especially rigorous analysis, if this is all that the 'happy ending' means, so be it. However, to have said this much is to have said very little indeed. Thus, while the broad notions of a 'favourable outcome' and 'pleasing results' will serve as guiding principles throughout this chapter, it is necessary to think in advance about their validity as definitional terms.

Let us look at Plantinga's formulation in a little detail. Regarding protagonists receiving a 'favourable outcome', we might relate this to Bordwell's uncontroversial characterisation of Hollywood narrative as being focused on 'characters acting to achieve announced goals' (Bordwell et al. 1985: 17). Could it be that the Hollywood 'happy ending' simply occurs when sympathetic protagonists of films made by major movie studios successfully achieve goals? If so, then the term describes equally well the conclusions of both, say, *His Girl Friday* (1940), in which an estranged husband achieves his goal of winning back his ex-wife, and *V For Vendetta* (2005), in which a masked freedom-fighter, though dead, achieves his goal of inciting a mass uprising against a totalitarian state. The ludicrous unhelpfulness of this proposal is due to the simple fact that, as Britton writes of Bordwell's approach to Hollywood narrative, 'both the goals and the success are placed in a complex total context which defines them as something more than actions that have been completed' (2009: 435). It is to such contexts that we must turn if we wish usefully to distinguish one ending that 'could be said to end happily' (Bordwell 1986: 159) from another.

We could bring similar provisional objections to bear on the possibility of defining the 'happy ending', from the perspective of reception, as a 'psychologically pleasing' conclusion. The aim of every magic trick might be said to be to amaze its audience, but it does not follow from this that scholars of the form should consider all magic tricks to be in any helpful sense equivalent. Equally, it has been claimed that one result of, say, modernist literary practice is that the reader becomes 'forced to interrogate his [*sic*] own codes, his own methods of interpretation, in the course of reading' (Wollen 1998: 111); yet few would suggest that this potential for a conventionalised response means that all modernist works are anything approaching interchangeable. In both cases, whatever broad similarities the effects may share, neither the phenomena's internal characteristics nor those effects will be enough alike across the board for us to refer to *the* magic trick or *the* modernist novel in ways comparable to what uses of the term *the* 'happy ending' are commonly intended to convey. This, clearly, is because the specific qualities of and reasons for the responses require us to differentiate judiciously between one amazing magic trick or reflexively challenging modernist novel and another. I propose that we might apply a similar logic to 'happy endings'.

Thus, while Plantinga's observation is reasonable in essence, where it may fall down is in its casual recourse to the concept of *the* 'happy ending' to help explain the processes it describes. This recourse tends to come troublingly naturally. It is very common to find scholarly references to '*the* happy ending' (e.g. Kracauer [1960: 268], Braudy [1976: 121], Thompson [1988: 114], Wood [1998: 37], Cooper [2003: 72], etc.), and I would suggest that this is almost certainly due in part to the continuing influence of often unacknowledged assumptions about what Hollywood cinema in general represents. My passing reference above to modernist literature was not wholly arbitrary. While discussions of modernist art are typically characterised by a focus on plurality, multiplicity, ambiguity, etc., the tendency to conceive of the 'happy ending' as fundamentally uniform is entirely in keeping with familiar presumptions about the fundamentally standardised nature of Hollywood filmmaking, and indeed popular culture, in general. This view perhaps received its most extreme embodiment in Adorno and Horkheimer's famous suggestion that 'under monopoly all mass culture is identical' (1972: 121). This is an example of the kind of generalisation that film studies has by and large moved away from in its discussions of Hollywood cinema. The 'happy ending', however, seems to be one subject towards which it is still usually acceptable to be almost as roundly dismissive as Adorno and Horkheimer were of popular culture as a whole.

Of course, generalising can be a useful tool – it is what permits the potentially invaluable (and, in any case, unavoidable) process of categorisation. It is in fact sensible to identify family resemblances across magic tricks and modernist novels, and we must similarly be allowed to generalise about Hollywood cinema and its 'happy endings' to a degree (something this chapter attempts). Yet to do so productively we must also do so precisely. It is extremely surprising that film studies should not yet have attempted this in the case of a feature so frequently treated as so fundamental to Hollywood cinema. To invoke again the concept which the phrase 'family resemblances' most immediately evokes for film scholars, genre: it has long been accepted that a genre provides 'a context narrow enough for recognition of the genre to take place but wide enough to allow enormous individual variation' (Pye 1975: 32), and much genre scholarship has of course been dedicated to distinguishing between different members of genres for a host of reasons. One plea of this book and this chapter is therefore rather modest: that we logically begin to question the homogeneity of the 'happy ending' in the same way as we have for so many other Hollywood phenomena.

Continuing with the question of definition, it may also be useful at this early stage to try to construct a picture of what the 'happy ending' definitely *is not* – i.e. an '*un*happy ending' – in order to help enable a relational process of possible inclusion by exclusion. We might consider tracing notions of 'happy' and 'unhappy' endings back to the commonplace notion that, as Byron puts it, 'All tragedies are finish'd by a death / All comedies are ended by a marriage' (Byron 1831: 543). I would indeed provisionally suggest that it is uncommon for a film climaxing in a protagonist's death to sit easily under the term 'happy' (though in this chapter *Portrait of Jennie* [1948] offers a potential limit case). Perhaps we can agree, then (pending investigation by someone other than myself into what constitutes an '*un*happy ending'), that the conclusion of a film such as, say, *Vertigo* (1958) is fairly unequivocally 'unhappy'. Here Scottie's (James Stewart) obsessive love for Madeleine/Judy (Kim Novak) ultimately brings tragedy in the form of Judy's fall to her death. The possibility of a relationship definitively ended, one half of the couple dead and the other able only to look on after her motionless body from above, standing 'empty, desolate' (Wood 1989: 95), with no tangible possibilities for the future – this ending is surely one of the furthest from any reasonable definition of 'happy' imaginable. I will elaborate later on why exactly we might feel justified in saying this by drawing contrasts with what I will call comparatively 'happy' endings; but let us for now take this point as uncontroversial. Given its currently undefined nature, we must necessarily leave the meaning of the term 'happy ending' provisionally open. Yet, if we can agree that the term cannot be reasonably made to apply to an ending such as *Vertigo*'s, this at least partially narrows our field of enquiry.

Another fruitful way to direct the enquiry will be to define a relatively specific corpus of films for analysis. Because of the paucity of in-depth work on the 'happy ending', it has seldom been openly conceded that the kind of ending to which this term refers might regularly possess different properties depending on virtually any factors at all – say, genre, or even period. Shaking its homogeneous reputation *could*, then, merely consist of drawing attention to how different 'happy endings' can be in films of very different genres and historical contexts. One could demonstrate, for instance, what little sense it would make to view as interchangeable the endings of *The Lady Eve* (1941) and *Star Wars* (1977), *Mr. Smith Goes to Washington* (1939) and *The Karate*

Kid (1984), *Modern Times* (1936) and *Lethal Weapon* (1987). However, while demonstrating this fact in detail might itself serve to undermine the totalising tendencies which routinely characterise critical references to the 'happy ending', I also consider the undertaking unnecessary.

So, let us narrow our focus in the name of precision. Whereas the rest of this book will cast its net of enquiry somewhat more broadly, this chapter will discuss one loosely-defined type of romance film – what we might call the romantic melodrama – during one delimited time period, 1939–1950. This decision has been taken partly because examining films which share more family resemblances than do *Modern Times* and *The Karate Kid* allows us to make distinctions based on nuance as well as wholesale divergence. Tightening our field of reference also has the added benefit of rendering a broader net virtually superfluous. Even within the comparatively delineated field analysed here we will find quite enough variation to make it clear that, were we to expand our view to films of *all* periods and *all* genres, the problems of confidently defining the 'happy ending' would only increase. (In order to remind us of this, I will occasionally make brief reference to 'happy endings' that lie beyond our present corpus.) Still, having decided to impose limits, my particular choice of field requires some explanation.

ROMANTIC MELODRAMA, 1939–50

To focus initially on studio-era films seems a necessary measure, given the common assumption that 'the convention of the happy ending was almost universal in Hollywood during its classical period' (Neale/Krutnik 1990: 29). Further, to examine films of this particular period allows us to explore some of the influence of the Motion Picture Production Code, which was still at or near its height between 1939 and 1950 (prior to the 1951 revisions), and which is important to any account of the nature and determinants of classical Hollywood narrative. To span the years in which WWII began to become a recurrent subject for American cinema also permits insights into some of the historically-specific dimensions of the flexibility of 'happy endings'. Finally, to concentrate on films whose narratives are to a significant extent concerned with romance is a choice made by the book as a whole, for aforementioned reasons. Yet I have not decided to focus at this early stage on the kind of romance film that might be most immediately associated with the 'happy ending' – romantic comedy. This is due to the kinds of narrative conclusions one can usually expect from comedy and melodrama.

In romantic comedy the presence of a major component of what is regularly meant by 'happy ending' – i.e. a final couple – is almost guaranteed by the fact that the narrative tends to end with either the culmination of a courtship or a romantic reunion. In later chapters we will explore variations within even this most apparently formulaic of endings. However, the most essential properties of this aspect of the 'happy ending' are nonetheless clear: a couple begin or resume a romantic relationship in, or close to, a film's final moments. To use the romantic comedy as an initial testing ground for an attempt to define the 'happy ending' would thus narrow our field of enquiry prematurely and *too* far. As implied by Lang's list in the introduction (and indeed by the cross-historical, cross-generic titles invoked above), there are of course many ways to create endings that could be said to end 'happily'. Without departing from our central concern with romantic couples, concentrating for now on the romantic melodrama thus allows our investigation to begin with a more inclusive view of our subject than would romantic comedy. This is because the romantic melodrama has far more potential to eschew the final couple – perhaps by depicting marriage, by making the romance adulterous, or by focusing on other problems facing a burgeoning couple. Potentially (though not *necessarily*) severed from an aspect so routinely associated with the 'happy ending', such films thus challenge us to ask: what elements *are*, then, needed in order for us to feel comfortable calling an ending 'happy'? In this chapter we will encounter conclusions in which couples are created, cemented, temporarily separated, and even parted forever, and each permutation finds possible ways to leave its characters, or us, or both, 'happy'. If we wish to keep open the possibility that all these varied conclusions could be 'happy endings', as I argue we should, then this must be for reasons other than simply because they contain a final couple. Attempting to identify these reasons can therefore help cast light on factors which we might risk obscuring if focused purely on the final couple, whose common association with the 'happy ending' is already clear, even if not – as later chapters will show – exactly simple.

The moment one begins to speak of melodrama, however, one is on uncertain terrain. Unlike in the case of the 'happy ending', there has been a great deal of debate about the definition of this term – some critics, for instance, having treated it as a discrete genre, others as a mode, and still others as an industrial category (Klinger [1994] offers a useful overview of these debates). My own understanding of the term here is informed by critics such as Williams (1998) and Thomas (2000), the latter of whom takes as her starting point the fact that 'throughout the critical writing on comedy, melodrama and romance there is considerable slippage between the views of them as genres and as categories of a broader type', going on to argue that a Hollywood film usually employs either a melodramatic or a comedic mode – with accompanying kinds of fictional worlds and predominant moods – and that it may offer a romantic permutation of either (ibid.: 10). While conceptualising romantic comedy or melodrama as genres can also be valuable (indeed, I will be invoking these categories where profitable), one of the strengths of a modal approach is its relative flexibility, as well as its ability to acknowledge that, as Thomas says, 'it is not always easy to determine whether romantic films are essentially melodramatic or comedic, since to some extent many of them have aspects of both' (ibid.: 99). The films addressed in this chapter testify to this fluidity, their worlds at times seeming melodramatically 'repressive and full of danger', and at others appearing more comedically 'benevolent and safe' (ibid.: 9). Thomas' instructively loose understanding of the term thus allows us, firstly, to define a usable field for ourselves without becoming unnecessarily sidetracked by potentially endless generic debates. It also offers a particularly inclusive framework by which to understand the tensions between repetition and variation which lie at the heart of both Hollywood storytelling in general, and – I argue – the 'happy ending' in particular. As we will see, one way in which one 'happy ending' can differentiate itself from another is by emphasising either comedic or melodramatic impulses.

In another narrowing of focus, I will be concerning myself here with what I am calling *romantic* melodrama. Kathleen Rowe has written that there exist two Hollywood genres which are most commonly 'oriented toward the private': 'romantic comedy, which emphasizes love, or melodrama, which emphasizes loneliness and/or motherhood' (1995: 99). There also exist, however, many movies which are both melodramatic in a modal sense *and* more concerned with love than with isolation or female parenthood. For my purposes, romantic melodramas will be defined simply as predominantly non-comedic films whose central subjects are romantic relationships (rather than family, motherhood, homecoming, etc.) – what a 1942 *Public Opinion Quarterly* survey of Hollywood's output referred to as 'pictures with a purely romantic theme' (Jones 1942: 416), and what Mary Ann Doan calls 'the ordinary love story' (1987: 96). Such films are infrequently invoked in the critical work on melodrama-as-genre. Often adhering to a definition of melodrama as 'a range of films [. . .] which use the family and the social position of women as their narrative focus' (Shingler/Mercer 2004: 2), critics have usually concentrated on other permutations of the form.[1] Few of the films examined in this chapter have formed a major part of this critical history, and indeed few have ever been addressed in detail at all (or, if they *have* been, the terms of the discussion have been rather different to my own).[2] I have also chosen to concentrate primarily on films by directors (e.g. William Dieterle, Gregory Ratoff, Anatole Litvak, etc.) who are far from central figures in melodrama scholarship. Furthermore, while retaining a focus here on studio-era films, the historical moment I will be analysing (1939–1950) is not so critically privileged for melodrama as are the 1950s.[3]

These choices are partly motivated by a desire to avoid well-trodden ground, as well as because I discuss a seminal figure for 50s melodrama, Douglas Sirk, in Chapter 4. However, it is also central to this book's argument that a 'happy ending' need not be in some way exceptional in order to become of critical interest, but that the convention is more *routinely* flexible. Focussing on films that have been less discussed and championed thus allows me to demonstrate that the 'happy ending' seems to have potential for dynamism, not only in famously complex family melodramas or in the work of, say, Sirk, Ophüls, or Ray, but also in less acclaimed, possibly even run-of-the-mill, movies.

*

My discussion in this chapter concerns three broad issues: characters' happiness, matters of morality, and the affirmation of values – focusing increasingly closely both on individual films' details and on pertinent theoretical questions as the argument progresses. I will explain why I think it necessary to address these different topics in the relevant sections. Since it is doubtless in the interaction of *all* these key issues (and more) that the 'happy ending' – if such a thing exists – is to be found, there will also necessarily be a cross-fertilisation of ideas throughout what follows. The question driving my analysis of all these elements will be, essentially: what are the limits of this convention?

THE 'HAPPY ENDING' AND CHARACTERS' HAPPINESS

> I only know that fate has [. . .] offered us a new life: a wonderful, happy life. The only question we must answer is – 'Do we love each other?'
> – *September Affair*

If the term is not an utter misnomer, the 'happy ending' must surely require that either a film's characters, or its audience, or both, are left 'happy' at/by its conclusion. Characters' happiness and audiences' happiness are, however, two distinct issues, regardless of whether they intersect in specific instances. I will focus initially on the former, before addressing questions of the latter. As such, let us first attend to the relatively simple question of the emotional states of characters themselves at the ends of romantic melodramas.

Happiness and the final couple

Is the 'happy ending' merely a term we should apply when a film leaves its protagonist/s in a state of happiness? This is perhaps an even more pressing question for romantic melodrama than for other contexts. Unlike Westerns, adventures, thrillers, horror or gangster films – whose narratives are often concerned with whether characters will be able to live in safety, or even live at all – perhaps *the* key narrative question of most romantic melodrama is whether protagonists will achieve personal fulfillment, however defined. Given this, characters in these films often invoke this very matter: in *Intermezzo* (1939), Anita (Ingrid Bergman) defends her decision to engage in an affair by saying, 'I *know* we can be happy'; similarly, in *September Affair* (1950), David (Joseph Cotten) rationalises his decision to leave his wife by saying, 'We never made each other happy – isn't *that* important?' Such instances are typical of films discussed in this chapter. This might suggest that if this goal – roughly, happiness – is achieved, then a film can be said to belong to the category 'happy ending', and vice versa. In the type of melodrama upon which I have chosen to focus, the main factor pertaining to characters' happiness will usually be the success or failure of a romantic relationship. In which case, our next question might be: does the 'happy ending' require a final couple?

As we have seen, it is usual to assume that a final couple is necessary for the 'happy ending' of *any* Hollywood film. Yet it is surely uncontroversial to admit that a successful romance is not a *sine qua non* of the 'happy ending' in Hollywood cinema – certainly not, at least, to the extent that it is often taken to be in, say, a Renaissance comedy, whose comic conclusion is commonly said to be *defined* by such an ending (e.g. White [1981]). What happens, though, when dealing with a genre in which romance is the primary concern? We find, if we look attentively, that this issue can be complicated. As we shall see, apart from anything else, it is worth attending to the fact that the *nature* of characters' happiness may vary enormously – both within films that do end with a final couple, and those that do not.

Certainly, providing a final couple can be one way for an ending to appear fairly unambiguously 'happy'. One example from my corpus is *This Above All*, which tells the WWII story of Prudence (Joan Fontaine), a Women's Auxiliary Air Force member, and her romance with a soldier, Clive (Tyrone Power). The film ends after the two of them have achieved their 'goal' of marriage, the final scene showing the couple together, smiling and holding hands, looking forward to the future and speaking of the need to win the war – certainly both united and happy. Yet even here the matter is not entirely simple: Clive has previously deserted the forces, a crime for which he knows he will have to be tried. As well as this, he has been badly injured in a German bombing raid, meaning that both the marriage and the final scene take place whilst he is incapacitated in a hospital bed, with Prudence standing bravely by him. Here, then, we see an ending that surely *can* be defined as 'happy', and primarily because it *does* indeed feature a fulfilled final couple, yet is also markedly different – not necessarily less 'happy', but simply *differently* so – than endings which contain a mutually healthy and legally unburdened final couple; say, to pick an example almost at random, *The Awful Truth* (1937).

This Above All's ending does not feature Bordwell's image of a 'clinch', but those which do may often themselves present their characters' happiness as in some way ambiguous, or at least not in any significant sense *the same* as another example. The ending of *The Enchanted Cottage* (1945) is interesting in this respect. This film depicts a romance between a 'plain' girl, Laura (Dorothy McGuire), and an ex-fighter pilot whose face has been physically scarred by combat, Oliver (Robert Young), both of whom experience great unhappiness because of their 'ugly' appearances. The two meet and fall in love in a remote holiday cottage that turns out to have magical powers. The cottage casts a spell over the pair that causes them to see one another as beautiful, whilst to the rest of the world they still appear 'plain' and disfigured respectively – a fact the film conveys by presenting us sometimes with the magically-inflected appearances of the couple, sometimes as they truly are. This film ends as Laura and Oliver stand by the entrance to a party held by a mutual friend: at this moment pictured as their 'beautiful' selves, the couple are about to open the door but then, upon hearing music coming from inside, pause; they turn to face each other, wishing to savour their happy moment alone with their 'perfect' images of one another before encountering those who see them as 'ugly'. They embrace and kiss, and we fade out. The couple are certainly, again, both 'united' and happy here, but their happiness is made explicitly bittersweet by the fact that they know themselves to be suffering under a private illusion. Clearly, the happiness Oliver and Laura finally experience is thus of a very different kind to that of Prudence and Clive in *This Above All* – or, for that matter, of, say, 'The Man' and 'The Wife' in *Sunrise* (1927), who also conclude their film with an embrace in close-up. For this reason, if for no other, it is thus also a rather different image of a 'happy ending'.

We might also consider final couples who will, soon after the film ends, be parted. Both *Remember the Night* (1940) and *I'll be Seeing You* (1944) are about women who have been convicted of crimes and are about to go to prison for a number of years. *Remember the Night* sees Lee (Barbara Stanwyck), whose trial (for theft) is postponed for Christmas, fall in love during the interim with her prosecuting lawyer, John (Fred MacMurray), and he with her. The final scene takes place after she has pleaded guilty and been sentenced, despite John's efforts to throw the case; the two pledge their love, John promises to wait for her, and they embrace; 'The End'. Similarly, *I'll be Seeing You* tells the story of Mary (Ginger Rogers), halfway through a prison sentence (for manslaughter), being allowed out for a week – again, for Christmas – because of good behaviour. During this time she begins a relationship with Zach (Joseph Cotten), a shell-shocked soldier recently returned from war. The film ends after Zach, having earlier been repelled by the fact of Mary's criminal conviction, has accepted Mary and sworn to wait for her. The two stand outside the prison, embrace and kiss, then each throws a stone accurately at a nearby lamppost (an action previously associated with being of sound mind); 'The End'.

Although united and happy, neither of these pairs of lovers are unreservedly or uncomplicatedly so, since they are about to face considerable periods of time apart. This, again, means that these endings display a very different image of the final couple, and a very different depiction of conclusive happiness, from the endings of both *This Above All* and *The Enchanted Cottage* (or, to take another arbitrary example, from that of *An Affair to Remember* [1957]). Indeed, there are even significant differences between these two outwardly-similar endings in the degrees of happiness presented. In *Remember the Night* Stanwyck and MacMurray play the scene melodramatically, almost desperately: her clinging onto him and sobbing, he intense and earnest; *I'll be Seeing You*, by contrast, edges the mood to towards a more comedic tenor following Zach and Mary's embrace via some playful smiles and jaunty extra-diegetic music as the couple throw their stones. This is a measure of the extent to which details of dramatic action, performance, and film style can help clearly distinguish one 'happy ending' from another, even in cases featuring great overlap of narrative convention and generic motif.

Since all these films end in the manner Bordwell describes as 'the cliché happy ending', I can only assume that, were they featured in his 'unbiased sample', all the above endings would be considered as such – that is: as instances of the same type of ending. I would suggest, however, that even attempting to attend only to the various expressions of 'happiness' displayed in all these films' 'happy endings' has begun to cast doubt on the ability of this term to act as a meaningful category.

Happiness and the parted couple

I have so far briefly demonstrated some simple, immediately obvious differences between a few conclusions that depict what is commonly assumed to be the most standardised of Hollywood outcomes. There are, however, perhaps even more interesting challenges to the homogeneity of the 'happy ending' to be posed by films that see couples parted before a film's conclusion.

This separation may be purely physical, as in *The Clock* (1945) – another WWII romance, about a young woman, Alice (Judy Garland), and a GI, Joe (Robert Walker), who meet in New York during Joe's weekend leave. The pair enjoy a speedy courtship and are married within 48 hours, only for Joe to return to war the next morning. In the film's final scene the couple share a calm and upbeat farewell on the platform of Grand Central Station, before Alice walks off, alone but smiling, into a busy New York crowd. Of course, it is possible that Joe *may* never return, given that he is leaving for the bloodiest war the world has ever seen – a point made more relevant by the film finishing with Alice alone, rather than with the couple's final embrace and farewell (as in *I'll Be Seeing You* or *Remember the Night*). Nevertheless, the smiles of Walker and (particularly) Garland, and their final words to each other ('see you soon'), imply strongly that these characters truly believe that they will be reunited upon Joe's return, and are happy and confident at the moment of their parting. This kind of happiness – one reliant upon a strong leap of faith – thus constitutes another distinct approach to a 'happy ending', and one which is quite manifestly significantly different again from those of *This Above All*, *The Enchanted Cottage*, *Remember the Night*, or *I'll Be Seeing You* (or indeed, to take another example from further afield, *Ball of Fire* [1941]).

If we move on to consider both physical and *emotional* separation, we none-theless discover a number of ways in which a film can leave its couple both dissolved and happy. Perhaps the most basic method is (following a romance's dissolution) by having one lover resolve to win the other back. The archetypal example of this is surely *Gone With the Wind* (1939), which concludes after Rhett (Clark Gable) has left Scarlett (Vivian Leigh), and she, a determined smile on her face, has nevertheless proclaimed, 'I'll find *some* way to get him back! After all, tomorrow is another day . . .!' Notwithstanding the huge dif-ferences in the characters' narrative situations, Scarlett's happiness here is somewhat similar to Alice's in *The Clock*, to the extent that it relies upon a belief in a precarious promise; yet it is also rather different, since it takes place after a relationship has been ended, not simply put on hold. This, combined with Leigh's wide-eyed, tear-streaked face, makes Scarlett's optimism appear not a little desperate, as opposed to Alice's, which is permitted to appear confidently trusting. On the other hand, the potential for *future* unhappiness inherent in *The Clock*'s ending (as Joe has noted, in 1945 a US soldier 'doesn't know what condition he's going to come back in; he may not even come back at all . . .') is rather graver, and would doubtless affect Alice more seriously than the potential undesirable future of *Gone With the Wind*'s relationship (i.e. that the couple will simply remain separated) would likely affect the ever-resilient Scarlett. Within these two final images of women whose happiness is founded primarily upon hope, we see again some of the significant variations avail-able even to one relatively tightly-defined approach to a character's ultimate happiness.

Another permutation involves a couple fully accepting their separation. Such a strategy is used by *Portrait of Jennie*, a fantastical romance in which a struggling artist, Eben (Joseph Cotten), meets Jennie (Jennifer Jones), who seems to have grown several years older in the space of a few days each time they encounter one another. Eben begins to paint Jennie's portrait during their infrequent meetings, and the two fall in love, despite Jennie being possibly a figment of Eben's imagination, a spectre of a real Jennie (who died some years ago), or something indefinable in between. Eben ultimately learns the time and place at which Jennie is destined to die at sea, and rushes to save her. As the waves of a huge storm crash around them, Eben holds Jennie close as she tells him rapturously, 'We'll have all eternity together, Eben . . . We're just begin-ning . . .' A few moments later, despite Eben's efforts, she is indeed dragged away by the sea. Recovering in bed later, Eben is at first distraught by having lost Jennie. However, upon seeing her scarf, which washed up with him on the shore, he becomes happy, a relieved smile crossing his face as he says, 'It's alright – I haven't lost her. Everything's alright now'. We then briefly flash forward a number of years to a point in the future when Eben has become a successful artist, a group of schoolgirls standing in a museum, looking admiringly up at his now-famous 'Portrait of Jennie'.

In their final moments, then, both Jennie and Eben are shown experiencing feelings of happiness despite their separation. During her farewell Jennie appears genuinely optimistic about death, which she sees as only the 'beginning' of the couple's romance, smiling confidently and reassuringly as she delivers these words. Eben's happiness is also undeniable, communicated partly by his faraway smile and reaction to Jennie's scarf, but also implied by the news that he becomes a successful painter, thus achieving the ambition with which he began the film. Of course, it is especially significant that it is his 'Portrait of Jennie' which (we are told by the page of an art book marking the ellipsis) constituted the transition into his 'later period', which is considered 'greatly inspired'. The suggestion is that, although he has lost Jennie, she became a muse that allowed him to achieve his artistic potential (the portrait is also granted great rhetorical significance by being the only image in the film which we see in Technicolor). This ending thus presents us with a couple who are parted (indeed, by death – a trope suggesting tragedy), though neither partner is finally left unhappy by this parting. We may note – again – that the manner in which this is achieved makes these characters' final happiness seem extremely different from relatively secure final couples (*This Above All, The Enchanted Cottage*), or those about to be parted (*I'll Be Seeing You, Remember the Night*), or indeed those who are *not* by each other's sides at their films' ends (*The Clock, Gone With The Wind*). Though all 'could be said to end happily' (Bordwell 1986: 159), the more variations we add to the equation, the less it might seem helpful to consider all these conclusions as examples of a single type of ending.

Unhappy characters

It will doubtless have been noticed that – although varying greatly in degree and approach – all the films I have so far examined *do* end with either one or both members of a central couple in a state that it makes sense to call happiness. If we were to agree that all offer variations on the 'happy ending', then this might seem to suggest, after all, a simple taxonomy, at least within this corpus: whether a couple is united or not, conveying a protagonists' happiness at the close of a film creates the 'happy ending' – however different those individual forms of happiness may be. However, this approach itself may not prove workable if applied to films in which central characters are *not* ultimately shown to be happy.

'Noble sacrifice' is a familiar trope in melodrama, and endings relying upon it often prove interesting in relation to the 'happy ending'. I will be discussing this further in connection with considerations of morality later, but I would like first to analyse one film whose ending famously deals in this theme – *Casablanca* (1942), whose romance plot will be my primary focus here.[4] I might begin by saying that, although its central couple is famously parted, this is certainly a film whose ending cannot fail to put a smile on *my* face. What follows is an attempt to tease out why this might be.

In the film's final scene – despite the love Rick (Humphrey Bogart) still feels for Ilsa (Ingrid Bergman), and she for him – Rick has arranged for Ilsa and Laszlo (Paul Henried) to escape Casablanca together so Laszlo may carry on his freedom-fighting work with the woman who 'keeps him going' at his side. Rick explains to Ilsa that this is the only right thing to do; although there are tears in her eyes, she agrees. As their plane prepares to take off, Rick shoots the Nazi Major Strasser (Conrad Veidt) as he attempts to prevent the departure. Casablanca's chief of police, and Rick's perennial verbal sparring-partner – Louis (Claude Rains) – covers for Rick by ordering his men to 'round up the usual suspects' for the crime. The plane leaves, and Louis and Rick walk away across the runway, making plans to leave for a Free French garrison in Brazzaville; 'Louis,' says Rick, as they walk off together into the fog, 'I think this is the beginning of a beautiful friendship'.

Unlike most films I have looked at so far, *Casablanca* constructs a 'love triangle', featuring two potential romantic couples: Rick/Ilsa and Ilsa/Laszlo. However, it is beyond doubt that Rick and Ilsa are the film's central protagonists and that it is *their* romance that is suggested to be primarily at stake for us: they are played by the two biggest stars in the film, receive the most screen time, and at one point are even provided with a flashback to detail their romance's past. By contrast, the inner contours of the Ilsa-Laszlo romance are alluded to only in occasional lines (e.g. Ilsa telling Rick how she fell in love with Laszlo, Laszlo briefly telling Rick of the depths of his love for her, etc.), meaning that their romance necessarily assumes a less central significance. (This, clearly, is an issue of point of view – a matter that will concern us in the next chapter.) Given this, assuming for now that protagonists' happiness translates to an ending's 'happiness', it would seem that Rick and Ilsa's fates are likely to dictate whether the film has a 'happy ending'. The next question must therefore be their respective happiness at the film's outcome.

First let's look at Ilsa. When Rick tells her she must accompany Laszlo she is shocked and distraught, her eyes wide and voice trembling; she pleads with him, confused and frightened, exclaiming: 'No, no! Richard, what has happened to you?' However, as Rick explains his logic she begins to soften, and eventually a sad smile crosses her face as she looks into Rick's eyes and shares their private ritual ('Here's lookin' at you, kid . . .') one last time – though the smile is accompanied by welling tears. As Rick speaks with Laszlo before their departure, we actually see Ilsa twice furtively using a handkerchief to wipe away her tears, her back turned to both men, who miss the gesture: once when Laszlo returns from loading his luggage, and again as Rick is handing over the letters of transit. Moments later, in our last image of her, she and Laszlo walk across the runway; Laszlo gives her a smile, which she returns – though rather mechanically, without holding his gaze. We now track in closer to her face to see what she is truly feeling, her features falling into a forlorn expression as we see the streak of a tear on her cheek.

Rick is harder to read emotionally, given the characteristically restrained manner with which Bogart embodies his role. During the conversation with Ilsa he appears strong, earnest, convincing – certainly not openly upset (even giving a reassuring smile on 'Here's lookin' at you, kid . . .'), his gaze, expression, and tone of voice firm. Nevertheless, a slight crack in the armour reveals itself when telling Ilsa and Laszlo 'You'd better hurry or you'll miss that plane', his eyes darting nervously between the couple, and a small – quintessentially Bogart-ian – twitch crossing his face, suggesting some sharp feelings of loss he may be repressing. After shooting Strasser (more on this in a moment), he and Louis walk across the runway; as they do, Rick looks to the sky, and the twitch returns. As for his famous final pronouncement of 'the beginning of a beautiful friendship', it is difficult to grasp its precise meaning: its tone, in the context of these men's banter throughout the film, suggests it cannot be taken without any flicker of irony, but – even if we were to understand it as entirely sarcastic (which certainly would be taking the matter too far) – it would still testify to Rick being in good enough humour to make such a dry remark.

Neither lover, then, is finally presented as being *happy* after the couple's parting – Ilsa emphatically not so, and Rick more ambiguously, though he is certainly distraught to a degree. With this in mind, we may ask how this ending avoids making the audience (or at least *this* audience member) share in this unhappiness. To answer this question we need to remember that two other key events take place in the film's final minutes: the killing of Strasser, and Louis' response to it.

Other factors: mood and continuation

Strasser has been unreservedly established as a villain: he is a Nazi, his smooth talk has hidden malevolent intentions, and he has threatened characters with internment in concentration camps. As such, his death has the status, within the world of the film, of an unequivocally good thing (a question of morality, clearly, which I will be addressing shortly). In itself, though, this is still not quite an invitation to an uncomplicatedly cheering conclusion, since it could lead to Rick's arrest; consequently, there is no triumphant smile from Rick as Strasser collapses. What *does* cause a flicker of a smile to flash across his face, however, is Louis' subsequent protection of him when the police arrive. Louis has been an ambiguous character throughout: eminently charming and funny, though proudly unscrupulous, preferring always the ethical path he deems most personally beneficial. Louis' display of solidarity is thus hugely edifying for Rick, as evidenced by that rare, brief smile after Louis' instructions to the officers, as well as another – even broader and warmer – one as the police move off. Yet this slight shift in Rick's own emotional state is certainly not all that allows this ending to appear 'happy'.

The business with Louis also creates the sense of a shift in *mood* – away from the high melodrama of a tearful goodbye and violent shoot-out, towards the lighter comedic atmosphere that has characterised much of Rick and Louis' earlier interactions. This drift towards the comedic is one of the most important ways in which the ending is able to appear 'happy'. Both the command to 'round up the usual suspects' and Rick's reference to the bet regarding Laszlo's escape ('This doesn't make any difference about our bet: you still owe me 500 Francs') mark a return to the mischievously flippant attitude towards serious issues of life and death that Rick and Louis have enjoyed previously (something like what Freud speaks of when describing the functions of humour: 'Look! Here is the world, which seems so dangerous! It is nothing but a game for children – just worth making a jest about!' [1961: 166]). Furthermore, the last-minute return to this frivolous attitude sees it by this point stripped of a potentially troubling apathy by both men's preceding noble actions; the film is now in a position to invite us to view such an outlook as unproblematically, rewardingly *fun*.

Indeed, it is to a great extent the sense of fun accompanying Rick and Louis' departure ('I could use a trip,' says Rick) which creates this ending's surprising levity: two likable men, each a match for the other's wits, escaping the oppressive atmosphere of Casablanca and embarking on a new, sauntering adventure towards the vaguely mysterious, somewhat utopian, Free French garrison – the word 'free' conjuring up notions of both political and personal liberation. Particularly when combined with the final triumphant scored blast of 'La Marseillaise', this concluding image feels, in fact, in its sense of freedom, almost as if it belongs to the world of comedy more than to the restrictive world of melodrama, as Thomas defines them (2000: 119). We might in this respect note that a shift towards the comedic is also used by *The Clock* and *I'll be Seeing You* in final moments that follow melodramatic partings: the former through a call-back to the running gag involving Joe and children, and the latter through its playful inflection of the previously serious matter of throwing stones at lampposts.

Still, it is not just important that the closing action allows for a small change in Rick's emotional state, nor in the film's mood: the final images and dialogue also importantly communicate *continuation*. The suggestion of the characters' lives *going somewhere particular* after the movie ends seems an important way in which this ending, and many others, achieve a sense of what we call 'happiness'. Rick leaving for somewhere else rather than simply returning to his life in Casablanca means that we are offered formless but conceivable images of him in the future, continuing to live – whether it be as a committed freedom fighter, or (perhaps more likely) in the largely nonchalant manner in which it is pleasurable to imagine a character played by Bogart living. Continuation also seems key to the endings of most of the other films I have been discussing: *This Above All* has Prudence and Clive looking forward to Clive's recovery, and to the Allies eventually winning the war; *I'll be Seeing You* and *Remember the Night* finish with the promise that their male characters will wait for their partners; *The Clock* sees Alice waiting for Joe's return, imparting the words, 'see you soon!'; *Gone With the Wind*'s last line ('Tomorrow is another day . . .!') explicitly acknowledges the future and its possibilities for Scarlett; and *Portrait of Jennie* sees Jennie promise that her death is only the 'beginning', as well as Eben's later artistic career, which benefits from creating the impression that, as Joseph Cornell once put it, 'in art there is the possibility of eternity' (Blair 1998: 124).

A sense of promised continuation, then, may be important for 'happy endings'. Conversely, it is exactly this sense that is so sorely lacking in our earlier example of an unequivocally 'unhappy ending', *Vertigo*, whose conclusion is nothing if not final, offering no possibility for future happiness: no future of any kind for Madeleine/Judy, and no prospects for Scottie – the only representative of any sort of life outside his romantic obsession, Midge (Barbara Bel Geddes), having exited the film some time previously. That continuation should be important to the 'happy ending' can perhaps partly be explained by the simple fact that it stands for *possibilities*; indeed, it may be worth mentioning that an audience research project into *Gone With the Wind* found that many spectators 'express exhilaration at the "open, forward-looking ending"' precisely because it offers 'a sense of possibility' (Taylor 1989: 143). I will be returning to this matter in some detail in subsequent chapters.

We have so far begun to see that the kinds of happiness displayed by final couples can vary greatly, and that a final couple need not in fact be present (even in romantic melodrama) in order for characters to be left happy at a film's close. I have also begun to suggest, however, that the emotions felt by characters should by no means be treated as the only pertinent factor in creating what might add up to being an ending's relative sense of 'happiness'. Whilst not dispensing with the matter of characters' happiness altogether, I will now move on to address other issues that may be relevant to the achievement of a 'happy ending': the possibility of 'moral satisfaction', and the affirmation of values.

THE 'HAPPY ENDING' AND 'MORAL SATISFACTION'

> I grant you your *emotions* were probably strong and sincere, but there's no vacation from *decency*.
>
> — *September Affair*

Morality, endings and the Production Code

It sometimes seems to be a film studies truism about studio-era Hollywood that 'in virtually all Hollywood films [. . .] virtue had to triumph, even if only in a tacked-on coda. This practice was made law in the Production Code of 1934' (Lang 1989: 47). For roughly thirty-three years (1934–1967), in a well-documented 'attempt to bind movies to Judeo-Christian morality' (Vaughn 1990: 39), the Production Code did indeed seek to ensure that movies' narratives would not transgress, in its own words, 'moral standards' (Maltby 2003: 593). Particularly relevant for our current purposes is the Code stricture that 'the sanctity of the institution of marriage and the home should be upheld. Adultery [. . .] must not be explicitly treated or justified or presented attractively' (Maltby 2003: 595). As the Lang quotation suggests, the most important part of a film, as far as the Code was concerned, was often its ending since – due to the rhetorical power of endings in general – this had the potential to be the moment at which 'virtue' was either ultimately rewarded or renounced once and for all. Richard Maltby even tells us that, in the early years of the Production Code, campaigners for censorship reform would criticise the industry for having 'invented the perfect formula – five reels of transgression followed by one reel of retribution' (ibid.: 484). If considering this in relation to our subject, one might well imagine that 'the Breen office virtually legislated the happy ending' (Gianos 1998: 52). This is a proposition that requires addressing. Having looked at characters' happiness, let us now ask whether the 'happiness' of an ending might lie in its ability to satisfy a viewer that the 'triumph' of 'virtue' presented at a film's end is something to be admired – something like Seymour Chatman's model of a plot in which '[a] good hero succeeds, causing us to feel moral satisfaction' (1980: 85).

Certainly, inviting 'moral satisfaction' can be one way for an ending to elicit a *viewer's* happiness, as distinct (potentially) from a protagonist's. Arguing from a cognitivist perspective, Murray Smith suggests that classical Hollywood films demand 'moral resolution', which in turn requires a 'moral centre' or 'locus of positive moral value' (1995: 213) in the form of characters with whom our moral sympathies are 'aligned' (ibid.: 187). This, he says,

> is perhaps even more fundamental than the 'happy ending' of the classical Hollywood film, since the latter is dependent on a moral centre. That is, for a happy ending to be recognised as such, we must have previously identified a morally desirable character and outcome. (1995: 213–14)

I would provisionally agree that any film does indeed likely require a 'locus of positive moral value' if a viewer is to recognise its ending as unproblematically 'happy' (or, indeed, 'unhappy'). *Casablanca*, for example, delivers a veritable barrage of moral triumph in its closing moments, made possible by its 'moral centre', which is designed, I would argue, to satisfy the spectator. First there is Rick and Ilsa's noble sacrifice, to which I will return in a moment. Equally, Laszlo has been established to be an effective freedom-fighter dedicated to opposing fascism, meaning that helping him escape will likely aid a great many other people, and perhaps even contribute to winning the war. There is also Rick's shooting of Strasser, which is particularly morally edifying since it conforms to the convention of noble killing established by so many Hollywood films (particularly Westerns), i.e. Rick shoots in self-defence, Strasser having already drawn his pistol. Finally, there is Louis' protection of Rick, which shows a previously proudly amoral character acting for the benefit of another good man. The film has tacitly established its vision of a 'morally desirable outcome' to the extent that we understand all these events as moral within the terms established.

However, what the Production Code deemed a 'moral' conclusion is not necessarily the same as a 'happy' one. This can be demonstrated by even a cursory look at, say, many movies featuring criminal protagonists. An ending in which 'virtue' is rewarded and 'evil' punished may easily produce a conclusion such as that of *You Only Live Once* (1939), which sees both its central lovers – Eddie (Henry Fonda) and Joan (Sylvia Sidney), who have been forced into crime because Eddie was accused, *almost* certainly falsely (though see Wilson [1986: 16–38]), of robbery – shot dead by the police as they are about to escape into Mexico. Joan and Eddie may be criminals, and we may not have been encouraged to admire them exactly (they often act foolishly), but their lost dreams of a 'normal' life, their tragically bad luck, and their continuing victimisation by the social order have assured that, by the film's end, we at least feel invited to extend to them our sympathy. Their climactic deaths are thus unlikely to strike us as anything other than a sad, wasteful shame, despite being 'moral' according to the Production Code (and, indeed, US law: Eddie was previously bound for the electric chair). Simply put, then, what the Code deems a morally correct ending *need* not translate to a 'happy' experience for audiences.

This is both because a film can align our sympathies with characters who must ultimately be punished, and also due to the basic fact that spectators have moral beliefs of their own, which may or may not run counter to those officially-sanctioned by the Production Code. Without entering into philosophy's oldest debate, we can acknowledge that moral concepts such as 'virtue' and 'evil' are not monolithic, and that their specific character necessarily varies depending on innumerable factors. A related point is often made in discussions of the relationship between censorship and reception; as Francis Couvares puts it: 'although undeniably powerful, neither Hollywood nor the other culture industries controlled the contexts within which their products were consumed. They therefore fully controlled neither the meaning nor the effect of that consumption' (1996: 3). This is clearly to invite consideration of the ideological operations of art in general – a debate which must wait until Chapter 4 to be addressed in any detail. For now, it is enough to remind ourselves that individual films need not rhetorically affirm the moral framework of the Code to which they were required to adhere. Needless to say, this fact can have an important bearing on the relative 'moral satisfaction', and thus perhaps 'happiness', of an ending.

Looking at *Casablanca*, it is clear that its ending is 'moral' in terms of the precepts established and enforced by the Production Code. Yet I would argue that it is not this, *in itself*, which makes the ending 'happy'. The combined facts that Laszlo is a good man, that Ilsa cares for him, and that he loves her enough to sacrifice his life for hers ('Yes,' he has told Rick, 'I love her that much'), are allowed to assume far more significance than the fact that he and Ilsa are man and wife. Were he an unloving beast, and Ilsa to despise or fear him (as in, say, *Caught* [1948]) the ending would likely appear morally dubious. It is also questionable whether we would be so willing to accept the dissolution of the Rick/Ilsa relationship were it not for the added moral weight supplied by Laslzo's position as a freedom fighter. Without Laszlo having been presented as such an overwhelmingly good man, the ending would still be morally sound according to the Production Code, but it would certainly not seem uncomplicatedly so in terms of the relative moral weight granted by the film to marriage *per se*. This is the kind of situation we are faced with in a film like *You Only Live Once*: that Joan and Eddie were forced (in Eddie's case, *back*) into crime by circumstances beyond their control is more significant than the fact that they are technically criminals; thus, their eventual deaths – although just in terms of the Code – are more than likely to appear unjust to us. I venture that it is this kind of moral evaluation – dictated both by a film's own rhetoric and a spectator's prior assumptions – which provides the degrees of moral satisfaction available to a viewer. Furthermore, I maintain that it is this kind of process (combined, of course, with issues addressed previously and others still to come) which can create the sense that one ending is more 'happy' than the other. Let us pursue this matter further in relation to some other films from our corpus.

Morality and romantic melodrama

It has often been acknowledged how fundamental issues of morality are to melodrama (see, for instance, Brooks' excellent *The Melodramatic Imagination* [1976]), and our romantic melodramas offer no exception. As we will see, the issue of 'decency', or doing 'the right thing', recurs almost as frequently in these films as does the matter of happiness. Specifically, it is unsurprising that it is usually characters' love that is most commonly made subject to issues of morality in these films. 'Oh, I shouldn't, I shouldn't: it's *wrong* . . .' exclaims Kitty (Ginger Rogers) as she considers running away with her married lover in *Kitty Foyle* (1940); 'Wrong to be *happy* . . .?' comes her lover's reply.

Often such a conflict between romantic love and moral obligation is made overt, with the two being placed in virtually binary opposition via an adulterous romance (on which more in a moment). As *Casablanca* demonstrates, if this opposition results in the sacrifice of romance for moral reasons, this *may* offer one way to leave an audience satisfied by a film's ending, and thus one way through which a conclusion might appear 'happy' even whilst its characters are not. In other instances the relationship between moral codes and romantic love is more implicit. The ending of *The Clock*, for example, is influenced by an historically-specific moral logic established in many WWII films wherein, as the Bureau of Motion Pictures' report on *Casablanca* puts it, 'personal desires must be subordinated to the task of defeating fascism' ('Bureau' 1942: 1). Were Joe to shirk his responsibilities, go AWOL, and run away to live a loving life with Alice at the film's end, the conclusion would be likely to appear morally unsatisfying and therefore rather less 'happy' (particularly, we might assume, to a contemporary Allied audience). Indeed, we might compare this hypothetical conclusion with that of *This Above All*, which is made 'happy' in moral terms partly by the fact that Clive, who previously *did* desert, has by now turned himself in, and come to the conclusion that 'we've *got* to win this war . . .' Joe and Alice's parting thus tinges the ending of *The Clock* with some melancholy, but the reason for it (the need to combat Fascism) is implicitly presented as morally sound enough to appear just, and is thus unlikely to upset our satisfaction. In this film, as in *Casablanca*, the sacrificial repression of the desire for immediate happiness may paradoxically help to make an ending 'happy'. Such, incidentally, is the way that the morality of 'happiness' may plainly change with historical context: whereas the rejection of army service can be treated as an honourable – if doomed – impulse by the time of a post-Vietnam film such as *Hair* (1979), it would have been unthinkable for a mainstream WWII movie to present it in such terms.

I'll Be Seeing You and *Remember the Night* also establish moral reasons for their couples' separation, here via their female characters' jail sentences. There is, however, a question over whether these separations can seem as morally convincing as that of a wartime romance such as *The Clock*. In *I'll Be Seeing You*, for example, we learn that Mary's crime is the accidental manslaughter of her boss, who tried to rape her but fell from a window when she fought him off. In *Remember the Night* Lee is guilty of stealing a necklace, but we learn that her compulsion to steal probably stems from the deeply unhappy childhood she suffered at the hands of her unforgiving mother. Once we learn their contexts, these women's crimes seem to a large degree forgivable according to the 'moral centre' the films establish, particularly when Mary and Lee have fallen in love – an indication of how moral evaluations change depending on shifting contexts. We may at least say that the fact that these characters must serve time at the end of their films is not morally satisfying *in itself*, and thus does not contribute significantly to the 'happiness' of the conclusions – unlike, that is, the partings in *Casablanca* and *The Clock*, where the need to fight the war manages to trump characters' desires. Nevertheless, what *is* satisfying about these *I'll be Seeing You* and *Remember the Night*'s endings is that the women's incarcerations allow the men to make admirable promises, based on love and more *personal* senses of morality, that they will wait for their lovers' releases. This both provides the sense of specific future promise I have suggested is helpful for a 'happy ending', and acts as a moral gesture communicating that the men accept and love these women, no matter how they are viewed by the American justice system. Like *You Only Live Once*, then, these endings – which are, again, of course required by the Production Code – do not satisfy their audience directly through their officially-sanctioned 'moral' narrative outcomes. Unlike *You Only Live Once*, however, both then find *other* ways by which to create a 'happy ending'.

Casablanca and *The Clock* thus manage to achieve 'happy' endings that stem to a great extent from their particular navigation of the Production Code's moral dictates. *I'll Be Seeing You* and *Remember the Night*, on the other hand, achieve their 'happy endings' almost *in spite* of the same guidelines. I now wish to look in some depth at two films that seem positioned somewhere between these poles. These films – *Intermezzo* and *September Affair* – apparently end in a very similar manner, both concluding with the morally correct (in Production Code terms) parting of adulterous couples. Yet the films inflect their endings with subtly, but importantly, distinct moral tenors, which in turn affects the degree of 'happiness' each seems to offer.

Intermezzo and *September Affair*

Intermezzo tells of a famous concert violinist, Holger (Leslie Howard), who leaves his wife, Margit (Edna Best), and their two children to embark on a romance with his daughter's piano teacher, Anita (Ingrid Bergman). The two move to France and live happily for some time. However, partly due to advice from their mutual friend, Thomas (John Halliday), and partly because Holger clearly misses his daughter, Anita comes to feel the affair is wrong. Although still in love, she eventually abandons Holger, leaving him only a letter of explanation. Following a period of mourning, Holger travels back to his old home to visit his family, intending to leave again soon thereafter. During his visit, however, his daughter is hit by a car, causing him to stay on whilst a doctor visits. After learning that she will recover, and apologising to his son for abandoning the family, Holger prepares to leave the family home; just as he is on the threshold, however, Margit descends the stairs and tentatively, but with full feeling, utters the words 'Holger, Welcome . . . home.' Holger moves back inside, closing the door behind him as the two move towards one another; 'The End'.

September Affair follows David (Joseph Cotten) – an unhappily married American engineer with one son – and a concert pianist, Manina (Joan Fontaine), who meet on a plane from Italy to the US. Their plane lands in Florence, and later departs without them on it, before subsequently crashing. Assumed dead by the outside world, David and Manina begin a new, secret life in Italy. Before long, however, David begins to show signs that he is missing his son, and his wife Catherine (Jessica Tandy) learns he is still alive. Although Catherine eventually agrees to the divorce David desired since before the film began, Manina has by now realised that it is best that the affair end. After a successful piano concert, Manina takes David to an airport and tells him she is leaving for South America. She explains that, although she still loves him (and he her), she knows David needs his son in his life. She then walks off across the runway as David looks sadly after her; 'The End'.

These films seem, on the surface, extremely similar in the way they satisfy the Production Code's requirement that extra-marital affairs must not survive a film's conclusion. The specific manner in which this necessary ending is dealt with, however, is different in each film, and in a way that must affect the satisfaction and 'happiness' offered by the films' conclusions. This can be suggested in relation to various factors, some of which relate to characters' happiness, and others to matters of 'moral satisfaction'.

Characters' happiness

In both films the moment of separation itself is equally painful for the characters. In *September Affair* the farewell sees Manina on the verge of tears, though seemingly sure she is doing the right thing, whilst David is stone-faced and solemn throughout. In *Intermezzo* the presentation of Anita's farewell letter on screen is preceded by a shot of her in despair on a train, and followed by one of Holger appearing crestfallen with the letter in front of him. One fundamental difference between the two endings, however, is that, while *September Affair* ends at this moment, *Intermezzo* continues for some time *past* this point – about ten minutes in screen time and several months in the film's world. This means that neither *Intermezzo*'s characters nor the audience are left with the sense of loss that inevitably accompanies the dissolution of romance in both films, but are rather presented with events (the daughter's accident, the apology to the son, the re-acceptance of Holger by his wife, etc.) which make available different emotional possibilities – for characters and audience – to those in *September Affair*.

The moment immediately after Holger learns that his daughter will survive is crucial in this respect. When hearing the words 'She'll be well,' from the doctor, Holger immediately seems relieved and happy, exhaling, smiling and looking up in the direction of his daughter's room upstairs. After the doctor has left, however, his eyes drop as it dawns on him that he must leave again the house in which he once lived. His following movement towards the door is extremely slow, his head lowered, his shoulders hunched – an important detail, since it depicts him feeling unhappy because of his imminent departure from his former home, rather than because of his separation from Anita, which had previously been the cause of his suffering. This in turn means that Margit's gesture of reacceptance when he is at the door is given the chance to mean a great deal. He does not exactly *smile* when he hears the words 'Holger . . . welcome . . . home' – rather he appears nearly incredulous, as if this is the last thing he expects to happen. There do seem, though, to be the beginnings of upward movement in his cheeks, and his eyes – directed up towards Margit on the stairs – suggest that he is not *only* shocked, but also rather grateful. In short, he does not appear at all to dread the idea that he is indeed 'home'. His emotional state, then, is *somewhat* ambiguous at the film's end, yet it is certainly much closer to happiness than is that of David at the end of *September Affair*, who must end the film merely looking longingly after Manina as she walks out of his life.

The possibilities for *future* happiness for the films' male characters are also rather different. Other than communicating the sadness he feels upon leaving his former home, the main way *Intermezzo* allows us to feel that Holger may be happy in future is that the film already showed us, in its opening, Holger and his family enjoying a happy home life. After returning from a concert tour, the third scene depicts Holger in his house, his wife and daughter by him, as he says, 'There's better air to breathe in this room than anywhere on earth. [. . .] If you knew the times I'd thought of this moment: back home, with you.' Although he is perhaps exaggerating his feelings slightly (we later learn that, even before he meets Anita, he feels a little restless in his marriage), he is nevertheless shown here seemingly happy at home with his family – a fact that makes it far easier to imagine him regaining something like this in the future. (Interestingly, the original Swedish version of *Intermezzo* [1936] places far less emphasis on showing Holger to have been contented at home, repeatedly suggesting instead that he is a man who, as his wife puts it, 'can't be and shouldn't be tied down'.)

David's marriage, by contrast, is already on the rocks by the opening of *September Affair*. This film's first scene sees David receive a letter from Catherine telling him she does not intend to go through with a divorce upon which they had agreed, causing David to become visibly aggravated. Although it later becomes touchingly clear that Catherine is probably still in love with David, we get few hints of reciprocal feelings on his part, and are instead consistently reminded that, in his words, 'we never made each other happy,' or, in Manina's, 'she was making him miserable' – a strong hint, within the limits of the Code, that their marriage was almost certainly a sexless one (this sense is heightened by the casting of Jessica Tandy – a less obviously sensual actress than Joan Fontaine). Our impression of this marriage is thus overwhelmingly negative throughout, and as such there seems little hope that, were the couple to attempt to rekindle it after the film ends, it would be anything other than, at best, a loveless grind – certainly when compared with the passionate relationship David and Manina shared. It is true that both male protagonists miss their children (both figuratively adopt characters who seem to represent children during their affairs abroad: the young girl Anne-Marie for Holger, and a young GI for David); in *Intermezzo*, however, we are given the sense that Holger's rekindled relationship with his wife may also bring him some future happiness, whilst in *September Affair* we are permitted no such hopes.

The future happiness suggested as likely or possible for the female characters, meanwhile, seems rather the inverse of their male counterparts, revealing the varied ways in which the retribution demanded by the Production Code may be nuanced in practice. About halfway through *Intermezzo* Anita is awarded a much-desired scholarship by a distinguished music college in Paris, but decides not to take it since it would mean being apart from Holger. It would be very easy – indeed, *logical* – for her to take up this place upon the dissolution of the relationship; there is, however, no suggestion that this will happen. Neither in her final conversation with Thomas nor in her letter to Holger does she say anything of what she will do upon leaving. Although we could infer from the shot of her on the train that she may be on her way to Paris, there is pointedly no confirmation of this, and the extreme sadness of her expression and slumped posture perhaps even imply the opposite: that she has *nothing* waiting for her. After this moment she is then not seen again for the remaining ten minutes of the film. (Again, the original *Intermezzo* provides a contrast: here we *are* shown a sign for Paris on the side of Anita's train.) At the end of *September Affair*, on the other hand, Manina has just given a successful concert performance – a reminder, as in *Portrait of Jennie*, that artistic expression can to some extent fill the gap left by a lover (something seemingly denied Anita). Even if we do not know what exactly awaits her in South America, we are thus permitted to make at least modestly optimistic predictions for Manina's future.

Whilst *Intermezzo* permits Holger the potential for future happiness, then, Anita's treatment by the film (no promised future, exclusion from the film's remaining minutes) gives one the uncomfortable sense that she is being punished for being 'the other woman'. She is condemned, essentially, to narrative oblivion, denied any sense of a life continuing – a measure of the extent to which the figure of the female 'home-wrecker' can become a scapegoat within the 'repressive, hierarchical world of melodramatic films' (Thomas 2000: 14).[5] By contrast, in *September Affair* David is left with a very uncertain future, while Manina is suggested to have more awaiting her. It is also important that – despite the unspecified nature of her journey – it is made clear, as in *Casablanca*, that Manina is on her way to a *somewhere* that has a name, and which the audience can conceive of as a place where she can live out some kind of positive future. Although suggesting nothing like the degree of comedic freedom that Rick and Louis' departure embodies, Manina is nonetheless offered an escape of sorts; David is emphatically not.

Thus differentiated in terms of characters' happiness, these films also convey rather different attitudes towards the morality of their endings.

Moral satisfaction

Although *Intermezzo* makes clear that the couple's affair causes Holger to miss his daughter and Anita to sacrifice her career (and may thus bring both some personal unhappiness), what is stressed far more strongly is that their affair must end because it is *morally* 'wrong'. Before they have even begun their romance proper (but after they have realised they are in love), Anita invites Holger to look at the image of the two of them in a mirror as they sit in a restaurant, asking him 'How do we look to you?', before answering herself: 'We look the way we feel: like two guilty people'. Later, after they have absconded to France, Thomas encourages Holger to sign divorce papers, telling him, 'You must try to think a little of Margit . . .'; Holger responds with 'I suppose you think I've behaved despicably' – a reference both to his abandonment of Margit and his living with Anita 'in sin'. The fact of the relationship's moral impermissibility is often thus stressed, meaning that the narrative tension of the film basically turns upon when the couple will face up to the their romance's immorality. A key point comes in a conversation in which Thomas tries, in a kindly way, to convince Anita of the 'immoral' nature of the relationship:

Thomas:	I wonder if anyone has ever built happiness on the unhappiness of others.
Anita:	*Oh*, what should I *do*?
Thomas:	Only you can answer that, my dear. And whatever you decide I know that it will be the *right* decision.

The reminder that their happiness causes unhappiness to others, combined with the particular stressing of the word '*right*', illustrates that what is at stake in this romance is that it must end because it is placed as immoral – *not*, necessarily, because it won't bring the lovers happiness. Anita goes on to echo this belief in her farewell letter to Holger: 'we know in our hearts that love like ours is wrong – that it drags itself down with remorse and fears, and the unhappiness of others.'

This letter ends with 'God bless you, Holger, and take you, some day, safely home'. This notion of Holger's *home* is constantly stressed throughout the film. We have already seen that the image of his home is emphasised near the film's opening, that the last words spoken in the film are 'Holger . . . welcome . . . home', and the final image is of the couple's front door closing. The idea of Holger's home only truly being with his family is also invoked strongly by Thomas both immediately following Anita's departure ('I hope now you'll return home'), and in his later letters to Holger ('Come home, Holger, come home'). All these references to home seem designed to encourage us to share the view Anita voices to Thomas when deciding to leave: 'We both know where Holger belongs.' They act to reinforce the binary opposition of the moral wrongness of the extramarital affair, and the 'moral centre' offered by the concepts of home and family. The daughter's accident and Holger's apology to his son, too, appear in this context to serve as moral punishments which Holger must endure before being permitted to return to his family.

September Affair, on the other hand – although certainly required to make some reference to David and Manina's romance in socially-sanctioned moral terms (Manina's friend, Maria [Françoise Rosay], tells her that 'What you're doing is selfish, cowardly and wrong') – seems far less concerned to convince us that it is for moral reasons that the affair must end. Instead, the film suggests that the relationship is wrong primarily because it will finally not bring the lovers *happiness*. We see a conscious shifting of focus from questions of moral frameworks to those of personal fulfilment early on, in the scene in which the couple first consider remaining together in Italy. Here David proposes competing moral codes (emotional honesty) and rationalisations (utilitarianism regarding his family's reliance on him) in order to steer the issue away from the morality of the affair itself:

> David: I wouldn't be being honest if I went back now, feeling the
>   way I do. [. . .] She'll never give me a divorce, we'll live like
>   strangers the rest of our lives.
> Manina: But you have a son . . .
> David: He doesn't need me: I was always too busy, he was away at
>   school. Next year he goes to college, and then he takes my
>   place at the plant; he'll have a fine life. I was younger when
>   I lost my father. [. . .] The only question we must answer is:
>   do we love each other?

From this point on the film stresses that whether or not the relationship should continue is predicated less on whether it is morally 'wrong' than on whether it will bring David and Manina happiness; as Manina later says: 'You must promise me that if I ever make you unhappy you must leave me.' Having established this condition, the film goes on repeatedly to suggest that, although they love each other, the affair *will not* ultimately satisfy them, irrespective of the unhappiness it causes others. David unwittingly reveals how much he misses his son when he takes a young American GI, Johnny (Jimmy Lydon), under his wing, enthusiastically offering him 'fatherly advice'; Manina discovers a desire to continue with her musical career ('You gave up your work after you had already found success; I gave up mine before'); and a significant subplot involves an engineering project David desperately wants to take part in but cannot. When David returns home, drunk after an evening with Johnny, Manina says, 'When I saw you with Johnny I suddenly felt how much you must miss your son – all the things you've given up. Are you sure we've made the right choice?' David does not answer, having fallen drunkenly asleep, but the unspoken answer is clear: no, they have not made 'the right choice'. Yet, significantly, here the choice is not 'right' in the sense that it will not make them happy – rather than the sense implied by Thomas in *Intermezzo*. Unlike *Intermezzo*, then, the narrative tension here revolves around when the couple will face up to the unhappiness their romance will eventually bring *them*, not others. These are the terms in which Manina is speaking when, in a farewell speech equivalent to Anita's goodbye letter, she tells David that 'our love was built on deception,' and 'we know it wouldn't be right'. All we have seen implies that 'deception' here refers more to a deception of their own feelings, and 'right[ness]' to the issue of fulfilment, rather than moral obligation.

Neither of these endings can reasonably be called uncomplicatedly 'happy', but attempting to untangle from the web of factors above which is the *more* 'happy' is also difficult, and involves juggling many different issues. (1) In both films the couples act 'morally' according to the Production Code, yet (2) only *Intermezzo*'s characters couch their actions primarily in these terms. (3) Both imply happiness and continuation for one character and not for the other. (4) Unlike *September Affair*, *Intermezzo* carries on past the point of its romance's painful dissolution and towards the establishment of a more hopeful status quo. Yet (5) this is only made possible through the wholesale evacuation of Anita from the final minutes – an inconclusive elision. (6) *September Affair*, meanwhile, does conclude at its moment of anguished separation, but also (7) makes the separation seem necessary because its avoidance would only mean eventual unhappiness for its couple; (8) *Intermezzo*, on the other hand, has not been concerned with convincing us of any such thing, because it has privileged the importance of 'moral obligation' over sexual and personal fulfilment.

Examining both the happiness of the characters *and* the implied 'moral satisfaction' offered by their actions, then, seems to leave us none the wiser about whether either film's ending is 'happy'. The only possible answer so far seems that both endings contain elements that contribute to the conclusions of *other* films seeming 'happy', but that these elements are not yet enough to allow us to feel confident in our judgement here. I earlier began to suggest reasons why a hypothetical taxonomy of the 'happy ending' based on characters' happiness alone would be unable to deal both with *degrees* and *kinds* of happiness, as well as with 'happy endings' featuring *un*happy characters. My analysis here has suggested that a similar fate might also befall a taxonomy based on implied morality – or, indeed, one that attempted to *combine* considerations of happiness and 'moral satisfaction'.

My discussion of *Casablanca* began from the starting point that the film's ending was 'happy' simply because I felt it to be so. Bringing the same unavoidable 'evidence of feeling' to bear on *Intermezzo* and *September Affair*: on first viewing I certainly felt that the former's ending was urging me to feel more 'happy' than was the latter's. I think that this response likely stems from the fact that *Intermezzo* establishes a new status quo – the restitution of the family – and, crucially, that the film rhetorically affirms this state of affairs (in Chapter 4 we will examine a film which ends with a similar status quo yet does *not* affirm it). In one sense, this could simply be understood as the film supporting the necessity for acting 'morally'. However, as I have said, 'morality' is not exactly a singular concept (however much a document such as the Production Code might attempt to suggest otherwise via references to monolithic notions such as 'moral standards' [Maltby 2003: 593]). What is going on in both films is in fact a clash between the conflicting demands of two different moral frameworks, with two different *values* at their heart: family and romantic love.

In the introduction we encountered Fritz Lang's recasting of the concept of the 'happy ending' as instead being a matter of the 'the *affirmative* ending' (1948: 29) – a useful term, and one we may relate to the problem of clashing values presented by the conclusions of *Intermezzo* and *September Affair*. Rather than continuing to attempt to conceptualise the issue at hand in terms of 'moral satisfaction' in a general sense, it may be helpful to slightly rephrase this issue in terms of how the endings of *Intermezzo* and *September Affair* confront a choice they both face: what value finally to affirm.

THE 'HAPPY ENDING' AND THE AFFIRMATION OF VALUES

We'll always have Paris.

– Casablanca

According to much conventional critical logic, both *Intermezzo*'s and *September Affair*'s conclusions should be examples of the 'happy ending', since both see the (potential) restoration of the family, and thus, in theory, a particular conception of 'normality' with which this institution is often associated. In keeping with assumptions about the ideologically conservative character of the 'happy ending', the convention has often been considered a means by which Hollywood films ensure that 'the "correct" family order [is] re-established by the end of the film' (Kaplan 1983: 45), and thus 'restore the original status quo' (Belton 1994: 22); in short, it affirms a particular set of *values*. Such ideological aims have also been attributed to melodrama, both as a mode and a genre: Carroll suggests that American film melodramas are ultimately concerned to communicate 'the "rightness" of the nuclear family' (1991: 184), while Cawelti argues that nineteenth- and twentieth-century literary melodramas share an 'emphasis on romantic love as an ultimate value, [and] the defense of monogamous, family-oriented relationships between men and women' (1991: 47). In Cawelti's characterisation, however, we find the seeds of potential contradiction. As often noted, melodrama can frequently find it difficult to ultimately affirm *both* these values simultaneously.

As Ellen Seiter puts it, speaking of recent film and television melodramas (though her words could equally apply to those of our corpus): while concerned with 'the naturalness and rightness of the nuclear family as a social arrangement, [melodramas] are also preoccupied with its disruption'; furthermore, she goes on, in particular 'sexuality has proven to be an unlimited source of narrative conflict' (1991: 528–29). The Holger/Anita and David/Manina relationships in *Intermezzo* and *September Affair* are certainly significantly bound up with sex: when David says that he and his wife 'live like strangers', we know to what he is referring. However, in the terms established by the films themselves, it seems appropriate to also align the affairs with Cawelti's notion of 'romantic love as an ultimate value' (romantic love and *amour passion* being, of course, distinct though not necessarily mutually exclusive cultural discourses [Giddens 1992: 44]). It is the films' conception of the value of romantic love that makes it so hard for them to adhere to the Production Code's injunction that 'the sanctity of the institution of marriage and the home should be upheld'. Although the Code may dictate that adultery 'must not be [. . .] presented attractively' (Maltby 2003: 595), the conventional value held by romantic love in romantic melodrama makes it virtually impossible for adulterous relationships such as these *not* to appear attractive – a fact that poses significant problems for these films' endings. So, let us now address 'love as a screen value' (Jones 1942: 421) – that is, its treatment as an idealised concept that is presented as highly desirable and of considerable inherent worth.

Romantic love as a value

In the films I have been examining, the romantic love felt between the two central protagonists may or may not be enough to keep them together until the end of the film but in either case the characters are usually still in love at the conclusion and – even more importantly – are never left in any doubt that *love itself* is still important. I would suggest that the conception of love that the characters in these films adhere to can, broadly speaking, be aligned with the view voiced by Clive in *This Above All*: that there is 'no more exultant, more beautiful, more noble thing than a man and woman who truly love each other.' This notion of (heterosexual) romantic love as representing essentially the highest form of human achievement seems sometimes to constitute not just a belief for our protagonists, but a virtual *belief system*, and may even offer explanations for global events in characters' worlds. In *The Clock*, for example, Alice reassures Joe that she knows he will not be killed at war because the pair are in love, and the world they in live (or, perhaps, God) is committed to maintaining this love:

> Darling, you're coming back; do you want me to tell you how I know? Two days ago you came to this city and you didn't know anyone: you didn't know me and I didn't know you; and now we're *married*. Now, we both know that that was meant to be. So, don't you see, whoever makes the arrangements for people is doing pretty well for us.

Similarly, in a line already quoted from *September Affair*, David tells Manina that 'fate has saved us from death and offered us a new life – a wonderful, happy life.' In a more literal, fantasy-inflected sense – the supernatural events in the worlds of *The Enchanted Cottage* and *Portrait of Jennie* appear to be governed by romantic love, or at least strongly influenced by it in particular instances, with love affecting the physical appearances of characters and the operations of time, respectively. Such suggestions that love is governed by, or perhaps governs, fate are extreme examples; nevertheless, it does seem to be taken more or less for granted by the characters in all these films that love is *at least* a valuable and desirable thing – if not *the* most valuable and desirable thing in their fictional worlds. All, clearly, are indebted to familiar cultural forms and conceptions offered by what Anthony Giddens has called the 'romantic love complex' – 'a specific cluster of beliefs, and ideals geared towards transcendence' (1992: 45).

Having established the innate worth of romantic love as a value, these films then tend to appear determined to reassure us that, regardless of the final status of the central romantic couple, the worth of love *itself* as a concept survives the film's ending. *This Above All* and *The Enchanted Cottage*, which both end with a final couple, easily allow us to assume that, though their couples will doubtless face difficulties (injury and court-marshals in the former, living with bodily 'defects' in the latter), they will confront them together because they are in love, which presupposes such unquestioning mutual support. However, in films with couples who are (or about to be) parted, the overt reaffirmation of the value of love becomes particularly important. Perhaps the archetypal instance of this is Rick's assertion to Ilsa in *Casablanca* that 'We'll always have Paris', the meaning of which is clear: though not continuing their relationship, the memory of their love, and their appreciation of its worth, will survive.

A similar approach is observable in virtually all the films that end with couples parting. In *September Affair*'s final scene, for example, David tells Manina that, 'What we have *mustn't* be lost,' to which she replies, 'It won't be: we'll keep it alive in our hearts'. Likewise, in *Portrait of Jennie* Eben's fear that, having found love with Jennie, 'now we have to lose it,' is quelled by Jennie's promise that, spiritually or emotionally, 'We'll have all eternity together, Eben . . . We're just beginning,' prompting Eben's later relieved exclamation, 'It's alright: I haven't lost her.' Inverting the wartime convention of waiting wives, *Remember the Night* and *I'll be Seeing You* both conclude with promises from their male protagonists that they will wait for their partners' releases because they love them, while *The Clock* ends with a similar promise from Alice to Joe. As we have seen, even *Gone With the Wind* has Scarlett announcing in the final moments that 'I'll find *some* way to get him back,' thus indicating that the ideal of love for which Scarlett has been striving, and which she eventually achieved (too late), is still something that holds as a central and vital value.

The survival of the characters' love is, in one sense, merely another way to provide the sense of continuation I have suggested is helpful for a 'happy ending'. It also, though, acts as a reaffirmation of love as a value. It is also worth pointing out that in many of these endings the value of love also seems to be implied *stylistically* via the connection of this theme with notions of, again, a kind of spiritual transcendence: we hear choirs at the ends of both *This Above All* and *The Clock*; *Portrait of Jennie* launches finally into Technicolor for its revelation of the painting; and several of the films' final images (under the superimposition 'The End') are of clouds or skies. (We will encounter similar strategies in *Sleepless in Seattle* in the next chapter.)

These sometimes near-desperate reassurances that the value and signifi-cance of love is not lost seem utterly rational in the face of the understanding of the concept presented in these movies. If love in these films' worlds truly is the highest form of achievement, then it makes sense that it not be deval-ued, or irrevocably lost, at the films' conclusions – *if*, that is, the films wish to provide an 'affirmative ending'. Were, say, *Casablanca*, or *Portrait of Jennie*, to end not only with their central couples parted, but also with the suggestion that their love affairs were a mistake, or not of worth, then it would surely be extremely difficult even to countenance the notion that they could be referred to as 'happy'.

Values and the 'happy ending'

This might, then, seem to suggest an additional factor for our hypothetical tax-onomy of the 'happy ending' – something along the lines of: if we can say that a romantic melodrama's ending reaffirms the value of love then we can say that it has a 'happy ending'. However, it is not difficult to see that this taxonomy would produce inaccurate, or at least certainly incomplete, results. How, for example, would tragedies fare if faced with the formulation? Clearly *Romeo and Juliet* features characters who love each other until their last breaths, and leaves us in no doubt as to the existence, power and value of love – but surely not even the most brilliant reading could convincingly argue it had a 'happy ending'? Moving our sights back towards Hollywood, how would, say, lovers-on-the-run crime pictures cope if faced with this hypothetical taxonomy? The aforementioned *You Only Live Once* touchingly conveys the deeply-felt love between its romantic couple, and that it survives undimmed till the film's final moments; yet, again, the ending of this film (which sees the murder of both protagonists by representatives of the state) surely cannot feasibly be called 'happy'.

Another potential objection against this taxonomy is that, as noted, there is seldom only one value at stake in a film. I have already mentioned that the ideological value of 'the family' may also play an important role, and indeed the conflict between this value and that represented by romantic love may con-stitute a central thematic tension. While some movies may make their 'locus of positive moral value' (Smith 1995: 213) eminently clear, others can be more torn. This fact is particularly relevant to the endings which previously caused such trouble: *Intermezzo* and *September Affair*.

As we have seen, *September Affair* concerns itself with reasserting the importance of romantic love right up until its closing moments. Interestingly, *Intermezzo*, by contrast, is uncommonly weak in this regard. Rather than *September Affair*'s final reassurance that 'what we have *mustn't* be lost', in *Intermezzo* the last reference the film makes to Anita and Holger's relationship comes in this brief exchange between Thomas and Holger:

> Thomas: I'm sure you will always think kindly of her . . .
> Holger: Kindly? I think my feelings will go a little deeper than that, Thomas. As time goes on I suppose the memory of her will grow vague in my mind, but in my heart will remain the image of her loveliness.

Although asserting that Holger's feelings will 'go a little deeper' than mere kindness, and that Holger believes he will remember 'the image of [Anita's] loveliness', the words spoken here appear unusually dismissive of the value of love when compared with the other romantic melodramas I have been discussing, and *September Affair* in particular. *Intermezzo* is in fact the only film in our corpus to suggest anything *like* the idea that the memory of a relationship will 'grow vague' over time – indeed, as we have seen, almost all our other films make sure to stress that this will *not* happen. Rather than laying a path for an 'unhappy' ending, however, this subtle downplaying of the importance of love seems to occur here in order to allow *Intermezzo*, in its final ten minutes, to move a different value to its 'moral centre': that of family.

Following Anita's departure, all of *Intermezzo*'s events are concerned with shifting focus away from the love affair and onto Holger's home and family: Thomas repeatedly urging Holger to 'come home', the daughter's accident, Holger apologising to his son for the pain he has caused, Margit's welcoming Holger home, and – perhaps most importantly – Anita's continuing absence. This also affects a change in what value is finally presented as holding primary importance. By the time of the film's final image – a shot from outside the family home depicting the slow closing of the front door as Holger and Margit move towards one another inside – it is absolutely clear what value is being reaffirmed most strongly. (In another contrast with its remake, the original *Intermezzo* ends not in the family home but in a hospital.) It is, I would argue, the pains taken here to make clear that a new value is being upheld which – when combined with the likelihood of happiness for Holger – allow this ending to appear more 'happy' than *September Affair*'s. Whether one accepts this ending and finds it satisfying despite the narrative evacuation and punishment of Anita, or whether it appears instead to be a mere ideological 'emergency exit' (Wood 2003: 63), is a question that can only be answered by each individual spectator (a matter to which I will return). Regardless, though, I believe that the strategies employed in the film's concluding minutes are clearly *designed* to facilitate our taking the ending as comparatively 'happy'.

It also seems important that the value of family is not just being *affirmed* by the end of *Intermezzo*, but that a manifestation of that value (i.e. the reconstruction of this family itself) is also finally *achieved*. Were the film to end, for example, with Holger merely experiencing an epiphany regarding the value of family and then *not* returning home (or being rejected when attempting to do so), the ending would of course be infinitely less 'affirmative', and thus doubtless less describable as 'happy'. Perhaps, then, the reason for the ending of *September Affair* seeming somewhat less 'happy' than that of *Intermezzo* is because, while it certainly reaffirms the value of love, it does not show the *fruits* of this value (i.e. a romantic relationship) being achieved, and *also* does not then go on to offer the reassertion of any other value in its place. This would also explain why endings such as those of *You Only Live Once* – or, say, *Romeo and Juliet* – appear 'unhappy': they reaffirm the value of love, but its rewards are beyond characters' reaches.

If we are convinced by this explanation, however, it is still necessary to point out that even *this* manner of determining 'happiness' may not be infallible, as *Portrait of Jennie* demonstrates. By the end of that film it is certainly the value of love that has been placed at its thematic centre, and – as with *September Affair* – the fruits of this value are not achieved; despite this, however, the film still does manage (via characters' happiness, promises of continuation, the painting of Jennie and its specific presentation in Technicolor) to conclude on a note that we would be hard-pressed not to call triumphant. Whether we would also wish to call it *a* 'happy ending' is another question, but one that also now seems less important than the fact that investigating value too has by this point surely offered us no obvious method of discerning what *the* 'happy ending' might look like.

It is not clear whether it would be possible to take as 'happy' an ending that *does* finally reject, or fail rhetorically to affirm, the values at its centre. Such a film might in fact be *Vertigo*: by the end of this film the concept of romantic love that has been so invested in by its characters has been corrupted beyond repair – having been either ignored (Midge's love for Scottie), or transformed into an obsessive need to possess and dominate. The final image of Scottie staring down from the tower not only conveys finality and stasis, but also utter absence of affirmation, complete defeat – not just for Scottie but for the positive values in the film's world, particularly that of romantic love. Without further work, I would not feel confident in saying whether it is possible for an ending to both delegitimise its central values and appear 'happy', though I am instinctively inclined to suggest that it is not.

However, answering the question of what constitutes an 'unhappy ending' was never the aim of this chapter. I have rather been concerned here to address the opposite question: what is the 'happy ending'? After examining the happiness of central characters at my films' conclusions, the sense of 'moral satisfaction' the endings appear to encourage, and the values they ultimately affirm, I am still unsure of how to answer this question consistently reliably – or at least *simply*. The considerable problems my analyses have encountered would seem to suggest that it may be time for us to begin rethinking common conceptions about this supposedly monolithic 'cliché'.

*

This chapter has aimed to suggest that common assumptions about the homogeneity of the Hollywood 'happy ending' may in fact misrepresent the potential complexity of this familiar convention. At the very least, what has been demonstrated is that it would be unhelpful to describe all the preceding conclusions as the 'same basic ending' – that is: as a single type of outcome to which it would be possible to 'retro-fit' a narrative (Altman 1992: 32). Slightly more ambitiously, I would argue that the difficulties of definition posed even by these handful of films should certainly give us pause before agreeing to presume that, say, 'the happy ending was almost universal in Hollywood during its classical period' (Neale/Krutnik 1990: 29). This is further attested to by the fact that the endings I have been exploring are largely taken from one loosely-defined type of romance film made over barely more than a decade: if there is this much persuasive evidence to suggest the comparative heterogeneity of the 'cliché' *here*, then we must assume that we would discover a great deal more diversity if the net of enquiry were cast more broadly.

The next question we necessarily face, therefore, is whether the 'happy ending' as commonly understood – that is: a formulaic, 'overly codified' (Neupert 1995: 35) conclusion that might very well recur consistently throughout Hollywood cinema – truly exists at all. This issue, it seems to me, largely comes down to precision of description. My discussions have necessarily presupposed that it is indeed possible for endings to appear 'happy' or 'unhappy'. Although the exact meanings of such descriptions have thus far been rather vague, given their wide acceptance and usage, it has seemed appropriate to continue to use them. Having accepted these terms, then, my analyses have at no point disproved that there is usefulness in the notion that a particular film 'could be said to end happily' (Bordwell 1986: 159), i.e. that we can refer to such a thing as *a* 'happy ending'. What this chapter has gone some way towards discouraging, however, is an unquestioning belief in the probable existence of such a thing as *the* clichéd 'happy ending'. A difference between definite and indefinite article could at first glance seem insignificant, but it may have potentially large ramifications for our thinking about Hollywood cinema.

Part of the aim of this chapter, then, has been to shake our faith in the category of *the* 'happy ending' – a necessary first step for any serious discussion of Hollywood endings. Its existence being thus in doubt, I will now abandon the use of inverted commas when making reference to a particular happy ending or happy endings, but retain them when referring to the 'happy ending' as a clichéd Platonic ideal (an important category in itself, as we shall see). That the discussion thus far has brought us to a point at which we are able to make this distinction is in itself significant. Also important, however, is the headway made into the issue of what happy ending*s* seemingly *do* have in common. My investigations – while certainly uncovering relative versatility – have by no means suggested that there exist *infinite* ways to create *a* happy ending. Although too diverse to add up to a cliché, or to make a definite article applicable, the approaches we have seen films take towards matters of characters' happiness, issues of 'moral satisfaction', affirmations of value, and promises of continuation, nevertheless have enough contours in common for us to continue referring to the *convention* of happy endings, and it will be necessary for us to keep these strategies in mind as we move into the rest of the book.

I will henceforth be addressing the relationship between happy endings and several features with which they are frequently assumed to have very particular relationships: closure, 'unrealism', and ideology. Needless to say, common assumptions about the innate relationship between these concepts and the 'happy ending' are also complicated by the shift from definite to indefinite article I have suggested. This is not to say that many happy endings will not prove themselves, say, 'closed', 'unrealistic', or 'conservative' when assessed individually, but rather that such individual assessment must replace automatic pronouncements stemming from assumptions about the feature's inherent homogeneity.

In part because most include a final couple, many of the happy endings we will be examining in the rest of the book may even appear more alike than do those featured in this chapter; yet all establish distinct relationships to the concepts being discussed in each case. Once we begin to question the assumption that the 'happy ending' is always largely the same and operates in largely the same way, and instead feel compelled to assess each happy ending on its own terms, we are far more likely to represent accurately the character of any conclusion under discussion. It is with such work that the remainder of this book will be engaged.

NOTES

1. E.g. the 'women's film' (Walsh 1984), which itself often encompasses the family melodrama (Schatz 1991), the maternal melodrama (Williams 1984), the melodrama of the 'unknown woman' (Cavell 1996), the 'fallen woman' cycle (Jacobs 1991), the 'persecuted wife' melodrama (Britton 2009: 30), and so on.

2. For instance, writing on *Casablanca* which assesses it primarily as WWII movie (e.g. Ray 1985), or work on *Gone With the Wind* which addresses its significance for the industry's history or for fans (e.g. Taylor 1989).

3. Even Andrea S. Walsh's book *Women's Film and Female Experience, 1940–1950* (1984) and Mary Ann Doane's *The Desire to Desire: The Woman's Film of the 1940s* (1987) discuss none of the films in my corpus.

4. Rather than, as is more common in scholarship (Shumway 2003: 114), its potentially propagandist nature (e.g. Ray 1985).

5. Jacobs (1991) has argued that the harsher punishment of female characters who indulge in either adulterous relationships or sexual relations out of wedlock was a common feature of classical Hollywood melodrama.

CHAPTER 2

Happy endings and closure

Happy endings are commonly treated as synonymous with closure, and final couples are commonly regarded as synonymous with happy endings. The logical extension of these assumptions also holds, meaning we often come across claims to the effect that Hollywood films tend to be 'closed by the [. . .] heterosexual couple' (Russell 1995: 6); likewise, Strinati speaks of closure entailing 'the coming together of the male and female leads in a romantic happy ending. This is a 'closed' narrative' (Strinati 2000: 217); Hayward, meanwhile, offers the simple dictum that, in Hollywood cinema, 'closure means a resolution of the heterosexual courtship' (2006: 83).

Final couples have certainly historically served an important role in the conclusions of a great many Hollywood movies, and part of this role has been to make a 'contribution towards narrative closure' (Mulvey 1989: 33). This much is undeniable, and will be explored in more depth in this chapter. It is also important, however, to offer a number of caveats to this rule of thumb. One of my aims here is to demonstrate that the final couple by no means always guarantees the same degree or kind of closure; another will be to attempt to present a more multifaceted picture of closure itself by drawing attention to factors that may contribute to its creation or repudiation, but which can often go ignored in discussions of the subject.

I have chosen this approach partly in order to expand upon the work of Richard Neupert's *The End: Narration and Closure in the Cinema*. Neupert's book is valuable for a number of reasons, not least because it grants the issue of form considerable significance, treating closure as the product of a 'dynamic relation between narrative discourse and story' (1995: 15). Neupert suggests that both story and narrative discourse must be resolved in order for films to be dubbed fully closed, erecting four categories into which they may fall: Closed Text (closed story and discourse), Open Story (open story but closed discourse), Open Discourse (closed story but open discourse), and Open Text (open story and discourse). Despite its usefulness, however, Neupert's study also has its limitations. One is the relatively cursory manner in which Neupert treats films seen as belonging to his Closed Text category – a banner under which he places every classical Hollywood film named in the book and which, he claims, simply 'adhere to conventional closure [. . .] wholeheartedly' (ibid.: 35). The book devotes just one chapter to this kind of film because, it is argued, 'we learn more about narrative [. . .] by devoting three-fourths of this study to films that challenge most actively conventional resolution and closure' (ibid.: 179). The unfortunate result is that the Closed Text film is merely cast in a contrasting role to the 'radical' tendencies of 'more modernist "art" films' (ibid.: 179). To focus discussions of closure around texts which seemingly 'resist' or 'refuse' the effect is a widespread tendency in the writing on this subject, as I will return to in my final chapter. D. A. Miller, for instance, whose book *Narrative and its Discontents: Problems of Closure in the Traditional Novel* is one of the most influential studies on literary closure, describes the 'failure of closure' as a text's 'most powerful and seductive effect' (1981: 164). As with the implausible 'happy ending', this intense investment in the processes whereby closure *does not* take place (see also, in literary studies: DuPlessis [1985], Rabinowitz [1989], Reising [1996]) has resulted in a context in which the workings of closure itself are continually in danger of being oversimplified or taken for granted.

A Closed Text, Neupert claims, 'struggles to limit and direct itself toward the eventual resolution of its structuring plot lines' (ibid.: 38) in an attempt to create a 'stable product' (ibid.: 36) possessing 'very complete and unified resolution' (ibid.: 38), which constitutes a 'logical, directed, and efficient conclusion to its narrative production' (ibid.: 40–1). In the book's conclusion Neupert mentions that the Closed Text film should 'never be considered as a monolithic group style or category' (ibid.: 179), and should therefore 'not be assumed to be either static or easily summarized' (ibid.: 179). Yet his previous characterisation of this film type has unfortunately repeatedly implied that we should draw precisely such assumptions. It seems to me that what Neupert might call Closed Text films offer nothing like one single approach to closure, as my analyses of the movies in this chapter will attempt to show. In this sense, I intend to take Neupert up on his parting invitation, sidelined in his own study, for 'future work with film endings [to] examine in far more detail the [. . .] parameters of Closed Text films' (ibid.: 179). Indeed, I will in a way invert Neupert's approach in this chapter by devoting the most space to the most 'closed' ending discussed – precisely because adequately explaining *why* it can appear so 'closed' is an extremely complicated matter.

Rather than treat closure simply as what happens when plotlines reach resolution, or even only as the product of a combination of narrative *and* narrational resolution, I think it useful to understand closure in the far more inclusive sense suggested by Barbara Herrnstein Smith in her early pioneering work *Poetic Closure*: as a name for the moment when a work 'creates in the reader a sense of appropriate cessation' (1968: 36). How to create this sense is the fundamental question faced by any narrative seeking closure, and it has been met with a great many answers. As Henry James put it, 'really, universally, relations stop nowhere, and the exquisite problem of the artist is eternally but to draw, by a geometry of his [sic] own, the circle within which they shall happily *appear* to do so' (1934: 5). When this circle, drawn by whatever geometry, feels complete despite the basic fact of the endlessness of human relations, we may speak of 'appropriate cessation' (I will be using this useful phrase often, and will thus henceforth drop the inverted commas). This, in other words, is the extent to which an ending is made to *feel like* an ending, and it may be created through a whole host of interrelated strategies. In this chapter I will explore the roles played by a number of factors whose closural powers are too seldom acknowledged in discussions of the subject. Specifically, I will be investigating the importance and interdependence of narrative resolution, thematic elements, style, genre, point of view, and implied narrative continuation. All these elements of a film of can be important in distinguishing the sense of closure invited by one ending from that encouraged by another. Thus, while I do not intend to propose here a new, coherent approach to the study of closure, I do at least intend to convince the reader that we should strive to keep the diverse nature of its determinants in mind.

In what follows I will move periodically between analysing individual endings and discussing theoretical issues surrounding closure and final couples more generally. My investigation begins with a film that might be said to offer an especially 'closed' final couple happy ending, *Sleepless in Seattle* (henceforth *Sleepless*).

THE FINAL COUPLE AND CLOSURE: *SLEEPLESS IN SEATTLE*

In its final moments *Sleepless* romantically unites two characters, Annie (Meg Ryan) and Sam (Tom Hanks), who live on opposite sides of the United States – the former in Baltimore, the latter in Seattle. The film ends with the success of Annie's plan, directly inspired by the plot of *An Affair to Remember* (I will be returning to this matter in Chapters 3 and 4), that she and Sam meet at the top of the Empire State Building on Valentine's Day. This ending is preceded by a brief version of the familiar romantic comedy 'Dark Moment' (Mernit 2000: 115) wherein it is suggested that the film's lovers may *not* end the film together. Here this moment occurs when Annie, having just broken off her engagement with her fiancé (Bill Pullman), rushes to the top of the Empire

State Building only to find it empty, Sam and his son Jonah (Ross Malinger) having just left. This is quickly resolved, however, when father and son return to reclaim a rucksack Jonah accidentally left behind. Annie and Sam introduce themselves, he takes her hand, and the three disappear together into a lift. The camera recedes from the Empire State Building and out into space; the end.

This ending clearly answers the film's key narrative question: 'Will Sam and Annie meet?' Furthermore, although we end only *with* a meeting – not a relationship, marriage, family home or future – this conclusion also to a large extent implies the resolution of the individual aims of each character: Sam's need to get over the death of his wife (made plain in the pre-credit sequence following the funeral, which shows his anger and listlessness), and Annie's desire for a 'magic' relationship (established in the post-credit sequence when she and Walter visit her family and Annie responds to her mother's belief in the importance of romantic 'magic' in a manner demonstrating that this is not what she feels for Walter). The satisfaction we are invited to take from these questions being resolved by the end of the film is what will often tend to be called narrative closure, while its lack will be called openness. It is a pleasure that comes from the sense of unquestionable completion: 'a feeling of satisfaction that the story's elements ended at their necessary spot, problems posed are resolved [. . .]; in sum, what was open is now closed' (Mortimer 1985: 15).

It is interesting to consider, however, that at least one potentially troubling question is left unanswered at the end of *Sleepless*: given that they live on opposite sides of the US, how will Annie and Sam pursue their relationship? We might answer that Annie will relocate, considering the earlier conversation in which she implied that this would serve as a kind of penance were she to pursue Sam ('It rains nine months of the *year* in Seattle!' / 'I *know*! I *know*! I do *not* want to move to Seattle!'); equally, from a purely utilitarian perspective, there is Jonah to think of. However, even if such assumptions exist in the backs of our minds, the film does nothing to remind us of them in its final moments, causing the issue in fact to be left ultimately unresolved. To put this in some context: in its irresolution, this ending stands in contrast to a romantic comedy such as *How to Lose a Guy in 10 Days* (2003), in which Ben's (Matthew McConaughey) last-minute declaration of love persuades Andie (Kate Hudson) not to move to Washington but rather stay in New York with him (similar conclusions are also found in *L.A. Story* [1991], *Win a Date with Tad Hamilton!* [2004], *Garden State* [2004], etc.) – or, indeed, movies that present us with an epilogue depicting a couple's future life following their final embrace (say, *When Harry Met Sally* [1989]; I will return to such epilogues later).

That this question of who will live where goes unaddressed is indicative of the broader fact that *Sleepless* does not just treat the beginning of a romantic relationship as its ending: it treats the moment when its couple *meet* as its ending (or meet proper: they have interacted face-to-face once before when they saw each other across a busy road and exchanged 'hello's). This is unusual: while love-at-first-sight has become a staple of the genres of romance, it is seldom used as a conclusion. I have chosen to use *Sleepless* as my opening example for this chapter for precisely this reason, since it distills a paradoxical relationship that final couples have with closure. Specifically, it allows us to examine the processes whereby a film can convince us that something that is so transparently a *beginning* is also a moment of appropriate cessation.

'The resolution of a film's story,' writes Neupert, 'requires that the driving action codes (defeating the bandits, finding a job, getting married) be completed' (ibid.: 20). This teleological approach, based on the often-invoked 'hermeneutic code' (Barthes [1977]) of question-and-answer, is probably the most common way in which closure has been understood. It is echoed, for instance, in a recent article by Noël Carroll called 'Narrative Closure', in which he describes closure as the 'feeling of finality that is generated when all the questions saliently posed by the narrative are answered' (2007: 1). Many other influential accounts of narrative, from varied theoretical backgrounds, presume that closure is secured primarily through first withholding, then finally providing, knowledge or answers: David Hume argues that narrative builds 'curiosity and impatience' before ultimately revealing 'the secret' (1998: 130), Edgar Allan Poe claims that novels are 'so arranged to perplex the reader and whet his desire for elucidation' (1994: 66), while Barthes believes narrative is made up of 'units whose function it is to [. . .] constitute an enigma and lead to its solution' (1977: 17). This definition also guides many important discussions of closure in film, such as those of Neupert (see above), Chatman, who dubs 'What will happen?' the basic question of narrative (1980: 48), and Bordwell, who speaks of narrative prompting 'a series of questions which the text impels us to ask' (1985: 39), leading ultimately to the 'closure effect' (1986: 159).

If we take something like 'getting married' to be the 'driving action code' of *Sleepless* (with some justification: the romance plot proper gets underway when Jonah rings a radio station because he believes Sam 'needs a new wife'), should it follow that the ending feels in some sense 'open' because it does not show us this marriage? No. While in the real world we would certainly be immediately troubled by the question of how Annie and Sam are going to pursue their relationship, in the context of *Sleepless* it is simply not one we think to ask. In order to explain why this is, however, we must be sensitive both to factors acknowledged by what we will call the hermeneutic approach, and some that are not. I want to argue that, while potentially significant narrative questions may be left unanswered by this film, they are caused to recede into virtual insignificance via a complex interplay of factors of which we should always try to remain cognisant in our discussions of closure. First, however, it is necessary to probe a little more deeply the relationship between closure and the convention of the final couple in general.

The final couple and continuation: time laid up in store

> All tragedies are finish'd by a death,
> All comedies are ended by a marriage;
> The future states of both are left to faith,
>
> – *Don Juan* (Byron 1831: 543)

The irony that final couples require a beginning to be treated as an ending has often been noted. In *The Future of the Novel* Henry James remarked that the strategy has caused marriage to become 'an immense omission in our fiction' (1956: 39). Similarly, towards the end of *Middlemarch* Eliot wrote, 'Every limit is a beginning as well as an ending. [. . .] Marriage, which has been the bourne of so many narratives, is still a great beginning' (Eliot 2003: 571). In one sense, it might indeed seem perverse to treat as an ending something that is in fact so clearly a beginning. One explanation for why this should have become a convention is ideological in character (e.g. Boone 1987: 8), and will be taken up in Chapter 4. For our present purposes, though, we first need to ask: how appropriate an ending is a newly-formed relationship for a narrative concerning romantic desire?

One answer might be that, given social convention, the true 'resolution' of romantic (as opposed to other forms of) desire is in fact the romantic *relationship* – precisely that which remains undepicted by ending at the moment of initial achievement; the philosopher Irving Singer, for instance, argues that in order for romantic love to serve its emotional and psychological function as the culmination of a 'search for harmonizations', it must constitute 'falling in love', 'being in love' and 'staying in love' (Singer 1987: 440). While this might be true, however, to question the convention of the final couple on these grounds is to ignore the fact that this kind of happy ending does not *elide* the ensuing relationship so much as *imply* it; as Herrnstein Smith says: 'the novelist or playwright is likely to end his work at a point when either nothing could follow (as when the hero dies) or everything that could follow is predictable (as when the hero or heroine get married)' (1968: 35). Usually absolutely central to such an ending is the sense that the couple do have a future ahead of them; the matter of what *kind* of future is what sets one ending apart from another. As V. F. Perkins puts it, 'if we end, as so often, on a prospect of a marriage we cannot leave with a guarantee of bliss, but we may be encouraged or forbidden to hope' (1999: 71). Endings that encourage us to make confidently optimistic predictions for their couples are likely to suggest that this future will include precisely both being and staying in love. At its most secure, this kind of ending can create a high degree of closure, and might be described with the famous phrase 'happily ever after'. This phrase is commonly invoked to describe Hollywood's final couple happy endings, and is even referenced in the titles of a high percentage of the few pieces of film criticism whose focus is happy endings (e.g. Lang [1948], Bordwell [1982], Deleyto [1998], Chauvin [2010]). Like the term 'happy ending' itself, it also crops up not infrequently in Hollywood films themselves (usually in reference to a naïve view of romantic love; see Chapter 3). It is worth considering what this phrase might mean, and how it might help us understand the kinds of closure potentially offered by final couples.

'Happily ever after' simultaneously communicates stasis and continuation. Acting as both ellipsis and full stop, it tells us that characters' *ongoing* lives will be *unchanging*, fixed in a single state. This point has often been applied to Hollywood endings. For instance, speaking of the musical, Rick Altman calls marriage 'the comic equivalent of apocalypse,' arguing that, 'by convention [. . .], marriage is that beyond which there is no more; it arrests discourse and projects narrative into an undifferentiated "happily ever after"' (1981: 197). Similarly, Robin Wood notes that 'films centred on the "romantic couple" traditionally *end* in marriage but are conspicuously silent about what happens next' (1998: 80). To an extent such arguments are valid: while a final couple implies 'what happens next', it is true that the 'next' will also usually be largely absent. To acknowledge this is to recognise that the concept to which 'happily ever after' refers has an inherently ambiguous relationship with closure – simultaneously constituting closure's most supposedly clichéd form *and* potentially challenging it through intimations of beginning. How is it, then, that such an ending could act as a reliable agent of closure?

Actually *showing* a 'happily ever after' is not something that has often been attempted in Hollywood cinema. It might be instructive, then, to briefly compare the ending of *Sleepless* with that of a film that *has* attempted something like this: Buster Keaton's *College* (1923). At the end of this film we see a couple being married, then, in a rapid series of shots, are shown images of the two growing old together until they eventually occupy neighbouring graves. Gilberto Perez has addressed this ending by replying to those critics who suggest that the epilogue sours the film's conclusion (e.g. Kerr 1975: 242):

> We'd have expected the story to end with Buster's getting the girl, but the epilogue merely shows that he gets to keep her: surely not the undoing but the exact fulfillment of his wishes. If the epilogue brings about a reversal of the happy ending, it does so by way of being a logical continuation of it, indeed a visual equivalent of those famous romantic last words: and they lived happily ever after. (1998: 93–4)

Probably unsurprisingly, *College*'s strategy did not become the norm for other films wanting to convey similar futures. One reason for this is surely that the phrase 'they lived happily ever after' would read rather differently if it became instead 'they lived happily until they died', which is essentially what *College*'s ending cannot help but convey. The gravestones mean, firstly, that the film's mood is unavoidably darkened by death in its final moments (however sweet the reassurance of a lifelong relationship may be). More importantly, however, they also close down the possibility of the ending conveying any sense what-soever of *continuation*.

As suggested in Chapter 1, the possibility of characters' lives extending beyond the film's final frames seems key to happy endings. It is worth pointing out in this respect that the words 'happily ever after' serve to elide the eventual death that is also their logical implication, putting the emphasis instead on the preceding happy years of living with no end in sight. By doing so, they manage to imply a sense of eternity, of *un*ending ('*for*ever'), that would be made impos-sible by any mention of that unequivocal end-point, death. I would argue that this sense of unending is important for the creation of most happy endings and that its lack at a conclusion like *College*'s is one of the main reasons Keaton's strategy might feel significantly unsatisfying. By this logic, we might say that if *College*'s ending is disconcerting then this is not so much because its end-point is *death*, but rather because death represents such an emphatic *end-point*.

We are used to hearing descriptions of closure that treat it as if it acted to close down all that preceded it and close off everything that might follow – understandable, in a sense, since the one incontrovertible thing we can say about endings is that they are the last moments of any work. There is, however, a danger that this emphasis can lead us to overvalue in every instance what is being finished at the expense of what is suggested as being *still to come*. It seems likely that this point is even more pertinent for endings desiring to be seen as 'happy' than for those that are 'unhappy'. This is something suggested even by the founding critical distinctions between comedy and tragedy, which, in their most paradigmatic form, end in marriage and death, respectively. It is no coincidence that marriage is an event explicitly marking a beginning, or in Frye's terms 'rebirth' (1969: 1), whereas death is nothing if not final, denying any chance of continuation – explicitly promising *nothing* for those who succumb to it. As Kracauer puts it, 'contrary to tragic death, the happy ending [suggests] that life will continue' (1960: 268). Promises of continuation mean narrative possibilities, and possibilities are likely to be beneficial if the future implied at a fiction's close seems in any sense positive. This is perhaps simply because, as Aristotle argued, 'all human happiness [. . .] takes the form of action; the end for which we live is a certain kind of *activity*, not a quality' (Aristotle 1962: 21; emphasis added).

As we have seen, to an even greater degree than most final couple happy endings, *Sleepless* ends by promising a great deal of activity for its lovers' futures. While virtually all romantic comedies end poised on the threshold of a new or resumed relationship, *Sleepless* goes further by remaining poised at a moment alive with anticipation for Sam and Annie *getting to know* one another. In this sense we might say that it is a powerfully 'front-loaded' ending, while *College*'s is emphatically 'back-loaded' – leaving open no possibilities for anything to follow. In this instance, the difference between these approaches seems to be the difference between a hopeful conclusion and an oddly troubling one. This is why to describe the kind of closure offered by a final couple as 'that beyond which there is no more', as Altman does, is to ignore precisely what allows it to function as a 'happy' ending: its sense of promise – what Larkin called, in a melancholy invocation of a past promise of young love, 'that certainty of time laid up in store' (Larkin 1980: 67).

When compared with an ending that covers the entire future lives and eventual deaths of its two protagonists, *Sleepless*' conclusion of Annie and Sam walking into a lift with no definite plans for the future might seem positively 'open'. Yet, in practice, *Sleepless*' ending seems nothing of the kind. I will now attempt to explain how this most putatively unresolved of final couple happy endings is able to make us feel that it is in fact far from 'open' and, on the contrary, that it has reached an especially satisfying moment of appropriate cessation.

The rhetoric of an ending

Michael Walker (2008) uses the phrase 'the rhetoric of an ending' to describe elements of imagery and style that recur with enough frequency at the ends of films (e.g. sunsets, helicopter shots, etc.) that their appearance can be used to help create a sense that the film is drawing to a close. Though not elaborated upon by Walker, other examples might include 'bracketing' – a film's end echoing its opening (e.g. *Grand Hotel* [1932], *Winchester 73* [1950], *Mr. & Mrs. Smith* [2005]); characters or modes of transportation departing from the camera (e.g. *Modern Times* [1936], *An American in Paris* [1953], *Jerry Maguire* [1996]); the camera receding from characters (e.g. *Since You Went Away* [1944], *The Father of the Bride* [1950], *Working Girl* [1988]); lovers kissing (e.g. *The Shop Around the Corner* [1940], *Sabrina* [1954], *Hannah and Her Sisters* [1986]); images of things closing – a door, a book, curtains (e.g. *Adam's Rib* [1949], *All I Desire* [1953], *Sliding Doors* [1998]), and so on.

Just as viewers must come to learn the function of any aspect of cinematic language through repeated exposure, so are they taught to associate endings with particular aesthetic signifiers of finality. This is achieved partly simply by the repetition itself – the learned knowledge that such motifs tend to be present at endings. It can also relate to the motifs' particular characteristics.

For instance, the image of a closing book, found particularly frequently at the end of films influenced by fairy tales (e.g. *Snow White and the Seven Dwarfs* [1937], *Sleeping Beauty* [1959], *Shrek* [2001]), of course cannot help but create an expectation of finality due to our real-life familiarity of what we do with books upon finishing them. Similarly for the 'bracketing' afforded by reprising settings, imagery, shots, or sounds from the film's opening – which, suggests Neupert, 'allows a fiction film to maintain a cyclical unity for its narrative' by '[proving] that the narrator knew where the story was heading all along' (ibid.: 22). For any appropriately conversant viewer, the appearance of a sunset, or a crane shot, or characters moving towards the horizon, is likely to encourage an intertextually-learned sense that this ending *feels like* an ending – an appropriate cessation – and thus feels 'closed'. To the extent that we may describe this as a process of persuading a viewer to accept an ending *as* an ending (just as segueing from a close-up of a character's face into a dissolve encourages us to take a flashback as a flashback), we may also describe it as constituting a cinematic rhetoric of the ending.

Such rhetorical stylistic devices can be hugely important to the creation of closure in any art form. As Herrnstein Smith notes, 'the experience of closure is the complex product of both formal and thematic elements,' and it is therefore 'difficult to examine the effects of either independently of the effects of the other' (1968: 40). *Sleepless'* conclusion makes use of the rhetoric of an ending in abundance. This begins in earnest when Jonah, Sam and Annie are in the lift: as the couple look at each other, Jonah turns towards the camera and smiles just as the lift doors shut. The self-conscious aspect of this action I will return to in the following chapter, but what the look to camera does first and foremost is to reinforce the sense of this moment's finality. Since it is in part Jonah who has brought about this meeting (by travelling alone to New York to meet Annie, thus forcing Sam to pursue him), it feels almost akin to a theatrical bow. As well as this, the doors closing are a powerful visual symbol of an end-point, sealing the characters into the film, their fictional lives now complete; they give the impression, to continue the theatrical analogy, of a final curtain closing on the completed drama. After this shot, however, the rhetoric of an ending is increased several degrees further.

As suggested, it is common in general for films' final shots to create distance between the audience and the fictional world, but *Sleepless* takes what Perkins calls the 'designedly recessional' nature of this convention to new heights (1993: 135). On the closed doors of the lift we see an outline of the Empire State Building; this outline then becomes reality as the screen dissolves to what initially seems to be a helicopter shot of the real building. We circle around the building before pulling up, craning back further and further, faster and faster, until we finally reach a version of the cartoon-like map of North America first encountered in the opening credit sequence (and which has since been used to illustrate the characters' travels, via dotted lines, across the country), now made up of hundreds of twinkling lights. There is more to come, however, when several fireworks shoot up to form the stars in the sky; finally, our view moves upwards again to focus on the stars, the song that is playing (sung by Jimmy Durante, who also sang over the opening credits – a further instance of 'bracketing') ends, and we fade out. This sequence is capable of creating an overpowering sense of closure, in part by so wholeheartedly employing a host of conventionally closural rhetorical devices one after another. If there is any chance of feeling that questions regarding what will follow for the couple have been left unanswered, these devices go a long way towards closing the film on the level of form.

In one sense, final couples can themselves be considered part of the rheto- ric of an ending: since they are found so commonly at the end of films their mere presence can aid closure by making one ending resemble other endings. Yet, as I have said, one final couple can be very unlike, as well as more or less 'closed' than, another. I will now expand on this by looking at a number of other important strategies that *Sleepless* uses to temper openness and embrace closure, before contrasting them with other ways of presenting final couples to different effects.

Themes: distance, destiny, and transcendence

Important here are a number of *Sleepless*' themes. The geographical distance between the couple has been repeatedly stressed throughout the film: it is set up in the opening credits via points on the map, referenced multiple times in dialogue ('There's like *twenty-six* states between here and there!'), and even represented in the film's famous poster, which sees Hanks and Ryan occupy- ing different time zones. However, seeing a cartoon-like US from space again in the final moments might remind us that overcoming distance in *this* fictional world can be as easy as dots moving, with regularity and efficiency, over a brightly-coloured map. This idea was first introduced during the opening credits when two stars lit up over the respective corners of the US where Sam and Annie live (accompanied by Hanks' and Ryan's names), and we have encountered it again in the dots indicating their flights back and forth across the States. The problem of bringing these two 'dots' together across such a great distance is thus highlighted only for it to be treated as nothing in the world of the film. Similarly, this distance has only been so emphasised in order to establish how difficult it will be for them to *meet* – a fact referred to in the film's last line: 'Sam, it's nice to meet you.' What that distance might mean in the *event* of this meeting has seldom been touched upon. Partly because such a great distance has had to be overcome in order for it to take place, and partly because its excessive deferral has made its eventual achievement all the more satisfying (more on this shortly), this meeting has thus been constructed very much as the end of this story. What happens afterwards might thus be said to become, in an important sense, moot.

This brings us to the issue of 'destiny' – a term used repeatedly by characters to describe the concept that people can fall in love because, as Annie puts it, 'in some mystical, cosmic way it was fated'. Seeing the map again at the end reinforces this suggestion that 'destiny' has had some part to play in bringing these lovers together, and thus acts to increase our certainty that the couple will likely overcome whatever difficulties they face in the future. Apart from anything, the extreme long shot from space seems to imply a benign force – be it destiny or a director – watching them from above and ensuring their happiness. Needless to say, the suggestion that the couple have 'destiny' on their side can only help banish any questions, such as who will live where, from our minds.

Furthermore, the invocation of 'destiny' is also only one part of a broader strategy whereby Sam and Annie's love is suggested to be (as in many of the romantic melodramas from Chapter 1) somehow transcendent. While fate and destiny have been repeatedly used to describe the love Annie is seeking, it is merely one facet of a more general conception of romantic love as something 'magic', 'all *trumpets* and *fireworks*'. It is also interesting to note that, while Annie's relationship with her fiancé Walter is almost entirely composed of planning the mundane details of their forthcoming wedding, the matter of being married (or, indeed, becoming a step-mother) is never mentioned in relation to Sam. One thing that this does is contribute to the sense that the 'magic' love associated with the Sam/Annie relationship is above the practicalities of wedlock and motherhood, thus further eschewing the question of what will happen after their meeting. A love so transcendent, the film implies, need not concern itself with such matters. Again, we clearly need to note both the helpful conventionality of precepts of the 'romantic love complex' here – wherein love's 'transcendence [. . .] promises triumph, a conquest of mundane prescriptions and compromises' (Giddens 1993: 45) – and the fact that rhetorically reaffirming the centrality and value of such a view of love encourages us to feel that the couple's future happiness is nothing less than ensured.

The ending's intimations of destiny and transcendence established, they now demand to be related to the extraordinary degree of emphasis that has been placed on Annie and Sam's meeting as a culmination not only of this particular narrative, but also of this *kind* of narrative.

The meeting as an ending: genre

In *The End* Neupert explains that he chose to use the film *The Quiet Man* (1952) as his only extended example of a Closed Text partly because this movie does not fit neatly into an established Hollywood genre, and thus allows his

analysis to 'side-step the risk of being limited to the conventions of one particular genre' (ibid.: 34). I would argue, however, that taking account of genre
should not be considered a 'risk', but should rather be seen as central to a full
understanding of any Hollywood film, and therefore its ending. As Britton
says, 'popular American movies presuppose an enormously sophisticated intimacy with the conventions of genre – an intense awareness of the logic of *this*
dramatic world as distinct from *that* one' (2003: 142). In the case of *Sleepless*,
the fact that the mere meeting of Annie and Sam has been the ultimate aim
of the film – and that what follows this meeting has been elided – demands to
be placed in the context of the conventions of closure in the genre to which
Sleepless belongs: romantic comedy.

In his book *Writing the Romantic Comedy*, Billy Mernit suggests that
'romantic comedy heroes and heroines are like questions waiting to be
answered – because they are starring in stories in which love is the ultimate
path to fulfilment' (2000: 17). Without forgetting that the degree to which this
statement is true will necessarily vary from film to film, it is true enough to
say that a romantic union, however enthusiastically or tentatively presented,
constitutes the vast majority of endings in this genre (notwithstanding films
such as *Roman Holiday* [1953], *Annie Hall* [1977], or *My Best Friend's Wedding*
[1997]). Our knowledge of this fact obviously creates certain assumptions
that we cannot help but bring to bear on an ending like *Sleepless*. Because a
viewer of *Sleepless* is likely to have seen so many romantic comedies end at the
moment of their protagonists' romantic union, s/he knows instinctively that
for *Sleepless* to do the same is a sign not of a significant elision of what follows,
but rather simply of the fact that it is operating according to generic convention. This is hugely important for our sense of how 'closed' this ending is,
since it allows us (or at least those of us who have seen our share of romantic
comedies) to feel that the film need not continue past the meeting in order to
be understood as complete. Other genres have comparable generic conventions that may act to in some sense 'close' what might otherwise appear 'open',
such as the cowboy riding off to an unspecified future in the Western, or the
final 'it's-still-out-there' scare in the horror film. Both these kinds of ending
might appear unresolved in other contexts, but their familiarity as closural
tropes ensures that they are felt to be less so in the genres which gave rise to
them; as Pinedo says of the slasher film: 'the genre's refusal of narrative closure
becomes through repetition [. . .] eventually anticipated' (1997: 66).

In the case of *Sleepless*, given learned generic expectations, it could in fact
seem somewhat superfluous for the film to include an epilogue that showed,
for example, Sam and Annie's marriage or future home life. Of course, a
romantic comedy can continue some way past the final union if it wishes (many
do, as I will address later). What is important, though, is that the expectations
experienced viewers bring to the genre ensure that *not* doing so is unlikely to

endanger their sense of an ending being adequately concluded. In subsequent chapters I will expand on what ending in this way might mean for a film's relationship to both 'unrealism' and ideology. For our present purposes, it is enough to point out that concluding at the moment when a romantic couple begin or resume their relationship is a staple technique of closure in the romantic comedy genre, and can thus be felt to be, in the context of *Sleepless*, a point of appropriate cessation.

Yet we must recognise that the feeling of appropriate cessation made possible by assumptions about genre is not quite like that accounted for by the hermeneutic approaches mentioned earlier. While *Sleepless*' narrative does certainly resolve its courtship plot to a significant degree (though not, as I have said, to the extent that it *could*), the film is not 'closed' only by 'all the questions saliently posed by the narrative [being] answered' (Carroll 2007: 1), but also by intertextually-learned assumptions about romantic comedies more generally. To acknowledge this is to admit that it is sometimes necessary to supplement – or even *supplant* – our hermeneutic understanding of closure with an awareness of the closural role played by genre.

Foregone conclusions

In the television show *Undeclared* (2001–2002), Roy (Seth Rogen) is introducing his friend Lloyd (Charlie Hunnam) to his favourite film, *You've Got Mail* (1998). Becoming increasingly bored, Lloyd makes to leave the room, prompting the following exchange:

Roy: Do you want me to pause it?
Lloyd: That's okay – I'll come back in a while.
Roy: But you're gonna miss what happens.
Lloyd: I *know* what happens, Roy.
Roy: *(Sarcastically)* Oh, you *know* what happens, Lloyd?
Lloyd: They meet in real life; she finds out he owns the book chain ruining her mom-and-pop operation; they continue their affair online, realise who each other are, and kiss right before the closing credits as some overused Louis Armstrong song plays in the background.

Lloyd is, of course, correct. In Chapter 1 we noted the great potential for complexity within the broad convention of the final couple in numerous romantic melodramas, and it is true that the precise handling and meaning of individual final couples need be no more monolithic or clichéd in romantic comedy (as we will see throughout this book). However, it is also important to note that the mere *presence* of a final couple – however it is precisely handled – is an undeniable fact of the vast majority of romantic comedies. Audiences' likely knowledge of and presumption of this fact – based on the convention's (rather too monolithic, but nonetheless influential) reputation – has significant ramifications for closure in the genre.

It is often pointed out that 'we know, with some certainty' (King 2002a: 53) that the final couple happy ending of particular kinds of romance narratives are 'foregone conclusions' (Glitre 2006: 16); as Neupert puts it, 'it does not take a PhD in film studies [. . .] to guess that Lucy Warriner in *The Awful Truth* will end up back with her nearly ex-husband Jerry rather than with Dan Leeson' (ibid.: 12). Equally, such 'near certainty of outcome' (King 2002a: 53) is commonly suggested to govern the ways in which we understand entire genres like romantic comedy, of which it is true to say that 'part of the joy for the audience is knowing that no matter the contrivances of the plot, the couple will end up together at the end' (Stillwell 2008: 27). Making this point succinctly, Kathrina Glitre opens her book *States of the Union: Romantic Comedy, 1930–1965* as follows:

> Everyone knows how Hollywood romantic comedies end: with a kiss. It is extremely rare for a romantic comedy to end without the union of a couple; it is equally rare for the union to involve people other than the two lead actors. In other words, we usually know how the plot will be resolved just by looking at the opening credits. (ibid.: 1)

Although I referred earlier to 'Will Annie and Sam meet?' as a key narrative question of *Sleepless* (and one with the potential for a definite yes-or-no answer), it is crucial to acknowledge that we absolutely assume to know the answer in advance. What does this foreknowledge of foregone conclusions mean for a hermeneutic conception of closure?

In his aforementioned piece, Noël Carroll uses the example of a romantic comedy to support his claim that 'narrative closure is the result of a narrative structure's answering of all the pressing questions it has stirred in the audience' (ibid.: 15):

> For example, arouse in the audience for a romantic comedy the desire to know 'Whether the young woman will marry the boy next door, or whether she will run off with the city slicker?' and then withhold the answer until the last reel. One may confirm the effectiveness of this technique – as well as the hypothesis that the audience is glued to the story by means of its curiosity – by shutting the projector down before that final reel unfolds. The viewers will jump up – as if from a trance – and demand to know who the young woman finally married. For, that was the question that had been organizing their viewing. (ibid.: 4)

A hypothetical (and apparently very conventional) romantic comedy seems in fact a quite disastrous example for Carroll to use in support of 'the hypothesis that the audience is glued to their story by means of its curiosity'. While these imaginary spectators might well be indignant were their film to be unceremoniously interrupted, it is difficult to believe that they would 'demand to know who the young woman finally married'. For any audience member conversant with romantic comedy convention, this is simply not a 'question' of whose 'answer' one could be unsure; as such, it would seem ill-equipped to the task of 'organising' one's viewing. A similar point is made by Deborah Knight when replying to another article by Carroll (1994) in which he addresses the ending of *Sleepless* itself. Responding to Carroll's claim that a question is raised as to whether Sam and Annie will finally meet on the top of the Empire State Building, Knight counters that 'the very framing of the question misrepresents the range of options available. [. . .] The implication that there is sufficient likelihood that they will *not* meet here is not a reasonable one' (1997: 355). This, as Knight says, is because when viewing such a romantic comedy 'the cognitive activities of spectators – in particular, their expectations – are not primarily driven by the particular story but by expectations about genre and plot as they are realized in the particular text' (ibid.: 344). Thus, as Glitre puts it, in romantic comedy the happy ending is 'determined by generic convention,' meaning that 'the very predictability of the ending undermines [. . .] cause-and-effect teleology' (ibid.: 16).

Indeed, romantic comedy may be the Hollywood genre in which a model of closure driven by 'curiosity' is most wholly undermined. H. Porter Abbott has adapted Barthes' definitions of the 'hermeneutic' and 'proairetic' codes (1970) to distinguish between narrative *questions* and narrative *expectations* in the detective story: 'at the level of expectations, we recognize that we are heading into the investigation of a crime and we expect that it will end with a revelation of the murderer. But at the level of questions, we want to know who did it' (2008: 61); learning this, she says, creates closure. In the romantic comedy, however, as Glitre points out, not only are our expectations for *how* the narrative will end often unambiguous from the outset (it will conclude 'with a kiss'), but questions of *who* will be involved in this ending are also usually irrelevant (it will be 'the two lead actors'). We can be so sure that Sam and Annie must form the final couple towards which *Sleepless'* narrative is undoubtedly leading in part because they are played by Hanks and Ryan (whereas Annie's fiancé is played by Bill Pullman), just as in Neupert's example above we can be sure that Lucy (Irene Dunne) will end up with Jerry rather than Dan because Jerry is played by Cary Grant and Dan is played by Ralph Bellamy. Indeed, the 'answer' as to who will be united in a romantic comedy can usually be confirmed even *before* the film begins if exposed to the film's poster/video/DVD cover, which, as Ewan Kirkland notes, 'frequently follow a visual template [of] one man, one woman, and, it would appear, one inevitable outcome' (2007: 1).

It should be said that expectations based upon star power are clearly histori- cally contextual and reliant on a spectator's ability to judge who in fact *is* the most prominent star. For instance, a modern viewer of *Sylvia Scarlett* (1935) might predict that Sylvia (Katharine Hepburn) will form a final couple with Jimmy, played by Cary Grant, rather than Michael, who is played by the now far less famous Brian Aherne. In fact, however, the opposite turns out to be the case, since in 1935 Grant was not the huge star he would soon become. Thus, a reliable way for a romantic comedy to make us more uncertain about its outcome is to exploit such preconceptions by having actors of comparable stature compete for the affections of a lead, as in *The Philadelphia Story* (1940), in which (for a time) both Dexter (Cary Grant, by this point near the height of his stardom) and Mike (James Stewart) seem equally capable of winning Tracy (Katharine Hepburn). This convention regarding star pairings also therefore plays a key role in creating certainty about how a romantic comedy such as *Sleepless* will end.

Despite earlier acknowledging the confidence with which we anticipate the final couple of *The Awful Truth*, Neupert writes in *The End* that 'a classi- cal film strives to make the obligatory reunion of the couple feel so correctly motivated [. . .] that the fact the audience was already aware of the ending [. . .] before entering the theatre may be forgotten or repressed' (ibid.: 73). This claim, however, does not seem equal to the task of explaining the interpretive processes required by a genre such as romantic comedy. It cannot explain, for instance, the practices of romance fans such as those interviewed by Janice Radway in *Reading the Romance*, who explain they will not embark on reading a romantic novel unless they can be *sure* it will have a final couple happy ending – to the extent that a number of readers admit to regularly checking a book's final pages *first* in order to be absolutely certain of it (1991: 200). The decision to read a book only if one *is* sure of the ending proves that satisfied hermeneutic desire need not necessarily form any part of the pleasures offered by certain kinds of romantic narrative. Though actually skipping to the end of a film is more difficult, I would suggest that the broad conventions governing most mainstream romantic comedy endings are predictable enough to make viewing films with comparable assurances as to the outcome an ever-present probability, if not a virtual certainty.

It is important to stress that being certain of an ending does *not* mean that we experience no sense of closure when it arrives, nor does it negate the fact that these kinds of narratives are still built, internally, upon the storytelling principle of question-and-answer. Such a film *not* answering the questions it raised would certainly upset closure – though precisely because this would mean that it did not conform to our very specific expectations about this *kind* of narrative. This form of closure is thus assuredly of a different sort than can be explained by classical models of narrative. In the case of a film like *Sleepless*, engagement in the narrative cannot be organised by a desire for Carroll's 'answers', Poe's 'elucidation', Hume's revelation of 'the secret', Barthes' solving of an 'enigma', or Chatman's 'What will happen?'

To explain the kind of closure afforded by such a film, then, we perhaps need to look to a model such as Patrick Keating's, which explains certain kinds of generic endings in terms of 'anticipatory emotions [. . .] based on certainty' (2006: 8):

> For instance, suppose I have a daughter in school and I have been told ahead of time that she is going to win an award at tonight's award ceremony. My emotion is one of 'eager anticipation' – I await the ceremony with delight precisely because I am 100 percent certain that she will win. [. . .] There is no reason why narrative cannot play on these kinds of anticipatory emotions. [. . .] When we feel certain that the two lovers will kiss at the end of the film we can eagerly anticipate the scene. This anticipation will intensify our feelings of joy when the culminating scene of the kiss finally occurs. (ibid.: 8)

Questions can still be asked, answers still given, and satisfaction still experienced, even when we are '100 percent certain' of where a narrative is ultimately leading. Yet if closure is experienced in such cases, it is predicated not primarily on the hermeneutic code, but on an emotional satisfaction that results from receiving an outcome that we consider to have been promised us. This closure need not by any means be weaker than that provided by, say, a detective story – it will merely be *different*. Indeed, far from undermining closure, being given a final couple happy ending which we have been expecting since the film's opening credits may in fact tend only to heighten our sense of appropriate cessation when it arrives, since an ending is never likely to feel more like an ending than when it appears to be the *only one* available to its narrative.

Yet, in spite of the common certainty about how generic narratives may end, not every final couple happy ending is figured as being quite as inevitable as is *Sleepless'*. Explaining why this film's ending feels as much like an ending as it does requires that we move our attention away from intertextual expectations, and back to a consideration of the internal qualities of *Sleepless* itself, in particular the expectations created by its approach to point of view.

Point of view and dual-focus narrative

Sleepless begins with Sam and Jonah attending the funeral of Sam's previous wife, Maggie (Carie Lowell), in Chicago. Three short scenes then establish

Sam's grief and his decision to move to Seattle in an effort to escape his wife's memory: he acts distractedly while his sister tries to give him tips on domestic life alone; a scene with a work colleague ends with Sam concluding that he needs 'a real change – a new city'; finally, he and Jonah are at the airport, he expressing doubt that he will find another love like that he had with his wife ('It just doesn't happen twice'). Following the credit sequence, an intertitle informs us that we have jumped forward eighteen months, and we are now introduced to Annie in Baltimore as she prepares for a trip to her parents' home with Walter, her new fiancé.

Immediately, then, *Sleepless* establishes that its narrative will follow these two characters, and as the film progresses we can soon surmise that it is also dedicated to following *only* them. Although they are separated by thousands of miles geographically, the film has nevertheless connected them for us, therefore creating expectations that their lives will come to be linked. This is a question of point of view, a concept that I take to refer to 'the ways in which a form of narration can systematically structure an audience's overall epistemic access to narrative' (Wilson 1986: 3). This is a famously broad and complex aspect of narrative, but one of its elementary functions is to structure our visual access to the fictional world in such a way that we build up a sense of what we can reasonably expect to be shown of that world – in part, in other words, a process that establishes a set of particular expectations concerning *who* and *what* a film is 'about'. By following only its central couple (introducing us to Sam before the credits, Annie immediately after), *Sleepless'* point of view conveys, very early on, that this is a narrative about Sam *and* Annie. Melding matters of point of point of view with considerations of genre, the film also sets up that its subject will be romantic relationships: Sam, we learn, has lost his wife, and Annie, we learn, is about to acquire a new husband. Such processes of point of view are key to creating expectations about how, and when, any film will end.

In the case of *Sleepless*, a main function of point of view is to create strong expectations that the two 'dots' in the opening credits will ultimately be brought together. Having been established as our protagonists in the first few minutes, the rest of *Sleepless* proceeds to provide us with roughly equal access to both Sam and Annie, as well as continually paralleling their lives in the process. For instance: after seeing Annie and Walter celebrating New Year's Eve together we cut to Sam and Jonah doing the same; we move from Sam and Jonah brushing their teeth in preparation for bed to Annie and Walter preparing Walter's night-time allergy medicines; we see Annie discussing relationships with her brother Dennis (David Hyde Pierce) then cut to Sam discussing relationships with his friend Jay (Rob Reiner); while 'Bye Bye Blackbird' plays on the soundtrack we cut between images of Sam and Annie both wandering outside alone and sitting on a bench next to bodies of water, and so on. While more and more parallels are taking place, the likelihood of

Sam and Annie meeting is also increasing: Annie first writes Sam a letter, then travels to Seattle to spy on him, before they finally both end up in New York on Valentine's day. In this way *Sleepless* enacts in a particularly stark fashion an approach to point of view that Rick Altman (1987) defined as dual-focus narrative, originally in relation to the Hollywood musical. This model offers a useful framework for understanding how the endings of many romantic fictions, and in particular romantic comedies, are *prepared for* by their narratives.[1]

Offering dual-focus as an alternative to the hermeneutic classical narrative schema proffered by theorists such as Carroll and Neupert, Altman argues that musicals usually structure their romance narratives not according to cause-and-effect, but through the continual paralleling of one scene featuring a male lead against one featuring a female lead, repeatedly using 'one character's actions to establish the context of another character's parallel actions' (1987: 22). Thus, he explains, 'each segment must be understood not in terms of the segments to which it is causally related, but by comparison to the segment which it parallels' (ibid.: 20). According to Altman, dual-focus narrative is ended by the moment when 'the alternating following-pattern [. . .] is eventually suspended by reduction of the text's two constitutive foci to one' (2008: 84). This reduction is effected through 'a merger of the two sides' (ibid.: 84); in other words, usually, via a final couple happy ending.

We might say that the most fundamental epistemic effect of dual-focus on romantic narrative is simply that it grants the opportunity for a point of view that is split pointedly, and more or less equally, between two members of a couple.[2] When combined with generic expectations, this in turn means that, because our perception of the world's time and space is structured around this pair, we also assume that they must eventually come to share the *same* time and space. Even if the couple are separated by a great distance, as they are in *Sleepless* (and in, say, *Fools Rush In* [1997], which begins with one character in New York and the other in Las Vegas), or given pointedly contrasting lifestyles (as in *Two Weeks Notice* [2002], which uses an opening montage to tell us that one half of the pair is an anti-corporate activist, the other the head of a corporation), the effect of dual-focus is to suggest that the narrative is actively and visibly working towards their final union. The closural significance of this structure thus lies in its potential to create a sense of inexorable direction and momentum that acts to heighten anticipation for an ultimate, expected 'merger of the two sides' (ibid.: 84).

Most dual-focus narratives (including Altman's case studies) in fact only *begin* with a split point of view before having their couple meet relatively early in the film (e.g. *It Happened One Night* [1934], *That Touch of Mink* [1962], *Last Chance Harvey* [2008]). *Sleepless*, however, continues its parallel plotting throughout the entire narrative by delaying its couple's meeting until the very end (an unusual strategy, though *Next Stop Wonderland* [1998] provides another example). This means that the 'anticipatory emotions [. . .] based on certainty' (Keating 2006: 8) created by not just genre, but also the film's point of view and parallelism, are permitted to increase until the last minute, thus heightening the sense of satisfaction and appropriate cessation when the final couple ending ultimately arrives. A dual-focus, then, can serve as another elegant and effective solution to the perennial problem faced by romance narrative: how to persuade us that a final couple constitutes an appropriate end-point.

*

I have so far introduced a number of issues that are too seldom addressed in relation to narrative closure (genre, continuation, point of view, etc.) as well as a number of more well-established closural devices (style, the hermeneutic code, etc.). My analysis of *Sleepless* has demonstrated that these devices may be employed in a manner that allows an extremely strong sense of closure to be created even in the case of this final couple, which has the *potential* to appear rather 'open'. I will now argue that using such devices in different ways can create final couple happy endings that feel significantly less 'closed' – or, at least, 'closed' in significantly different ways.

THE FINAL COUPLE IN A BROADER CONTEXT: *THE BEST YEARS OF OUR LIVES*

I have suggested that promises of continuation are key to the creation of happy endings. This, however, is a matter of degree. While a film such as *Sleepless* concludes at a moment alive with a great deal of promise, this is promise of a particular kind. Because so much emphasis has been placed on their meeting as a culmination, although Sam and Annie are implied to have a future, this future may as well be, as Altman puts it, relatively 'undifferentiated'. This is because all the strategies I have been discussing have been dedicated to making us view this film's final couple *as an ending*. By comparison, the happy ending of *The Best Years of Our Lives* (henceforth *Best Years*) uses a number of strategies to create a sense that it is *not* in fact an 'ending', but rather perhaps a beginning, or simply an ongoing middle.

Following three servicemen as they re-enter American society after WWII, *Best Years* is usually discussed in scholarship either as a 'prestige' film (e.g. Cagle [2007]) or a 'social problem' film about veterans and disability (e.g. Gerber [2000]) (or else in connection with Bazin's famous 1948 essay on Wyler's directorial style [Bazin [1997]]). However, while it does dramatise an explicit social theme, the film also makes plain early on that a central stake for its ex-servicemen's reintegration will be their romantic relationships. For instance, Homer (Harold Russell), who lost his hands in combat and has had them replaced with metal hooks, makes clear on the plane home that his main worry is how his childhood sweetheart Wilma (Cathy O'Donnell) will cope with his disability ('Well, you see: I got a girl . . .'); the ex soda-jerk Fred's (Dana Andrews) employment troubles would be nowhere near so problematic were it not for the dissatisfaction they cause his wife, Marie (Virginia Mayo), which in turn contributes to his growing attraction towards the very-different Peggy (Teresa Wright); the anxieties Peggy's father, Al (Fredric March), feels towards 'rehabilitation' are expressed repeatedly in terms of his relationship with his wife Milly (Myrna Loy) and their children. Accordingly, the end of this film too is dominated by matters pertaining to these relationships.

The film concludes during the wedding celebrations of Homer and Wilma. Referring to these characters, David A. Gerber writes that *Best Years* 'culminates in a conventional happy ending, their marriage' (2000: 71). I wish to argue, firstly, that this marriage is not in fact a greatly important element of the happy ending in terms of 'conventional' closure; and, secondly, that *Best Years* offers an excellent demonstration of what a broad church a 'conventional' final couple happy ending can in practice be. Explaining these points involves considering the ending both in hermeneutic terms and in terms of point of view – both of which ultimately involve appreciating the significance of the fact that (unlike *Sleepless*) this is a multi-protagonist film, that is: a film featuring 'a multiplicity of characters of similar narrative relevance' (Azcona 2010b: 2).

Hermeneutic closure

The reason I say that Homer and Wilma's wedding is relatively unimportant to the happy ending in hermeneutic terms is because the questions relating to this romantic plotline have already been answered in a scene that occurred fifteen minutes previously. In this earlier scene Homer invites Wilma to his bedroom to witness the removal of his hooks – a display for her benefit of the level of his dependency, which lies at the root of his anxieties about marriage. Wilma rises to the occasion, helping Homer by buttoning up his pyjamas and straightening his collar – a dress rehearsal for the marriage bed to come. Once this scene has taken place there can remain no reasonable doubt in our minds that the couple will be married, since it overcomes the two possible barriers to the romance: that Wilma might not be able fully to accept Homer's disability, and that Homer's insecurity may sabotage the relationship. This scene has thus made the final wedding itself as hermeneutically unnecessary as the implied-but-unseen future that lies beyond *Sleepless*' final couple. (Equally, the earlier scene will also likely have served as the culmination of any potential 'anticipatory emotions [. . .] based on certainty' the film may have raised [Keating 2006:

8].) That is to say: it is not the wedding's vows of 'for richer, for poorer' that conclude this plotline, but the earlier scene's declarations of love (Wilma's 'I'm never going to leave you', Homer's 'I love you, Wilma. I always have and I always will.'); similarly, it is not the kiss that the couple share following the reverend's pronouncement of man and wife that provides us with closure, but their embrace in the bedroom scene. In this sense, the wedding appears to be less this couple's end-point (as Sam and Annie's meeting in *Sleepless* is made to seem) than an early stage in an already-established, ongoing relationship.

The specific placement of the wedding within the film's structure also guarantees its difference from that category of romance endings that hastily attach a wedding to a concluded courtship narrative. The end of *Notting Hill* (1999), for instance, brings its couple together, then immediately uses a montage to show us, firstly, their wedding, and next the pair some time later, when Anna (Julia Roberts) is revealed to be pregnant and William (Hugh Grant) is sitting by her side. Many other films use variations on this convention – that is: offering final secure images of the couple's continued happiness in an epilogue (e.g. *Mannequin* [1987], *Serving Sara* [2002], *Dan in Real Life* [2007]). As epilogues, such final images usually function broadly as 'a brief celebration of the stable state achieved by the main characters' (Bordwell 1986: 159). Thus, since they immediately follow the achievement of a final couple, they act as extensions of these conclusions – offering images of continuation, yes, but also shoring up the sense of closure already created (more on this in Chapter 3). The wedding in *Best Years*, by contrast, is separated from the 'true' resolution of Homer and Wilma's plotline by fifteen minutes, and several scenes. The world of *Best Years* thus continues past a moment of romantic closure that could, under other circumstances, have been offered as the film's conclusion, allowing the wedding to exist in some sense *beyond* the completed romance plotline rather than merely constituting an epilogue to it.

Homer and Wilma's marriage, then, is not relied upon significantly to bring closure to the film, since *their* 'happy ending' has, in a sense, already taken place. In other words, they are not this film's final couple. For this, we need to look elsewhere in the wedding scene; specifically to Homer's friend, Fred, and Peggy (the daughter of Al, the third returning veteran, to whom we will return in a moment).

The relative closural importance of the Homer/Wilma and Fred/Peggy unions is in part conveyed stylistically. At three points during the ceremony we cut to a shot that uses Gregg Toland's famous deep-focus photography to frame Fred in the immediate left-hand foreground, looking at Peggy in the background, turning his face towards her in a parallel of Homer and Wilma's pose on the right-hand side of the image. We also cut away from the marrying couple during the vows themselves, transferring the importance of their words onto this second couple. This pattern culminates when the rites end,

Homer and Wilma kiss, and the wedding guests throng around the couple, leaving Fred and Peggy the entire left-hand side of the image to themselves. As Hugo Friedhofer's score strikes up, rising and yearning, Fred slowly crosses the room and, without words – as if the vows have already spoken for them – takes Peggy in his arms and kisses her. We cut in to a close-up of the embrace concluding. Peggy looks up at Fred, initially seeming nervous as to what the kiss means, only for a look of joy and love to spread gradually across her face as he delivers the film's final words: 'You know what it'll be, don't you, Peggy? It may take us years to get anywhere; we'll have no money, no decent place to live; we'll have to *work*, get kicked around . . .' After Fred's warning has trailed off and he has smiled, she throws her arms around him and they kiss once again, her hat falling from her head; we fade to black; 'The End'.

Fred and Peggy are the other potential couple about whose fates we have been encouraged to speculate throughout this film. By the end, they have overcome obstacles such as Fred's unhappy marriage to Marie, and Peggy's father Al forbidding Fred from pursuing the relationship out of concern for his daughter's feelings. These obstacles having been surmounted by a dissatisfied Marie leaving Fred, the final couple that Fred and Peggy form is thus the culmination of this plot strand, answering the perennial question of courtship narratives and in this sense offering hermeneutic closure. Nevertheless, rather than emphasise the finality of a courtship's end, Fred's speech to Peggy about the hardships they may face in the future stresses a sense of *beginning*. At its most basic level, this once again gives the lie to the common assumption that – even if on one level providing hermeneutic closure – the final couple needs to stress finality at the expense of continuation. In this case, the significance of the promise of continuation clearly cannot be fully felt without reference to the historical context in which the film was made. Fred's cautious predictions for his and Peggy's happiness can be understood as also being related to the future of the post-WWII United States – a central concern of this film. The film has of course been in large part concerned to dramatise the key contemporary social issue of ex-servicemen's problems of reintegration into the American workforce and family life, and has also earlier made pointed references to what the film implies to be widespread fears for the country's future – caused by, for instance, the fact that the 'war boom' was perceived by many as fading, and to widespread uncertainties prompted by living in a post-Atomic world.[3] As such, the film suggests, any honest assessment of the country's prospects in 1946 would necessarily have to be tentative at best. To that extent, Fred's speech vocalises a historically-qualified optimism rendered more symbolically in the Homer/Wilma wedding ceremony, with its image of the traditional placement of a ring onto a bride's finger being carried out with difficulty by a man who has lost his hands for his country.

Yet, while the uncertainty expressed in Fred's words is important, we must also grant it only as much rhetorical emphasis as the film itself does. It is only Fred and Peggy's external circumstances, not their relationship itself, of which we are encouraged to feel unsure: while they may 'have no money, no decent place to live,' there is nothing here to suggest that they will ever not have one another. Indeed, Fred's predictions and Peggy's enthusiastic acceptance of them in fact speak well of the couples' chances according to terms established by the preceding film: Peggy's acceptance of this future is key in distinguishing her from Fred's ex-wife Marie who, after being reminded that marriage involves standing by each other 'for better, for worse,' had impatiently asked 'Well, when do we get going on the "*better*"?' Equally, it is important that during the speech we are focused not on Fred, but on Peggy: he is turned away from the camera, meaning his predictions of a hard life are accompanied not by a concerned look from him, but by a close-up of Peggy's adoring expression. The film also concludes with a very conventional element of the rhetoric of an ending – a kiss – a final image always likely to make an ending appear more 'closed' than it might otherwise.

By raising questions about a potentially troubled future, then, this final couple qualifies its hermeneutic closure more than some others, whilst still exploiting elements of the resolution that will frequently accompany the convention. We find further complications regarding the overall closure offered by this film's happy ending, however, if we turn to the film's third couple: Peggy's parents, Al and Milly.

That the hermeneutic questions raised by Al and Milly's plotline are left significantly less resolved than those of Homer/Wilma or Fred/Peggy is due in part to the nature of their relationship. Unlike the other two couples, Al and Milly are already married by the time the film begins. The usual question of a courtship narrative – whether X and Y will form a relationship – contains the possibility for one yes-or-no answer (even if in many cases we assume to know it ahead of time). A marriage plotline, by contrast, cannot concern itself with this kind of clear-cut, answerable question. Furthermore, since divorce is never raised as an issue for Al and Milly (as in some other films concerning pre-established marriages, e.g. *The Awful Truth*, *Penny Serenade* [1941], *The Happy Ending* [1969]), neither can this plotline be structured towards answering whether they will *stay* married. In this sense, it cannot quite be understood in terms of goals, questions, and answers, and thus cannot follow the classical Hollywood narrative schema whereby 'the story ends with a decisive victory or defeat, a resolution of the problem and a clear achievement or nonachievement of [. . .] goals' (Bordwell 1986: 157). Instead, what constitutes our investment in Al and Milly as a couple is rather the more amorphous question: what is the *state* of their marriage? Within the scope of this question, however, come some potential complications faced by Al and Milly, which we can indeed assess in terms of their degree of hermeneutic resolution. Other than questions surrounding Fred's relationship with Peggy, the two problems that we might say the Al and Milly couple faces are (1) that Al may not have remained faithful while in the service, and (2) his drinking habits.

The first of these arises only once, and somewhat obliquely, during the men's first night back in Boone City. In Butch's bar, a very drunk Al is dancing with Milly when, suddenly seemingly revisiting a memory, he slurs, 'You're a *bewitching* little creature. In a way, you remind me of my wife . . .' Apparently immediately understanding her predicament, Milly plays along: 'But you never told me you're *married*.' 'Oh yeah,' says Al, 'I got a little woman and two kiddies back there in the States.' 'But let's not think of them *now*,' replies Milly, exaggerating her role. 'No, you're so *right*!' exclaims Al, 'This night belongs only to *us* . . .' As Al spins her round, we now see Milly in close-up: surprisingly, she is smiling. Never brought up again, this intriguing moment is nevertheless allowed to hang over our understanding of the marriage – partly informing, for example, the sheepish affection Al displays towards Milly the next morning. Since it is not developed during the rest of the film, this suggestion of infidelity is never quite allowed to become a fully-fledged narrative *question* (akin to, say, 'Will X and Y form a relationship?'), but is nonetheless what we might call a narrative *issue*: a matter about which we may expect to receive no definite answers, but which we are still permitted to register as either more or less resolved.

Al's drinking is treated similarly, if more openly, and with a certain amount of humour. Throughout the film we (and Milly) have the opportunity to notice that Al seems to have returned from the war with a drinking problem. From his first night back on the town, it is clear that Al treats alcohol in something more than a recreational manner, continually drinking more than needed, and encouraging others to do the same (at one moment surreptitiously switching his empty glass for Milly's full one then innocently asking, 'Not drinking?'). In this scene and others, Milly's acknowledgment of Al's habit is largely communicated through subtle glances, gestures and lines – as, for instance, in the scene before the company dinner, when, upon spying Al reaching once again for his tumbler, Milly reminds him, 'You'll probably have to make a speech . . .' ('It's my plan to meet that situation by getting well-plastered,' is his deadpan reply). While granted greater focus than the possible infidelity, this suggestion of alcoholism too is something more of a narrative 'issue' than a question: it is never discussed openly, and the relative lightness with which it is treated means it does not lead down the potentially more melodramatic path available to such a plotline, which would require it to be confronted more explicitly. Unlike the implied infidelity, however, this issue is referred to during the film's final scene.

Standing on the porch with Homer and Fred, Al is drinking from a glass;

'I've been sampling the punch,' he tells them jovially, 'I presume it was made for the *kiddies*.' He offers the drink to Homer and Fred, who both decline, assuming it to be alcoholic. Milly emerges from the house and sees the glass, commenting disappointedly, 'Al, you promised you *wouldn't* . . .' 'Now listen, darling,' protests Al, 'you take a sip of this and you'll realize that there isn't a headache in a barrel of it.' He puts the glass to her lips: 'Here, see for yourself.' She tastes it, then gives him a very ambiguous look: somewhat suspicious, it turns into a faint smile just before we cut away, though still not one of obvious relief. This moment in fact constitutes the couple's last significant appearance in the film; given this, to what extent does it offer resolution to the issue of Al's drinking? We finally cannot be sure what the punch contains. While Al's confidence in offering it to Milly suggests he is telling the truth, the earlier discussion of its contents (particularly with Homer, whom we might reasonably expect to know what has gone into the drinks at his own wedding), could imply otherwise. Similarly, Milly's reaction is so inscrutable as to allow us to draw no definite conclusions. At the very least, we can say that the film is not overly concerned with reassuring us of Al's innocence. It is for precisely this reason that the inclusion of this ambiguous moment in the final scene is important.

The film seems interested in representing Al and Milly's relationship as one about which there can be no final resolutions; it is rather constantly evolving, allowing for mistakes, continual renegotiations, built to withstand its share of conflict. This point is made poignantly in an earlier speech Milly makes to a lovelorn Peggy after the latter has resentfully claimed that Milly and Al's marriage 'never had any trouble of any kind':

> We 'never had any trouble' . . . [*To Al:*] How many times have I told you I hated you and believed it in my heart? How many times have you told me you were sick and tired of me – that we were all washed up? How many times have we had to fall in love all over again?

The repeated stress placed here on 'how many times . . .?' pointedly emphasises the developing, shifting, accommodating quality of a marriage *over time* – akin to what Stanley Cavell calls 'the mutual willingness [. . .] for a sort of continuous reaffirmation' (1981: 142). This image of renegotiation and renewal stands in direct contrast to the timeless picture Peggy has painted of their supposedly serene married life: 'Everything has always been so *perfect* for you,' she has proclaimed: 'you loved each other, and you got married in a big church, and you had a honeymoon in the south of France . . .' Of course, what Peggy is describing here is in fact, quite explicitly, the *beginning* of a relationship – or, put another way, an imagined 'happy ending'. Al and Milly may have in some sense momentarily experienced this 'happy ending', but, during the twenty years that followed, they have clearly learned to reject a conception of romantic love as static and forever 'perfect', instead building themselves a marriage that allows for changes, *issues*: a potential infidelity, for example, or a struggle with alcoholism.

Viewed in this light, the final scene's ambiguous treatment of the couple's interactions seems entirely appropriate, since it reaffirms in a particularly potent fashion a value that is central to the film, and thus – in keeping with my discussions in Chapter 1 – plays its part in making this conclusion a happy ending. This value cannot be summed up by the 'undifferentiated' romantic future invoked earlier by Peggy; instead, it is closer in spirit to the potentially difficult, yet still loving, futures predicted for the Fred/Peggy and Homer/Wilma unions; it affirms the value of understanding marriage as not only being 'for better, for worse,' but as something for which its members 'have to *work*, get kicked around . . .'

Each of the film's three romantic strands, then, incorporates important degrees of continuation. Just as important as this, however, is the very fact that all these different 'endings' are made to exist within the ending of one film. This is because *Best Years* is a movie that is focused equally (or thereabouts) on the romantic lives of not just one couple, but three – a fact with significant consequences for the closure of its happy ending.

A multi-protagonist happy ending: point of view

While discussing *Sleepless* we encountered Billy Mernit's claim that 'romantic comedy heroes and heroines are like questions waiting to be answered,' because 'they are starring in stories in which love is the ultimate path to fulfillment' (2000: 17). This formulation speaks to two main ways in which closure is offered by *Sleepless*' happy ending in particular: Annie and Sam effectively appear as (1) questions who have been answered (via their meeting) because they are (2) *starring* in their film's narrative. I have already discussed ways in which *Best Years*' romance plotlines are treated in such a way that their individual final couples do not appear to offer complete answers. What is also important to the closure offered by this ending, however, is the way this film complicates the notion that the members of these couples are 'starring' in their stories; this too can be illuminated by a contrast with *Sleepless*.

Few films – even romantic comedies – focus quite so narrowly on their lovers' relationship as does *Sleepless*. For instance, neither Sam's nor Annie's friends are given romantic interests of their own (unlike, say, *Down To You* [2000], *Failure to Launch* [2006], *Did You Hear About the Morgans?* [2009]). Equally, the couple's careers never create any challenges or deadlines that must be met (unlike *His Girl Friday*, *Intolerable Cruelty* [2003], *The Proposal* [2009]); nor do their parents receive any significant focus: we only meet Annie's mother and father briefly near the film's opening, and never hear of

Sam's (unlike *Moonstruck* [1987], *Runaway Bride* [1999], *Kissing Jessica Stein* [2002]). By the same token, the couple's 'unsuitable partners' are granted comparatively little attention: Annie's scenes with Walter are concerned either with reinforcing his unsuitability or with wedding plans, while Sam's date, Victoria (Barbara Garrick), is required mainly to exhibit her undesirability (she disgusts Jonah), and her planned weekend getaway with Sam is entirely forgotten, never to be mentioned again, in the excitement following Jonah's disappearance. (We might compare this to films in which 'unsuitable' partners have much larger roles to play, e.g. *Picture Perfect* [1997], *Sweet Home Alabama* [2007], *Definitely Maybe* [2008].)

If a film desires it, the strategy of reducing its number of plotlines can offer a marked degree of closure simply by virtue of how few questions it requires the narrative to answer. Certainly, a film can increase its finality by resolving more than one narrative strand at once (see Bordwell 1986: 158); we might think, for instance, of 'backstage musicals' combining the resolution of their romance plot with the success of a production (e.g. *The Bandwagon* [1953]; see Feuer 1993: 82). Similarly, in romantic comedies, secondary plotlines may be resolved at the same time as the romance narrative, be they related to work (e.g. *His Girl Friday*), friends' relationships (e.g. *Double Wedding* [1937]), family (e.g. *She's the Man* [2006]), or otherwise. Nevertheless, it will always be true that the greater the number of plotlines, the more questions will be raised, and the greater number of answers needed to bring about closure. As such, in the context of multi-protagonist films, we are necessarily '[forced] to look at the resolution of each of the narrative lines in the context of the wider perspective that the film offers' (Azcona 2010: 156). In *Best Years* one outcome of this wider perspective is that it allows the film to leave each of its couples' plotlines at different stages of hermeneutic completion, as we have seen. We are thus here unable to experience the sense of closure that can be yielded when one conclusive narrative answer coincides with the end of the film itself, as in *Sleepless*. As well as being a hermeneutic matter, however, the wider perspective of this happy ending is also a matter of point of view.

Perhaps the most significant aspect of multi-protagonist films is that their point of view is simply broader than that of a movie featuring only one or two protagonists. This expanded focus means that our view of the film's fictional world, and – particularly importantly for my present purposes – our perception of the limits and functions of that world, also expands. This in turn has consequences for the extent to which we perceive the narrative of a film such as *Best Years* as being one that it would be even *possible* to 'close' via a final couple in a manner comparable to *Sleepless*.

It is of course worth remembering that, as Thomas points out, 'so-called happy endings [. . .] are rarely happy for everyone, especially where romance is concerned' (2000: 21). One measure of this, as Thomas points out, is the afore-mentioned romantic comedy convention of 'unsuitable' partners – potential romantic mates whom we are encouraged to consider incorrect matches for the film's protagonists, and whom we fully expect not to form part of the final couple (ibid.: 20). Our final impression of the unsuitable partners in *Sleepless*, for example, is certainly less 'happy' than for Sam and Annie: we leave Walter disappointed but stoic at the moment that Annie gives him back her engagement ring, and the last reference made to Victoria comes when Sam is preparing for their weekend break, which will in fact never take place, since Sam instead rushes to New York to retrieve Jonah. Part of the usefulness of Thomas' observation is that it draws attention to the fact that, were the emotions of peripheral characters like Walter and Victoria taken into account, it would likely be difficult to dub the ending of virtually *any* film truly 'happy'. As Thomas says,

> Seeing how a narrative's [. . .] resolutions feel from the point of view of a character who is not centrally located within the spatial, narrative and ideological structures of a film [. . .] may provide insight into the extent to which a film's melodramatic or comedic atmosphere is dependent upon the minimizing of [. . .] countercurrents to its resolution in these terms. (ibid.: 20)

We already saw an example of this strategy in Chapter 1 with *Intermezzo*'s abandonment of Anita on its way to its 'happy' resolution for Holger (to be revisited in Chapter 4). This process, furthermore, has significant ramifications not only for what allows a happy ending to feel '*happy*', but also for what allows it to feel like an *ending*.

Let us conduct a thought experiment similar to that suggested by Thomas. What would the ending of *Sleepless* look like if it incorporated a view of Walter and Victoria's lives at the moment we leave the film's world? Walter might be back at his hotel, probably upset that Annie has left him; Victoria, meanwhile, would probably either be stranded and confused at the Holiday Inn where she had arranged to meet Sam, or, if Sam found time to cancel the trip, she would simply be feeling mildly put-out at home. Importantly, not only would these images of Walter and Victoria's lives at the moment Annie and Sam meet not look particularly happy, they would also not look particularly like endings (or, at least, could only look like endings to a very different kind of film). We could continue the experiment further, incorporating views of Sam's work buddy Jay, or Annie's brother Dennis, and so on. Of course, what would become increasingly clear the wider our perspective became is that Sam and Annie's is but one potential story in this film's world, and that their meeting would certainly not be enough to adequately 'close' the film were its point of view to encompass so many other manifestly unconcluded lives.

We might remind ourselves here of James' words: 'really, universally, relations stop nowhere, and the exquisite problem of the artist is eternally but to draw, by a geometry of his [sic] own, the circle within which they shall happily *appear* to do so' (1934: 5). This notion of relations stopping nowhere is true in terms of time, which forever keeps moving, but it is also true in terms of *perspective*, which can always expand further. In order to reach a happy ending that feels not only happy but also like an ending, *Sleepless* organises its world and our view of it into a 'circle' that appears almost purpose-built to bring its two protagonists together, something which requires the ultimate exclusion of figures like Victoria and Walter. That the beginning of their relationship should feel to us so satisfyingly like an ending is due in large part to our understanding of what *matters* in this film and world: the meeting is essentially what, we are encouraged to feel, that world, and film, are *for*. In order to grant us this sense, *Sleepless* has had to limit its point of view to the extent that Sam and Annie appear to be the only 'questions' requiring 'answers' in the film's world, and it has done this by ensuring that they are 'starring' in the only story that finally matters to our perception of its world.

By contrast, the problems caused for narrative closure by expanding the numbers of central characters, and thus point of view, have often been recognised by critics – in literature, and more recently in film (see Bakhtin [1984] Garrett [1980], Quart [2005], Bordwell [2006: 72], etc.). Of course, the multi-protagonist film is itself far from a singular or homogeneous type, and one such movie need not always guarantee anything like the same degree of irresolution as another. Without entering into an in-depth discussion of the form, we can comfortably assert that the degree of closure will always depend upon a great many different factors. Necessarily important, however, will be the number of protagonists since, as Azcona puts it, 'the wider the perspective, the more difficult it becomes to ascribe an absolute meaning, or to describe in a coherent and unified way a set of events or their narrative resolutions' – a fact which unavoidably 'problematises [such films'] sense of an ending' (2010: 157). The fact that this narrative form's potential resistance to the 'sense of an ending'[4] is always likely to come into play can be seen by looking even at a film with so comparatively few protagonists as *Best Years*.

In *Best Years* the Fred/Peggy couple carries less closural power than *Sleepless*' in part because the film's broader point of view has ensured that it is presented as being far less the accomplished purpose – or the 'absolute meaning' – of its film's narrative and world. We have been granted a view that requires us to consider that more *matters* than simply whether Peggy and Fred will embrace in the final moments: Homer and Wilma's embattled future matters too, as do Al and Milly's ongoing marital issues – as, indeed, does the future of the post-war United States in general. This is because the world of *Best Years* has been constructed to serve not just one main purpose (say, bringing together a couple), but several, having been simultaneously a portrait of returning veterans, a romantic narrative about coping with disability, an exploration of a marriage, a courtship plot, and so on. The film's final scene acknowledges this.

While the fact of Homer and Wilma's marriage itself may not be especially significant in closural terms, the wedding ceremony is more so, since it permits the film to bring together its characters in the same space for a common purpose. At the same time, though, we are encouraged throughout the closing sequence to register the film's strands as both interconnected and distinct. First we witness Al and Milly's ambiguous exchange on the porch, then move inside to see the marriage of Homer and Wilma (during which Al and Milly become simply two among many faces of the gathered guests), before finally shifting our focus to Fred and Peggy's union. These characters and their stories have been linked in numerous ways – by a professional past, by a man's relationship with his friend's daughter, by a mutual concern for a new couple's happiness – and when we leave them they are all in the same room for the same ostensible reason. Yet throughout the movie, and now at its conclusion, we have also been invited to view their lives and narratives as distinct and various, their combined stories *together* making up our view of this fictional world. The ending can certainly be seen to draw its own 'circle' – we *do*, after all, leave the world with the enactment of a final couple (and not, say, two years into Fred and Peggy's marriage). Yet this circle is considerably more inclusive, and less neatly-rendered, than that of *Sleepless*. Placed in the context of the multi-protagonist movie, whose conventions can suggest that 'life goes on, that this is just one part of the story, that there are more stories like this' (Azcona 2010: 157), the final couple here loses some of the links with final, unambiguous closure so often so casually ascribed to it.

We might add, in addition, that point of view is also thus a matter of genre. Douglas Pye writes that 'genre brings with it complex, informing expectations [. . .] that have a bearing on point of view' (2000: 12), and it would be equally true to say that point of view has a determining bearing on genre (see Deleyto 1992). This is a point made by Thomas when drawing our attention to the entirely unseen real mother in *Bachelor Mother* (1939), who must have abandoned her baby in order for Polly (Ginger Rogers) to find it: 'a shift in point of view from the heroine to the mother could have pushed the film towards melodrama rather than towards comedy' (2000: 19). Just as expanding our point of view to peripheral characters in *Sleepless* would make it harder for Sam and Annie's final couple to adequately 'close' their film, so would narrowing *Best Years*' point of view to only Fred and Peggy help their union bring closure to theirs. What this would also do, of course, is make *Sleepless*

feel somewhat less like a 'romance' and *Best Years* feel rather more like one –
that is: it would make these films appear either more or less like the *kinds* of
films for which a final couple can most comfortably constitute a moment of
appropriate cessation.

Our next film, however, allows us to see that a virtually opposite strategy
than *Best Years*' may have a similar effect on the closural powers of the final
couple.

A NARROWED VIEW ON THE HAPPY ENDING: *THE GRADUATE*

The Graduate ends with the escape of Benjamin (Dustin Hoffman) and Elaine
(Katharine Ross) from the church where Elaine has just been married to an
eligible young man of her parents' choosing (Brian Avery). Having barricaded
the irate congregation inside using a handy crucifix as a makeshift lock, the pair
run from the chapel and flag down a passing bus. Once on the back seat, the
bus pulling away, they fall about laughing at the stunt they have pulled. As this
initial euphoria passes they look at one another and smile, before turning and
facing forwards. At first they each grin intermittently, but before long both
begin to grow more pensive; the plaintive strains of Simon and Garfunkel's
'Sounds of Silence' begin to play on the soundtrack. Elaine turns to look
at Ben; he is still facing forward; she looks away. Their smiles now faded,
they stare blankly ahead until we cut to a shot of their bus receding from the
camera; fade to black.

The ending of *The Graduate* has become famous for lacking the secure
closure of other final couple happy endings. Many have suggested that 'the
ending is left ambiguous' (Denisoff 1991: 165), its final moments ensuring
that 'a certain sense of unease lingers' (King 2002b: 184), with it often being
noted that 'the camera holds on the seated couple for an interminable amount
of screen time, leaving us to wonder – as, it seems, are they – "What the hell
now?"' (Kipnis 2003: 100). Often, the implication in such accounts is that this
final couple would be unproblematically 'closed' if the film's final moments
did not act to 'open' it stylistically – a strategy described by Tim Hunter
as 'Nichols' muting of the otherwise conventional happy ending' (1967: 1).
Thus, Neupert claims that 'the happy ending is subverted by [the actors']
performances, the soundtrack' (ibid.: 178); Rowe writes that the happy ending
is undercut because the film 'exploits the possibilities of wide-screen compo-
sition to show the distance between them' (Rowe 1995b: 195); and Colwell
argues that it is because we are left with medium shots of the characters rather
than a recessional image that the 'apparently happy conclusion' is sabotaged
(1981: 47) – this last argument being rather negated by the fact that the final

shot *is* in fact a recessional image: the bus departing from the camera. The view of this happy ending being somehow *deceptive* is now so well established that the romantic comedy *(500) Days of Summer* (2009) explains its protagonist's overly-romantic beliefs as having 'stemmed from [. . .] a total misreading of the movie *The Graduate*' – a misreading we are invited to surmise is grounded in his interpretation of the film's ending.[5]

It is possible to see why *The Graduate*'s ending has often been characterised in this way. Apart from anything, there is the deeply ingrained assumption (encountered in the introduction, and to be revisited later) that a final couple happy ending is surely standardised unless it is being subverted. Equally, the notion that the ending slyly undermines a Hollywood convention is convenient for the way it seems to support the film's critical reputation as a key inaugural film of 'New Hollywood' (see, for instance, Krämer [2005: 12], who suggests that the film's 'ambiguous' ending influenced subsequent such films). I do not wish to deny that *The Graduate*'s handling of its final moments is very important to the way in which this ending works. Yet I also believe that an interpretation of the ending that rests purely on the film's last fifty seconds runs the risk of ignoring the not insignificant fact that other aspects of the film would necessarily ensure its relative 'openness' even *without* these final stylistic strategies. Explaining why this is, however, involves remaining sensitive to more closural factors than simply the mood of its final moments alone. In particular, as with *Best Years*, point of view is absolutely crucial for creating an ending that encourages us to ask, 'What the hell now?'

Narrowed point of view

What all the above critical accounts of *The Graduate* effectively presuppose is that, were it not for its last seconds, this film's final couple would serve as a moment of appropriate cessation for its narrative. In order to fully satisfy us of this, a film must convince us that its final couple has been prepared for adequately by the preceding narrative – that this is the end-point towards which it has been driving. One way a movie can confidently achieve this is via a dual-focus narrative like that of *Sleepless*. Another familiar method is to have the characters who will come to form a final couple meet (or re-meet) in an early scene. This helps because it immediately creates the sense that the ensuing narrative will be concerned with these characters' developing relationship, and thus perhaps their union. A neat variation on this convention, for instance, is for the couple to meet in an opening scene with complementary or conflicting needs, as in *Serendipity* (2001), in which John (John Cusack) and Sara (Kate Beckinsale) encounter each other in a department store both wanting to buy the same pair of gloves, or *Bluebeard's Eighth Wife* (1939), which begins with Nicole (Claudette Colbert) and Michael (Gary Cooper) meeting over the fact that he wants to buy a pyjama top, and she pyjama bottoms. Whether one half of the couple merely glances at the other from across a room (as in *Groundhog Day* [1993]), or they have an extended conversation (as in *My Man Godfrey* [1936]), introducing us to the couple early and more or less simultaneously is a way for a film to clearly indicate that it will be primarily about this couple, and that its ending must concern their relationship if it is to correspond to our expectations of how such narratives usually develop (see too, for instance: *A Foreign Affair* [1947], *I Was a Male War Bride* [1949], *Bell, Book or Candle* [1958]). By contrast, *The Graduate* is a film that does not appear to be about Ben and Elaine as a couple, but far more about Ben alone.

This is very much a film of two halves. In the first half we are introduced to Ben as he arrives home from college. We learn he feels unsure of what he wants from life, knowing only he wants his future to be 'different'. We meet his parents and their society friends at a party, during which Ben seems alienated from their upper-middle-class suburban existence. We are introduced to Mrs Robinson (Anne Bancroft), who has Ben drive her home as an excuse to invite him to begin an affair with her if he wishes. The film's next thirty-five minutes are concerned with their ensuing affair (e.g. the awkwardness of their first meeting, later problems of intimacy), Ben's attempts to keep it secret (e.g. lying to cover his absences), and the continuing sense of 'just drifting' that he says he feels while at home with his family (e.g. the montages and swimming pool sequences). It is not until his mother (Elizabeth Wilson) and father (William Daniels) force him to take Mrs Robinson's daughter, Elaine, out for a date that we meet this character who will come to form the other half of *The Graduate*'s final couple; this is fifty-two minutes – just over half-way – into the film.

Ben and Elaine's first courtship lasts for around twelve minutes on screen, covering the period from the beginning of their first date to the moment when Elaine learns of his affair with Mrs Robinson the next day, and disgustedly orders him out of her life. There follow a number of scenes, covering about ten minutes, during which we follow Ben as he returns to his unfulfilling existence at his parents', pines for Elaine, and finally decides to travel to Berkeley, where she is studying, to ask her to marry him. This second courtship again lasts about twelve minutes, and is halted when Mr Robinson (Murray Hamilton) appears and forbids Ben from seeing Elaine. We now enter the final portion of the film, during which Ben discovers that Elaine is promised to marry the 'Make-out King' of Berkeley (Brian Avery), rushes to find her, and breaks up the wedding. This portion – combined with the 'moral satisfaction' offered by Elaine's repudiation of her parents (Chatman 1980: 85) – is perhaps the main reason why so many interpret the ending as a 'conventionally' romantic conclusion that is being subverted. Ben's last-minute dash has significant anticipatory power for the happy ending we finally receive, not least because romantic conclusions involving the interruption of planned or in-progress weddings are conventional in romantic comedy (e.g. *Girl Shy* [1924], *It Happened One Night*, *Dream Wife* [1953]). The question, however, is whether it is enough to make the final couple to which it leads an appropriate end-point for this narrative as a whole.

If a film desires to create the sense that a final couple could form a moment of appropriate cessation, yet delays the introduction of one half of the pair, it is common for it to either establish a dual-focus narrative beforehand, as in *Sleepless*, or divide its point of view between the two characters following their meeting. *Holiday*, for instance, begins as a story about Johnny (Cary Grant) meeting the family of his fiancée, Julia (Doris Nolan); yet, after Linda (Katharine Hepburn) has been introduced, we come to see as much of her problems with familial frustration and growing attraction to Johnny as of his increasing doubts about the forthcoming marriage. (Other films that delay introducing us to one half of a couple only to split focus later on include *Bachelor Mother*, *Murphy's Romance* [1985], *French Kiss* [1995].) This is also a matter of how long the introduction of the second partner is delayed. Linda, for example, is introduced at around the thirteen minute mark of *Holiday*, meaning that the film's narrative begins the process of becoming about its eventual final couple far earlier than does *The Graduate*, which is already half-finished by the time we meet Elaine. Not including the final scene, Elaine is on screen for around twenty-four minutes. The remainder of the movie's one hundred-plus minutes are focused squarely on Ben, his relationship with Mrs Robinson, and his sense of post-collegiate malaise.

Not only do we stay by Ben's side for the entirety of the film (he is present in every scene – an approach to point of view that Murray Smith calls 'exclusive attachment' [1995: 153]), but many prominent (and now famous) techniques are used to ensure our 'epistemic alignment' (Wilson 1986: 5) with him regarding his views of the world around him: literal point-of-view shots suggest his sense of detachment (e.g. through a scuba mask), peripheral characters stay out-of-focus while Ben stays sharp (e.g. his first scene with his father), and montage sequences organise the passing of time according to his experience (e.g. cutting from Ben hauling himself onto a pool inflatable to a shot of him on top of Mrs Robinson). These are also the terms by which the film makes us understand its satire of 1960s suburban life: as Leo Braudy notes, 'the film's point of view corresponds to the point of view of Benjamin [. . .] [The] satire of his parents and their milieu is easily understood as his idea of them' (Braudy 1976: 59).

An extension of this focus on Ben's subjectivity is that the romance with Elaine too is made far more about Ben's experience than about the couple *per se*. Firstly, we never spend time with Elaine without Ben present, meaning we are denied views of her that we might expect to receive were this truly a narrative about both halves of a pairing. We do not see, for instance, how she copes with the news of Ben's affair with her mother (only later do we discover she has been misinformed that he raped her), the process leading to her decision to enter Ben's room at night and agree to consider marrying him (she merely shows up, her feelings towards him already changed), nor – most ostentatiously – why she agrees to marry the 'Make-Out King'. We do not see these things because this is not a film about two people on a path to romantic union, but rather a film about a particular moment in one young man's life during which he happens to enter into a romance.

Of course, Elaine's presence is felt during periods when she is not onscreen via Ben's frustrated desire for her, but it is precisely the fact of these periods during which we have access only to Ben's view of the relationship that is significant. One result is a prominent motif whereby Elaine is seen, *Vertigo*-like, from a distance and from Ben's (experiential, if not always optical) perspective. Another is that we often stay with Ben before Elaine appears in scenes and after she leaves, as in a scene at the zoo: once Elaine's date has escorted her away we remain with Ben as he watches her leave and turns to look glumly at the caged chimpanzees; the same pattern is also used in the two scenes when Elaine visits Ben in his Berkeley rooms. Finally, there is the extensive attention given to Ben's attempts to learn where the wedding is taking place and his frantic journey there, which – as mentioned – we see at the expense of any of Elaine's preparations for marriage.

Having a romance narrative be told via 'exclusive attachment' to one half of a couple need not *necessarily* be a barrier to a film creating the sense that it may be dedicated to the creation of a final couple – as demonstrated by, say, *Annie Hall* (1977) or *Bridget Jones's Diary* (2001). However, the difference between these films and *The Graduate* is, again, that both raise the possibility of the central couple early enough (in these cases, their first scenes) to create the expectation that they (and their endings) must be concerned primarily with the status of this couple if they are to satisfy our expectations. In *The Graduate*, the late introduction of Elaine, her subsequent narrative marginalisation, and the film's continual preoccupation with Ben's point of view create a context in which the couple's romance does not appear to be the film's main focus, but rather simply another aspect of Ben's ongoing, confused twenty-something existence.

A sceptical point of view

That the romance *is* confused is also important, and is partly communicated through tone. In its latter portions the film begins to take a similar satirical stance towards Ben as was previously used to criticise his parents' world, meaning that we are placed at a certain ironic remove from the romantic quest he mounts to win back Elaine. Take, for instance, the scene in which Ben tells his parents, very matter-of-factly, of his marriage plans:

Mother:	When did you decide all this?
Ben:	About an hour ago. [. . .] Actually, she doesn't know about us getting married yet.
Mother:	Well, when did you two talk this over?
Ben:	We haven't.
Mother:	You *haven't*?
Father:	Ben, this whole idea sounds pretty half-baked . . .
Ben:	Oh, it's not – it's completely baked. It's a decision I've made.
Mother:	Well, what makes you think she *wants* to marry you?
Ben:	She doesn't. To be perfectly honest, she doesn't like me.

After speaking this last line, Ben promptly exits, leaving his parents dumb-founded into silence. His plans already placed as amusingly hasty and ill-considered, they are similarly satirised once he puts them into action. This happens mainly through a combination of Hoffman's deadpan performance and the corresponding stylistic deadpan of Nichols' direction. When Ben first proposes, for example, he utters the words, 'Will you marry me?' whilst also letting out a deep yawn. In the following scene, after Elaine has only conceded she 'might' marry him, Ben is already jumping several steps ahead: 'We can go down and get our blood tests tomorrow,' he flatly suggests as they walk through crowds of Berkeley students. 'Benjamin, I haven't even said I'll marry you yet!' is her quite reasonable response. Oblivious, he continues: 'We'll need our birth certificates – I happen to have mine with me . . .' The next scene con-tinues the ironic tone: 'I just don't think it would work,' Elaine tells Ben whilst entering a classroom and leaving him outside the closed door; 'Why *wouldn't* it?' asks Ben. A hall bell rings. Immediately cutting to a different angle of Ben outside the same door, another bell rings; Elaine exits the classroom, and we realise Ben has been standing stock-still in this spot for the entire length of a lesson; 'Why *wouldn't* it?' he asks again in precisely the same voice. These are not knowing gags Ben makes in an attempt to be charming, but gently ironic commentaries on his blind insistence upon marriage that are being made at his expense. Together, they have the effect of casting this whole second courtship as rushed and – particularly when combined with Ben's virtual stalking – not a little crazy.

These strategies are highly significant for the closure offered by *The Graduate*'s ending. Most importantly, a trajectory towards a final couple does not appear to structure the narrative as a whole, meaning that for much of the movie's running time we cannot *anticipate* it. Because the romance is only a strand of the second half it appears to be simply the next portion of Ben's life following his affair with Mrs Robinson. Indeed, the way the film presents the romance encourages us to view it as being not greatly dissimilar to the earlier affair itself, which Ben has described as 'just this thing that happened along with everything else.' The film thus begins as a narrative about young adulthood in crisis and presents the affair that develops as a component of that crisis. Given this, the late appearance of a new potential romance cannot turn *The Graduate* into a story about the creation of a couple – something Tim Hunter notes in his contemporaneous review of the film: 'Structurally, the last hour resolves a conflict, but unfortunately not the conflict set-up in the first hour' (1967: 1). Returning to the relationship between point of view and genre, we might say that the emergence of the Elaine plotline and Ben's run to the wedding do not shift the film's point of view to the extent that it becomes a 'romance' narrative. Furthermore, the fact that the second courtship is to a significant extent ironised should reinforce our sense of the film ultimately remaining essentially a satire (both of middle-class mores and, now, of youthful romanticism) rather than persuade us that it has transformed itself into a narrative whose proper end is a final couple. We might say that, although *Ben* may come to see Elaine as the *Bildungsroman*-like 'solution' to his problems, the film he is in does not present the relationship as such.

The received wisdom that *The Graduate*'s happy ending would be uncomplicatedly 'closed' were it not for its final seconds is thus unconvincing. Although 'a certain sense of unease lingers' (King 2002a: 184) over the final couple, this is far from the only reason. True to typical accounts of the movie, in *The End* Neupert briefly mentions the film as one which would *seem* to be a Closed Text, except that its ultimately 'somber tone' (1995: 178) transforms it into an Open Story; thus, despite the fact that 'the story certainly has resolved the major hermeneutic of Ben's goal' (ibid.: 178), we are ultimately made to feel that 'he does not seem satisfied with achieving that goal' (ibid.: 178). This reading is symptomatic of Neupert's relatively narrow treatment of 'goals'. *Best Years* has taught us that it is not enough merely to register that questions have been answered or goals achieved: we must also ask, for instance, how much emphasis is placed on one answer when a number of *other* questions have also been posed. Likewise, at the end of *The Graduate* we must be aware not only of the fact that a 'goal' has been achieved, but also of *when* that goal was formulated, and of what *attitude* we have been encouraged to take towards it. As we have seen, although Ben does achieve an aim, this does not appear to be the 'aim' of the *film*. Thus, if we do indeed wish to call this film's final couple relatively 'open', then it must be for reasons other than simply because the ending holds a shot too long, allows its couple's mood to change, and concludes with a plaintive song.

In fact, acknowledging that the film treats this ending as merely another moment in Ben's unfocused and ongoing life allows us to understand these stylistic features more deeply. Simply put: unlike in a film like *Sleepless*, it would not *make sense* for this movie to present its final couple as a 'closed' happy ending. It thus does not do so, and instead uses its last moments to remind us that this narrative has been about a young man in a restless time of his life. The reprise of 'Sounds of Silence' is not just important for the way it tempers the mood of Ben and Elaine's escape, but also for its connection with the film's opening, when the song accompanied Ben's lonely journey into LAX airport. Similarly, the extended shot of Ben and Elaine looking blankly forward mirrors the opening shot of Ben on the plane, as does the fact that they are being passively carried along on a mode of transportation. This 'bracketing' (a convention here dissociated to an extent from the strong closural functions *Sleepless* imbues it with) reinforces the fact that this narrative has been Ben's all along, and that the moment of escape cannot be seen as a definitive end-point. Things may have improved for Ben: he is now travelling with a partner rather than alone – this is what allows the ending to feel nominally 'happy' (it is what Plantinga might call a 'favourable outcome' [1994: 12]) – but they are a long way from *concluded*.

*

It would be possible to describe all the endings examined in this chapter in a manner that made them sound equally 'closed'. Each contains a final couple, and each employs familiar closural imagery. I hope I have convincingly argued, however, that they work in significantly different ways, and that we should not assign them to categories marked simply 'open' or entirely 'closed'. This in turn has allowed us to see that the relationship between closure and the heterosexual, final couple happy ending is far from predetermined. It is true that our very familiarity with the final couple as a feature of so many endings likely ensures that it will indeed always make some contributions towards closure – perhaps significant ones: it is often used, after all, as part of the rhetoric of an ending. Because it *is* so common a feature of Hollywood conclusions, it can be tempting to assume – particularly when emboldened by preconceptions about happy endings and closure more broadly – that it will always usher in an equally 'closed' ending (unless, of course, it is 'subverted'). Yet I would suggest that this very prevalence should itself encourage a contrary assumption: that the convention will serve varying closural functions depending upon the varying needs of different films, and that these functions will be dictated not by the final couple's mere presence, but by its employment. This assumption will be important to bear in mind as we move on to discuss other functions final couple happy endings are commonly taken to serve, relating to 'unrealism' and ideology.

NOTES

1. While the pertinence of dual-focus to romantic comedy is occasionally acknowledged (Krutnik [1998: 26]; Cook, [1999: 213]), its centrality to many films in the genre has in my opinion not yet been adequately recognised.

2. Altman has in fact attempted to distance his approach to narrative from the issue of point of view (2008: 26). This, however, is because he interprets point of view as 'always [involving], however transitorily, the use of a character as a secondary filter of information (as opposed to the Olympian narrator [. . .])' (ibid.: 22). I, however, am using point of view in a much broader sense, which can absolutely accommodate dual-focus patterns.

3. As Wilma's father has put it, 'As I see it, we're headed for bad times in this country. [. . .] Next year, in my opinion, we'll see widespread depression and unemployment'; equally, both Butch (Hoagy Carmichael) and Al's teenage son have expressed concerns about nuclear weapons to the effect that, 'We've reached the point where the whole human race has got to find a way to live together, or else . . .'

4. Frank Kermode's (1967) phrase, to which we will be returning in Chapter 3.

5. These words are spoken over a shot of the movie's male lead, Tom (Joseph Gordon Levitt), as a boy, enraptured by the film's ending on television (we hear Ben's cries of 'Elaine! Elaine!' from the wedding scene emanating from the television). Tom will later take the far less romantic Summer (Zooey Deschanel) to see the film, whereupon the bus scene moves her not to joy, but to tears.

CHAPTER 3

Happy endings and unrealism

When the term 'happy ending' is spoken in Hollywood movies, it is usually being debunked for promulgating idealism in the face of life's true hardships. One of the most bitterly ironic uses of the phrase, for instance, comes in the WWII romance *Waterloo Bridge* (1940) when Roy (Robert Taylor), unaware that his fiancée has been forced into prostitution via a combination of economic circumstance and erroneous news of his death, tells her upon his reappearance, 'Darling, don't cry – it's a happy ending . . .'; almost fifty years later, at the somber and amoral conclusion of *Crimes and Misdemeanours* (1989), Judah (Martin Landau) says simply that, 'If you want a happy ending you should go see a Hollywood movie.' Repeatedly, in all kinds of films, the term 'happy ending' is compared to fantasy and illusion, and contrasted to the comparative harshness of the real world.[1]

This is the same basic pattern that tends to govern movies' uses of the term 'happily ever after', which will commonly be mocked for referring to a naïve, 'fairy tale' view of life, and romantic love in particular. Sometimes this point is made in reference to specific relationships: in *The Awful Truth* Lucy tells a judge during her divorce proceedings that she and Jerry 'thought we had better get married; that way we were able to give Mr. Smith [their dog] a better home and live happily ever after – until now . . .'; in *Caught*, jealous husband Smith (Robert Ryan) angrily taunts his wife about the affair he presumes she is having: 'You thought you'd live happily ever after and I'd pay for it'; recently, in *Mamma Mia* (2008), divorcee Sam (Pierce Brosnan) warns the teenage daughter of a former flame that 'I've done the big white wedding and believe me it doesn't always end in happily ever after.' The phrase may also be made to refer explicitly to false romantic dreams propagated by popular culture; in *He's Just Not That Into You* (2009) Gigi (Ginnifer Cooper) laments that 'There's always a story about some girl getting married and living happily ever after. But that's the exception, and we're not the exception – we're the rule'; in

Only You (1994), Kate (Bonnie Hunt) responds to the question 'Life's not like it is in the movies, right?' with 'No, it's not. Although from day one everyone conspires to tell you it is [. . .] – dreams come true, the good guy wins, people live happily ever after – all that crap.' These are the terms in which Hollywood movies themselves routinely characterise the notion of 'happily ever after'.[2]

One thing these uses tell us is that, in Hollywood movies at least, the concept of the 'happy ending' is usually treated as 'unrealistic' – as opposed, perhaps, to 'realistic'. The virtual truism that 'happy endings are [. . .] notoriously "unrealistic"' (Maltby 2003: 269) is the focus of this chapter. This is indeed an extremely common criticism of the convention in cinematic, public and journalistic discourse, though it has been rather less widespread in film scholarship – a fact stemming in part from the intellectual history of political modernism (Rodowick 1994), to which we will return, which cast 'realism' itself as 'nothing but an expression of the prevailing ideology' (Commoli/ Narboni 1971: 30). Nevertheless, the association can sometimes be suggested implicitly. While a critic such as Peter Wollen did not name the 'happy ending' in his famous categorisation of the 'seven deadly sins of cinema', the fact that this list included 'closure', 'pleasure', and 'fiction' – as against counter-cinema's 'seven cardinal virtues', including 'aperture', 'unpleasure', and 'reality' (1998: 501) – means we may be sure which side of the divide between 'fiction' and 'reality' our convention would belong (see Rushton [2011] on the often tacit survival of political modernism's approach to 'reality' in contemporary film theory). Another way in which scholars may obliquely associate the Hollywood 'happy ending' with fantasy or 'unrealism', already encountered, is by linking it with the fairytale via the phrase 'happily ever after' – a common association to which we shall return.[3]

What, though, could 'unrealistic mean? Simply not 'realistic'? (This is the last time I will use quotation marks for these terms; though their meanings are neither obvious nor stable, I will explain the particular uses I intend for them as we progress.) While I am less concerned here with the controversial concept of realism than with its untheorised colloquial counterpart, it nonetheless seems necessary to begin by placing these two terms in some kind of relation to one another. Realism is a famously fraught term that has historically constituted, as Andrew Tudor puts it, a particularly 'roomy catch-all' (1972: 27). Unless willing to risk a major misnomer, however, we must surely relate the word in some way to what Harry Levin called the 'willed tendency of art to approximate reality' (1966: 3). Yet there are a multitude of possible reasons for concluding that a particular artwork or convention approximates reality – or that it does *not* do so. The uses the above films make of the terms 'happy ending' and 'happily ever after' imply one common framework for such a judgment.

UNREALISM AS WISH-FULFILMENT

Happy endings do not impress us as true but as desirable.
                                          – Northrop Frye (2002: 152)

'In the casual, everyday sense in which we identify one movie as more "realistic" than another,' Maltby tells us, '"realism" implies that its conventions more closely resemble those we pessimistically assume operate in the world outside the cinema' (ibid.: 29). The view that happy endings are unrealistic because they are wish-fulfilling – because they are somehow 'happier' than real life – is bolstered by the perceived symbiotic relationship between happy endings and Hollywood more generally. Publically, Hollywood cinema 'has usually been equated with fantasy and escapism' (Thompson 1988: 201), while the concept of realism 'has passed much of its history in a state of opposition to fantasy of all kinds' (Tallis 1988: 191). According to one view, happy endings do not 'approximate reality' because reality is simply less 'happy' than Hollywood happy endings allow.

In search of a usable theoretical framework through which to discuss our subject, I think it wise immediately to dismiss the premise that happy endings are unrealistic simply *because* of their happiness, i.e. due to the fact they provide sympathetic characters with a 'favourable outcome' (Plantinga 1994: 12). This dismissal is particularly necessary in the case of the final couple: it is, needless to say, a far from uncommon life event for people to fall happily in love (however long the ensuing relationship may or may not *last*, of course – a matter to which we will return). Bluntly put: there is thus nothing less 'life-like' about ending a film with a joyful wedding than, say, a tragic death, since each event occurs countless times in the real world every day. I suspect, though, that the happiness of happy endings is often conceptualised as unrealistic because of the cumulative picture apparently painted by Hollywood endings taken as a group, with the logic going something like this: certainly life contains its share of happy moments, but not the overwhelming majority share repeatedly granted by the conclusions of Hollywood films ('we're not the exception, we're the rule'); judged together, happy endings therefore collectively portray life, wishfully, as 'happier' than it truly is. Quite apart from the fact that this argument takes us a considerable way down a radically unresolvable path of conjecture, it should also be clear that it has little bearing on the unrealism of the final couple as a convention in and of itself. If we do indeed wish to pursue the idea that this convention is unrealistic, we must look elsewhere for our rationale.

Unrealism as excessive conventionality

The good ended happily, and the bad unhappily. That is what fiction means.

— *The Importance of Being Ernest* (Wilde 1990: 58)

There is perhaps something to be said for the claim that, if the final couple happy ending is unrealistic, then this is partly because of its continual repetition – though not quite for the reasons laid out above. One persuasive reason for calling the final couple unrealistic may be not because it is necessarily unrepresentative of reality, but because it is routinely viewed as *so* representative of fictions.

In Hollywood movies, when it is not having accusations of wish-fulfillment leveled at it, it is unsurprising to find that the term 'happy ending' is also often used in relation to fictions that exist within the world of the film. In *Make Way For Tomorrow* (1937), Lucy (Beulah Bondi) reports that a movie she saw at the cinema was 'a little sad in places, but it had a happy ending'; in *Must Love Dogs* David (Colin Eggersfield) says of *Doctor Zhivago* (1965), 'When they remake this they've got to add a happy ending'. The same is true of 'happily ever after': *The Ghost and Mrs. Muir*'s (1947) titular character (Gene Tierney) at one point says that she has 'just finished a novel in which the heroine was kissed in a rose garden and lived happily ever after'; in *Kate and Leopold* (2001), Kate's secretary (Natasha Lyonne) is asked of the romance novel she has just read, 'Did it end happily ever after?'; while Alex (Luke Wilson) in *Alex and Emma* (2003) explains what stage he is at with his latest novel by saying, 'Adam needs a fortune so he can live happily ever after with his true love'.[4]

Clearly, the reason for the constant use of these phrases in connection with fictions is that final couple happy endings are seen as an exceedingly common feature of fictional narratives, and particularly Hollywood movies. Nowhere can we see this more plainly than in how movies themselves have chosen to parody Hollywood endings. A relatively early example of this comes in *Sherlock, Jr.* (1924), in which Keaton, standing in a cinema's projection booth with a woman he is courting, takes cues on romance from the movie playing in front of him: the onscreen hero kisses his heroine's hand, prompting Keaton to kiss *his* girl's hand, and so on. This continues until the film-within-a-film shows its onscreen couple kiss, dissolves immediately to a shot of hero and heroine holding several babies, and (we have every right to presume) promptly ends; the final image of *Sherlock, Jr.*, meanwhile, is of Keaton looking decidedly puzzled by this chain of events. *The Dancing Cavalier*, the film-within-a-film in *Singin' in the Rain* (1952), ends with a close-up of its central couple singing of their love for one another and kissing. In *Paris When it Sizzles* (1964), Richard (William Holden), a screenwriter, tells Gabrielle (Audrey

Hepburn), his secretary, that a Hollywood film necessarily ends with 'that ultimate and inevitable moment: the final, earth-moving, studio-rent-paying, theatre-filling, popcorn-selling *kiss*. Fade out. The end.' This film itself goes on to end in precisely this way: speaking of the new script Richard is writing, Gabrielle asks, 'It will have a happy ending, won't it?', before intoning his earlier words ('Theatre-filling, popcorn selling . . .') then falling into a passionate embrace as the words, 'Kiss. Fade out. The End.' are typed onto the screen.

Furthermore, assumptions about the final couple's ubiquity in fiction are hardly confined to the cinema and, on the contrary, are a longstanding feature of popular opinion regarding narrative more broadly. 'When one writes a novel about grown people,' Mark Twain wrote, 'he knows exactly where to stop – that is, with a marriage' (Twain 1980: 237). Equally, from the world of theatre, there is the aforementioned line from *Love's Labour's Lost*: 'Our wooing doth not end like an old play; Jack hath not Jill'. For hundreds of years it has held true that, as David Shumway says, 'the love story is so familiar in our culture that we rarely give it a second thought. [. . .] 'Boy gets girl, boy loses girl, boy gets girl back' is exhibit A of standard plots in all fictional media' (2003: 157). While perhaps exaggerated, this assumption nonetheless reflects an undeniable truth about the final couple's prevalence (even if not its total monopoly), and this assumption, however oversimplified, has great significance for discourses surrounding the unrealism of final couples.

It is here that the distinction between cliché and convention again becomes important. Realism, as we are often told, is 'an effect created by [. . .] an artwork through the use of conventional devices' (Thompson 1988: 197). That is to say: rather than being an objective, static quality, realism is a shifting, historically- and culturally-specific attribution whose conventional signifiers are arrived at discursively rather than fixed for all time. Of course, it is only through repetition that fictional conventions become both formed and associated with particular effects. However, if repeated and experienced enough times, a convention can come to gain the status of a cliché, and from here it is not difficult for its conventionality to be viewed instead as *artificiality*. When any convention becomes this familiar it can come to seem *excessively* conventional, something dictated only by the demands governing certain kinds of representation – rather than, perhaps, something appearing to 'approximate reality'. This can happen even for conventions once considered realistic. For instance, contemporaneous champions of Italian Neorealist cinema would often praise the movement's 'open endings', and would 'motivate and justify their failure to resolve by appealing to a realistic aesthetic' (Neupert 1995: 75). However, as Thompson says, writing of *Bicycle Thieves* (1948):

> By now the open and unhappy ending has become a cliché of the
> modern art cinema, but we should bear in mind that *Bicycle Thieves*
> was one of the first widely seen films that used it [. . .]. Subsequent
> usage has pointed up the conventional nature of a device that must have
> conveyed a strong sense of realism to postwar audiences. (1988: 211)

A feeling of over-familiarity alone, then, can be one cause for a device coming
to be viewed as unrealistic, where unrealism here refers to the sense of excessive conventionality that may accompany cliché. In their study of clichés in
literature, Amossy and Lyons note that 'the cliché points not to the real but
to language' (1982: 41); we need not sidetrack ourselves with the concept
of 'cinematic language' in order to acknowledge that something similar can
be said of filmic conventions that have come to be regarded as clichéd. This
process is what Anton Zijderveld in his book *On Clichés* calls 'the supersedure
of meaning by function' – an original meaning or representation increasingly
appearing to be 'something stale and worn out by overuse' (1979: 8).

In the case of the excessively familiar cross-medium convention of the final
couple, we might even say we are dealing with a narrative device that points
not to 'the real' but to something as general as '*fictional* language' (Bordwell
claims that 'the final clinch' was 'a device which became considered clichéd by
the second half of the teens' [1985: 268]). If the process whereby 'traits [. . .]
become automatized by repetition' (Thompson 1988: 199) might be said to
have taken place even for so comparatively recent a convention as the modern
art cinema's 'open ending', then the final couple's reputation for having been
repeated hundreds of thousands of times, across many hundreds of years and
virtually all forms of storytelling – to the point that it might be called 'exhibit
A of standard plots in all fictional media' (Shumway 2003: 157) – has doubtless ensured that the association with fiction has been enacted tenfold upon
this convention. In short, despite referring to something so common to real
life – beginnings of romantic relationships – the final couple's status as the fictional cliché *par excellence* has meant that its ability to seemingly 'approximate
reality' has been severely compromised.

Clearly, this understanding of unrealism as 'excessive conventionality' can
only be grounded in historically-specific intertextual expectations since, as
Adolphe Haberer puts it, 'there is no cliché outside of the context of its reception' (2005: 144). As such, this definition does not assume that there is something *intrinsically* unrealistic about a particular convention itself. Later in this
chapter I will ask whether the final couple might also be viewed as intrinsically
unrealistic in this fashion. However, this particular intertextual conception of
unrealism is absolutely fundamental to the historical reputation and cultural
meaning of happy endings, and demands to be addressed. As such, I will now
explore the potential problem faced by any film desiring to feature a final

couple: how to navigate this convention when its status as a cliché ensures it is so apparently tied to fiction, and thus – by one definition – unrealism?

PRETTY WOMAN: 'THIS IS HOLLYWOOD!'

Pretty Woman, famously, offers one answer to this question. This film follows Vivian (Julia Roberts), a prostitute working on Hollywood Boulevard, and her relationship with a client, Edward (Richard Gere), a corporate mogul from New York. A defining feature of this film is its frequent nods to other fictional romances: Vivian watches the ending of *Charade* (1963) on television, seeing Audrey Hepburn embracing Cary Grant; the couple attend *La Traviata*, itself concerning a romance between a prostitute and a rich man; asked for an example of someone for whom 'things worked out', Vivian's friend Kit (Laura San Giacomo) answers, 'Cinder-fuckin'-rella!'; more pervasively, the film's narrative is inspired by *Pygmalion*, and also features a variation on the horserace scene from *My Fair Lady* (1964). At one point, when the couple have grown closer, Edward offers to pay for accommodation for Vivian to get her off the streets; Vivian responds,

> When I was a little girl, my momma used to lock me in the attic when I was bad, which was pretty often. And I would pretend I was a princess trapped in the tower by a wicked queen. And then suddenly this knight on a white horse with these colours flying would come charging up and draw his sword, and I would wave, and he would climb up the tower and rescue me. But never in all the time that I had this dream did the knight say to me, 'Come on, baby: I'll put you up in a great condo.'

Vivian later tells Edward, 'You made me a really nice offer, but . . . I want more.' 'The question,' Edward says, 'is how much more?' 'I want the fairy tale,' she answers. Eventually the couple parts, Edward planning to return to New York and Vivian intending to finish school in San Francisco. In the final scene, however, Edward pulls up to Vivian's apartment in a (white) limousine, 'Amami Alfredo' from *La Traviata* blaring from the speakers, brandishing an umbrella as if it were the sword from Vivian's fairy tale. 'Princess Vivian!' he shouts, as she rushes to look from her upstairs window. Bouquet of red roses in hand, he ascends the fire escape, and the two embrace. 'So, what happened *after* he climbed up the tower and rescued her?' he asks. 'She rescues him right back,' she replies. As the pair kiss the camera cranes back and picks up the chorus-like figure of the 'Happy Man' (Abdul Salaam El Razzac), to whom we were introduced at the beginning of the film when he gave a variation on the movie's closing speech: 'Welcome to Hollywood! What's your dream?

Everybody comes here – this is Hollywood: land of dreams! [. . .] This is Hollywood: always time to dream, so keep on dreamin' . . .'; we wipe to black.

This final scene includes elements of the romantic fictions invoked throughout the film: Edward and Vivian kiss like Audrey Hepburn and Cary Grant, overcome class boundaries as in *My Fair Lady*, enact a version of the fairy tale, and are accompanied by the opera. The reason for this approach can be gauged by the words of the 'Happy Man', which serve, as director Garry Marshall puts it in the Region 2 DVD's commentary, to 'give us the idea that maybe this was all a fantasy'. In short, this is a version of what we have previously referred to as an implausible happy ending. Why this film should desire to suggest in its final moments that it is 'all a fantasy' is a matter worth probing, since it can tell us something of the relationship between perceived excessive conventionality and perceived 'unrealism', and the reputation of the 'happy ending' ending in particular.

Unrealism and the 'new romance'

Pretty Woman has often been treated as a key example of what romantic comedy scholars have come to call the 'new romance' (Neale 1992) – a cycle of Hollywood (and British) romantic comedies produced from the 1980s onwards which repeatedly display, amongst other things, a 'knowing embrace of the artifice of convention' (Krutnik 1998: 27). These kinds of films, whose strategies are still absolutely in circulation today (see Garrett 2007: 92), are characterised in part by the way they allude to previous romantic narratives such as films, books, or plays, often in a manner that allows them to contrast fiction with real life. The narratives or cultural discourses referred to might be romantic novels (e.g. *You've Got Mail* [*Pride and Prejudice* (1831)], *Serendipity* [*Love in a Time of Cholera* (1985)], *The Jane Austen Book Club* [2007]), theatre (e.g. *Moonstruck* [opera], *The Prince and Me* [2004] [*A Midsummer Night's Dream* (1600)], *Shakespeare in Love*), specific Hollywood movies (e.g. *When Harry Met Sally* [*Casablanca*], *Only You* [*Roman Holiday*], *Because I Said So* [2007] [*Love in the Afternoon*] [1957]), or Hollywood in general (e.g. *Notting Hill*, *America's Sweethearts* [2001], *Win a Date With Tad Hamilton!*). One mode referenced particularly frequently is the fairy tale – a story form now regularly implied to be *the* most representative of naïve romantic fancy (itself a problematic association; see Zipes [2006]). In *Kate and Leopold*, Kate (Meg Ryan again) cites the marriage of Charles and Diana as 'further proof [that] you can't live a fairy tale'; in *Music and Lyrics* (2007), Alex (Hugh Grant) upbraids Sophie (Drew Barrymore): 'You think life is this fairy tale, and when it turns out everything doesn't end happily you can't deal with it.' Meanwhile the contemporary real world of romantic relationships is accordingly repeatedly characterised by its *lack* of such romantic conventions; as Erica (Diane

Keaton) says in *Something's Gotta Give* of the ending to her play: 'I always wanted to end a play [in Paris]. People need romance, and if someone like me doesn't write it where are they going to get it? Real *life*?!'

I would agree with those critics (e.g. Krutnik 1998; Deleyto/Evans 1998; Garrett 2007, etc.) who explain this tendency at least partly in relation to postmodernism. Postmodernism has been defined according to almost countless tendencies, but one recurring theme of course has been its close relationship to the exponential increase in mass communication during the late twentieth century (e.g. Best/Kellner 1997: 124–194), and the accompanying rise of popular culture which knowingly pastiches, cites or otherwise alludes to the conventions and products of other popular culture (e.g. Hoesterey 2001: 45–78). Although such strategies are a very long way from being unique to the 'postmodern' period, perhaps even tending to emerge cyclically in cultures (see, for instance, Dyer 2007), certain unsustainable claims about their historical radicalism should not blind us to the fact that particular approaches to allusion do appear at least to have become *more* pronounced in American film during the last forty-or-so years (see Carroll 1982). With Jameson, we might say that what once may often have been 'residual' for the medium became a 'cultural dominant' (1991: 4); in the process, pointedly self-conscious intertextuality seemed to develop into one of the key features of popular filmmaking in general (see Booker 2007: 89–150), and of romantic comedy in particular.

It is not difficult to see why this process might have particular significance for those areas of culture concerned with representing romantic love. As mentioned, the conventions of romantic narrative have long been considered hackneyed, something that can be gauged by the sorts of parodies and pastiches noted above. In keeping with this, such practices in fact have a considerable history in romance texts: we could cite *Northanger Abbey*'s pastiche of Gothic novels (1818), or Shakespeare's parody of the conventions of romance sonnets in Sonnet 130 ('My Mistress' Eyes'), and so on. More specifically, the implausible happy ending itself has a long heritage: Elizabethan comedies, for instance, would not infrequently end with the spectator being 'invited directly or by inference to look at the bare bones out of which the play was made, to accept consciously the unashamed artificiality of its conventions' (Jagendorf 1984: 12). It is thus unsurprising that Hollywood too should long have desired to do something comparable, as with the aforementioned *Sherlock, Jr.* – or, for instance, *Platinum Blonde* (1931), which ends with a playwright describing the happy ending he is currently writing while he embraces the object of his affection. While thus far from offering something new, however, the self-conscious strategies of the 'new romance' do nonetheless seem to be indicative of an escalation in such approaches (Krutnik 1998).

Pastiche is an appropriate strategy for a cultural moment 'haunted by the overpresence of the "already said"' and its accompanying anxieties (Krutnik

1998: 28). This burden of the 'already said' is bound to be borne especially heavily by conventions which already shouldered a great deal of its weight. It is hardly surprising that, in a postmodern context, the already very over-familiar conventions of romance came in for particular scrutiny. As Charlie (Steve Martin) says to the titular *Roxanne* (1987): 'I'm afraid of words – they've all been used up in adverts. [. . .] How can I use the same words about you that someone uses about a *stuffing?*' The main point to make about this for now is that this excessive over-familiarity could not help but accelerate the process of a diminishing appearance of realism, whereby meaning is superseded by function and conventions become 'automatized by repetition' (Thompson 1988: 48). The 'new romance' can thus be seen as a sustained attempt to deal with the corresponding appearance of heightened *un*realism of its genre's conventions – in particular, the final couple happy ending.

Unrealism and the implausible happy ending

As implied by the cycle's preoccupation with the fairy tale, the conventions of romantic narrative with which 'new romances' are especially concerned usually relate to *successful* romances. Of course, tragic romance has a long list of conventions of its own, but it is not these that appear to have become over-identified with fiction. Thus, despite featuring numerous tragic operas in its narrative, in *Moonstruck* Ronny (Nicholas Cage) nonetheless tells Loretta (Cher) that 'Love don't make things nice – it ruins everything. [. . .] The story books are *bullshit!*' Likewise, in *Sleepless in Seattle*, Annie and Becky watch *An Affair to Remember*, prompting the following exchange:

> Annie: Now, those were the days when people *knew* how to be in love – they knew it! Time, distance, nothing could separate them, because they knew it was *right*, it was *real*, it was . . .
> Becky: . . . A *movie*! That's your problem: you don't want to be in love, you want to be in love *in a movie*.

Clearly, there exist any number of 'story books' and Hollywood movies in which love does indeed 'ruin everything', and in which a great deal is capable of separating couples – say, *La Traviata*, which is featured in *Pretty Woman* (or indeed *An Affair to Remember*, which may end with a final couple, but depicts a far more troubled romance than *Sleepless*). Furthermore, given the post-1960s decline in romantic melodrama and rise in romantic comedy (see Preston [2000], Dowd/Pallotta [2000], etc.), it is precisely in the *past*, in 'the days' seemingly longed for by a character like Annie, that such 'unhappy' portrayals were more prevalent. Yet 'new romances' nonetheless almost exclusively align fiction with an imaginary cultural past made up of *successful* romantic narratives.

Given its reputation for ubiquity, it is unsurprising that the final couple happy ending should have been particularly affected by the 'overpresence of the "already said"'. Similarly, given the 'new romance' preoccupation with successful romantic culture, it follows that – of all the local conventions of romantic fiction – happy endings should have been treated by the cycle as romance's *ur*-convention, a virtual synecdoche for the genre. As such, they have also often been treated for this reason as the epitome of what the genre, in this context, is taken to stand for: unrealism. *Pretty Woman* is far from unique amongst its contemporaries for featuring a happy ending that is treated in a particularly self-conscious fashion. Sometimes these movies will include within them diegetic romance films, of which we are permitted to see only their ending (e.g. *Only You* [1994], *The Wedding Planner* [2001], *The Holiday* [2006]). In *Notting Hill*, when William goes to the cinema to watch Anna star in a romantic comedy, all we see of the film is what we can assume to be its clichéd ending ('In about seven seconds I'm going to ask you to marry me,' Anna's co-star tells her with absurd gravity); similarly, *Win a Date With Tad Hamilton!* (2004) begins with three of its main characters watching the final couple happy ending of a romantic movie in the cinema, prompting Pete (Topher Grace) to exclaim, 'What kind of desperate and pathetic emotional cripple would actually *buy* that as an ending?!'

This latter film also then goes on to practise what is the more common strategy, which is for a 'new romance' to suggest that its *own* happy ending may be implausible. Thus, *Win a Date With Tad Hamilton!* concludes by re-enacting the happy ending that opened the film, with a similar setting (a road at night), song (a modern update of the opening scene's jazz standard), dialogue ('Would you like to dance?'), camera movement (a final pull-out), and even the font for its superimposed words, 'The End'. Comparable examples can be found in *Something's Gotta Give*, which ends with a real-life re-enactment of the romantic scene in Paris written for Erica's play; *Romancing the Stone* (1984), which ends like the romance novel Joan (Kathleen Turner) has just finished writing; *She's All That* (1998), which precedes its final kiss with Laney (Rachel Leigh Cook) saying, 'I feel just like Julia Roberts in *Pretty Woman!*' *Sleepless in Seattle* offers one of the most overt examples of the tendency: firstly, when Annie and Sam meet on the Empire State Building, this moment is accompanied, not by music from *Sleepless'* composer, Marc Shaiman, but by the score of *An Affair to Remember*; secondly, as the lift doors are closing Jonah looks directly towards the camera and smiles; finally, the excessively long zoom-out, the cartoon map of the US, and the fireworks that shoot up into space, all help highlight the artificiality of the film's fictional world.[5]

Thus, while 'new romances' may cite other romantic texts or conventions throughout, it is at their happy endings that this strategy becomes particularly important. Prior to its ending, *Pretty Woman* on one level simply uses its inter-texts to imply its awareness of the clichéd nature of fictional romantic conventions. When Vivian explains that the knight in her imagined fairy tale never once said to the princess 'Come on, baby: I'll put you up in a great condo,' she is suggesting that her life – and by extension, at this point, the movie – is more realistic (partly simply because more *modern*) by comparison. Likewise, when she discusses her situation with Kit the pair jokingly contrast Vivian's life to a fairy tale:

> Kit: Maybe you guys could, like, get a house together and buy some diamonds and a horse; *I* don't know – it could work, it *happens*!
>
> Vivian: *When* does it happen, Kit? When does it happen? Who does it really work out for? Did it work out for 'Skinny' Marie or Rachel? No! [. . .] You give me one example of someone we know that it happened for. [. . .]
>
> Kit: Cinder-fuckin'-rella!

The simultaneously vague and exaggerated terms in which Kit lays out her imagined picture of Vivian and Edward's future implies the absurdity of the notion that anything like this could ever happen in 'real life': only in the world of fiction, the realm of 'Cinder-fuckin'-rella', is a romantic future featuring houses, horses and diamonds possible. The grimness of the world represented by fellow Hollywood Boulevard prostitutes like 'Skinny' Marie, by contrast, allows only for a *lack* of this fiction. This point is made again when Vivian is about to leave Edward's hotel and the kindly hotel manager (Hector Elizondo) enquires sadly, 'Then I gather you are not accompanying Mr. Lewis to New York?' 'Come on, Barney,' Vivian replies, 'You and me live in the real world – most of the time.'

Yet *Pretty Woman*'s ending does, of course, see things 'work out'. It does so, however, without relinquishing the film's earlier beliefs in the indissoluble link between the 'happy ending' and fiction. Rather than attempt to present the couple's union as a convincing solution to its narrative, the film instead uses the various elements of its implausible happy ending to reinforce its unrealism, ensuring that we are able to see it as nothing less than the fiction it now self-professedly is. This ending is associated with the combined fictional realms suggested by the fairy tale, *La Traviata*, and *Pygmalion*; more than anything, though, it is tied to the notion of 'Hollywood' to which the 'Happy Man' refers; as Robyn R. Warhol says:

> on the intradiegetic level, Hollywood is the town next door to Beverly Hills, the location of prostitution, drug addiction, poverty, and death;

at the extradiegetic level [. . .], Hollywood is the source of movies that confirm fairy-tale wishes for 'happy endings'. (2003: 69)

In its final moments if not before, the Hollywood in which the film is set becomes transformed from the geographical location into the ontological concept: the 'land of dreams' – the only place, the film seems to suggest, in which this happy ending would be possible. No longer is there a separation between the world in which the film's characters live and the world of fiction to which they have continually longingly referred: both are rendered equally unrealistic by this intentionally excessively clichéd happy ending.

This strategy is thus different than that used by a film such as, say, *Annie Hall*, towards the end of which Alvy (Woody Allen) writes a sophomoric play about his relationship with Annie (Diane Keaton). This play ends happily in a way that Alvy and Annie's actual relationship did not. After watching its final scene in rehearsal Alvy turns to the camera: 'What do you want?' he asks us, 'It was my first play! You know, you're always trying to get things to work out perfect in art because it's real difficult in life . . .' Allen's film then concludes by showing us what really became of this couple: a final platonic meeting, after which the two part ways. This film thus draws a clear distinction between the fictional world of happy endings and the world of real romantic relationships by offering what is essentially a gag about the inauthenticity of happy endings, albeit a tender one.

Pretty Woman's ending is a little more complex. Rather than maintaining *Annie Hall*'s distinction between 'art' and 'life', this film collapses it, self-consciously adopting the role of 'clichéd' fiction.[6] Nora Ephron, *Sleepless*' director and co-writer, has said of her 'new romance' that, 'Our dream was to make a movie about how movies screw up your brain about love, and then if we did a good job, we would become one of the movies that screwed up people's brains about love forever' (Maltby 2003: 19). That film's happy ending thus grants its characters their wish to not simply 'be in love' but 'be in love in a movie', wholeheartedly removing itself from anything that might be confused with reality. Likewise for *Pretty Woman*: at the moment Vivian remarks to Barney that she and he live in 'the real world', the ontological division her words imply is still putatively in place; by the time of Edward's ascent to her window to the strains of *La Traviata*, it has been dissolved.

In an article concerning the concept of realism in film studies, Christopher Williams writes that 'we need films to be about life in one way or another, but we allow them latitude about how they meet this need' (1994: 282). We might say that the implausible happy ending meets this need by drawing a particularly sharp distinction between 'life' and fiction. Representing one possible response to the close association of happy endings with unrealism, *Pretty Woman* enacts a traditional comedic fulfillment of desires, yet does so by announcing that this fulfillment is only possible in a fictional world. While comedic films tend, as Thomas puts it, to suggest that 'the social space within them is transformable into something better' (2000:14), *Pretty Woman* in a sense implies the impossibility of such a transformation – without, that is, a film retreating entirely into the realm of fiction, and sealing its happy ending forever inside.

As mentioned in the introduction, this general approach to the 'happy ending' is in fact the model that is most frequently discussed in film studies: the happy ending which, as Bordwell puts it, 'flaunts the disparity between what we ask of art and what we know of social life' (1982: 7). In its characterisation of the 'happy ending' as something that must always necessarily exist in opposition to, in Vivian's words, 'the real world', it is a strategy grounded in a conception of the convention in its clichéd, Platonic form. Doubtless, the reason it has proved so popular with both film critics and Hollywood cinema is precisely because it conforms so readily to the reputation of the 'happy ending' for being unrealistic. Yet, how deserved is this reputation? We have so far been treating the unrealism of the 'happy ending' as something caused by the convention's over-familiarity. By this rationale, *any* artistic convention could potentially come to be viewed as unrealistic. Let us thus now address the question of whether this convention *itself* appears to 'approximate reality' or otherwise.

Happy endings and innate unrealism: 'the dilemma of fiction and reality'

> We cannot say, surely, that any sequence of real events actually comes to an end, that reality itself disappears, that events *of the order of the real* have ceased to happen.
>
> – Hayden White (1981: 22: original emphasis)

We have established that realism and unrealism are always a matter of convention, but it is necessary to explore this notion further. Literary and film theorists have long tended to avoid treating realism as something which 'depends on a natural relationship of the artwork to the world' (Thompson 1988: 197). Instead, its conventional nature has been interpreted as meaning that the relationship between 'realism' and reality is also arbitrary. This is an interpretation that effectively relies upon a definition of 'convention' as

> . . . something adopted in the context where there are alternative ways of achieving the same effect and it is a matter of indifference as to which of the alternatives is adopted, such as driving on the left or right hand side of the road.' (Carroll 1988: 248).

Taken to its logical extreme, such a framework prompts recommendations such as Anne Jerslev's, that 'contemporary discussions of reality and the media seek to problematize any understanding of a relationship between the two concepts that is based on absolute ontological differences' (2002: 8). Yet the fact of realism's conventionality – that the concept changes according to different needs, and 'no one set of traits can define realism for all time' (Thompson 1988: 198) – should not necessarily lead us to conclude that the relationship between reality and what comes to be called realism (or unrealism) in media is either non-existent or arbitrary. Stressing the process of negotiated agreement that is innate to convention, Gilberto Perez writes in *The Material Ghost* that

> A soliloquy in the theatre is plainly a convention. But it is not arbitrary: it is motivated by its resemblance to the way someone we know might take us aside in life to confide his or her thoughts. And it is not a matter of indifference whether Hamlet's thoughts are expressed in the soliloquy Shakespeare gives him or written in Morse code at the back of the stage. (1998: 23)

In need of a device which implies taking the audience into confidence, it is not by chance that the theatre developed a convention that resembles how such an action is performed in social life. This convention in turn met with agreement from audiences thanks to that resemblance. This is simply to say that, while always a matter of convention, it will not be true that just *anything* can come to be viewed as realistic, or indeed *un*realistic. Given this, beyond its familiarity from fiction, what might be said to motivate the association of the final couple happy ending with an effect of unrealism?

If anything has the power to make the final couple happy ending appear innately unrealistic it is not, I think, the fact that it is 'happy', but rather the fact that it is an *ending*. 'A narrative has a beginning and an ending,' writes Christian Metz, 'a fact that [. . .] distinguishes it from the rest of the world' (1968: 17). It is a justifiable commonplace for both artists and critics to draw attention to the fact that, as Northrop Frye puts it, 'except for death, life has little to suggest in the way of plausible conclusions' (Frye 1963: 36), and that the true ending of a sequence of events is therefore something that can only exist in representation, and particularly in narrative (see also: Ricoeur 1984, White 1981, etc.). This tension between the endlessness of reality and the necessary endedness of narrative is another implication of Henry James' observation that 'really, universally, relations stop nowhere'; yet James also, as we have seen, describes the task of the fiction writer as being to draw 'the circle within which they shall happily *appear* to do so' (1934: 5). 'This,' says Frank Kermode – perhaps the critic who has done most to explicate this aspect of narrative – 'is what I crudely call the dilemma of fiction and reality' (1967: 131).

In his seminal book on narrative, *The Sense of an Ending*, Kermode draws upon the ancient Greek distinction between two different kinds of time: *chronos* and *kairos*. *Chronos*, he offers, is time in its true nature: simply successive, contingent, 'passing time', unordered and unmeaning (ibid.: 47). *Kairos*, meanwhile, is time as we experience it in narrative, 'filled with significance, charged with a meaning derived from its relationship to the end' (ibid.: 47). 'Normally we associate "reality" with *chronos*,' he goes on, and 'in every plot there is an escape from chronicity, and so, in some measure, a deviation from this norm of "reality"' (ibid.: 50). Kermode's argument in fact goes on to stress that the human mind itself also tends to flee *chronos* in favour of *kairos* via narrativising, in constant need as it is of 'organisation that humanises time by giving it form' (ibid.: 45). For now though, let us remain with this notion that endlessness and contingency constitute the closest description of how reality is ordered temporally, even if it may not be how humans themselves tend to perceive temporality.

Viewing the matter in this way means that, as David Lodge writes, 'ending a story at all – [. . .] tying up all the loose ends of the plot, settling the destinies of all the characters – comes to seem like a falsification of reality' (1982: 150). Every ending *is* an ending, and is also to that extent – by this definition – unrealistic. Given this, ends have often proved problematic for storytellers wishing to 'approximate reality'. 'Nearly all novels are feeble at the end,' wrote E. M. Forster, 'because the plot requires to be wound up.' (1962: 102). Likewise, George Eliot suggested that 'conclusions are the weak point of most authors, but some of the fault lies in the very nature of a conclusion, which is at best a negation' (2005: 102). Of course, both these novelists themselves played roles in pioneering approaches to narrative that operated on the assumption that, as Iris Murdoch later put it, 'since reality is incomplete, art must not be too afraid of incompleteness' (1977: 31). They did this partly by complicating precisely the process of 'tying up all the loose ends of the plot' – since, as Armine Kotin Mortimer asks, 'how can one pretend verisimilitude without encoding a lack of finality?' (1985: 185-6). Referencing James' comments on the subject, William R. Thickstun notes that during the nineteenth century novelists increasingly attempted to 'draw the necessary aesthetic circle in such a way that human relations shall happily appear *not* to stop within it, leaving the reader free to imagine that the characters go on living – as if they were real people – after the novel's close' (1988: 7).

Using this definition, the matter of how to avoid concluding a narrative unrealistically thus becomes similar to the matter of how to temper its sense of closure: it is a question of the extent to which an ending is made to *feel like* an ending. Like our previous definition of unrealism as 'excessive conventionality', this understanding of the term – schematically, as 'the illusory appearance of finality' – is again clearly very specific. However, to avoid accusations of

unwarranted idiosyncrasy, we might point out that something like this definition of realism and its opposite haunts even theoretical approaches to film
that have famously regarded realist approaches to cinema as 'eminently reactionary' (Comolli/Narboni 1971: 30). Perhaps simply because 'we need films
to be about life in one way or another' (Williams 1994: 282), we can see the
continuing appeal of realism's essential aims in the fact that many '*anti*-realist'
film theorists themselves do not abandon their search for forms that would
better 'approximate reality'. In his landmark article 'Realism and the Cinema:
Notes on Some Brechtian Theses', for example, Colin MacCabe criticises the
'classic realist text' – yet does so on the grounds that such a text is 'a heavily
"closed" discourse', which (in Marxist terms) "cannot deal with the real in its
contradictions' (1974: 16). Comparably, Peter Wollen has extolled the merits
of modernism on the following grounds:

> The world itself is an untidy place, full of loose ends, but the artifact
> can tie all these loose ends together and thus convey to us a meaningful
> truth, an insight, which enables us to go back to the real world with a
> reordered and recycled experience which will enable us to cope better,
> live more fully and so on. [. . .] All this is overthrown when we begin to
> see loose ends in works of art, to refuse to acknowledge organic unity.
> (1998: 117)

Like the most traditional champions of realism, then, what MacCabe and
Wollen in fact praise is a representational mode capable of conveying 'the real'
and 'the real world', respectively. Furthermore, they object to the tendency of
texts to appear 'closed' and to 'tie all [. . .] loose ends together', at the expense
of a view of reality which recognises the world as 'an untidy place' – however
one conceptualises such 'untidiness'. Proceeding from a completely different
set of assumptions than the authors and critics cited earlier, as well as offering different diagnoses and plans of action, such theorists nevertheless imply
strikingly similar conclusions about what constitutes both reality and one
typical narrative means of its distortion (see Rushton [2011] on political modernist film theory's underlying commitment to representational 'reality'). It is
thus instructive to note that even here (in a theoretical tradition to which we
will return in Chapter 4) we find 'the frequently evoked conflict between the
closed form of art [. . .] and the openness of life' (Miller 1981: xi). This adds
further persuasiveness to the suggestion that this conflict should be seen as a
key aspect of the 'willed tendency of art to approximate reality' – as well as the
tendency *not* to do so.

Temporal unrealism and the final couple

> If you want a happy ending, that depends, of course, on where you stop your story.
>
> – Orson Welles (Vidal 2002: 221)

How might the final couple relate to this conception of unrealism? A central issue of the preceding chapter was that an ending depicting the first few moments of a new relationship should be recognised as an image not of an ending, but a *beginning* – not an end of time, but of time laid up in store. This, though, is a matter of degrees. As I have said, what follows this conventional beginning tends to be not so much elided as implied; this, however, speaks again to the potential paradox at the heart of the final couple. As F. M. Dunn puts it in relation to theatre (though his words are equally applicable to film): on the one hand, final couple endings can

> suggest that human events have a life of their own, continuing beyond the end of the performance and still engaging our interest and curiosity. On the other hand, they show that the future offers simply more of the same, promising no new departure from the pattern of earlier events. [. . .] It's not really the end, but it might as well be. (1996: 67/8)

Despite the basic importance of continuation to the image of the final couple, it is possible for this continuation to be treated in different ways, and one of these ways is for a couple's future to be coded as entirely predictable, meaning that 'the event of marriage [becomes] the happy ending beyond which no comment is necessary because nothing happens: all is serene' (Boone 1987: 79). In such treatments, Altman writes, 'the couple is united, the film ends, and we must accept on faith the implied assertion that they live happily ever after. By convention, time stops when the couple kisses, and change is forever banished from their life together' (1987: 51). It is this notion of stopped time and banished change that is important for our current understanding of unrealism. Shumway puts the matter similarly:

> The ending leaves the couple isolated in their own bliss. [. . .] In other words, there is no possibility of a *post coitum triste*, but rather the explicit denial of the temporality of satisfaction. It is in this illusory eternity that marriage is rendered mystical, in spite of whichever of its realities the film has indulged earlier. (1991: 16/17)

It is this 'denial of temporality of satisfaction' that I would suggest is the primary way in which a final couple might reasonably be considered to have the potential for innate unrealism within our current terms. Virginia Wright Wexman has pointed out that there exists an essential contradiction between the nature of romantic love as an 'all-consuming passion that is by its very nature short-lived' and its position in modern societies as the building block for 'lifelong monogamous marriage'; she goes on: 'Hollywood film has elided this contradiction through the convention of representing weddings [. . .] as the culmination of its romantic-love fantasies; thus, romantic love after marriage need not be portrayed' (1993: 8). A happy ending that attempts to ignore this contradiction by suggesting that the happiness accompanying the *beginning* of a romantic relationship will go on to characterise the *entirety* of the romance might thus, in these terms, be called unrealistic.

We have so far been speaking, however, in broad generalities. Paradigmatic pronouncements such as Altman's or Shumway's may apply to some actual, existing endings, but not necessarily all. The final couple's potential for treating what is in fact a beginning as an ending undoubtedly does in itself (according to our current definition) reflect a somewhat unrealistic impulse. However, the extent to which final couples actually *do* this will vary from film to film. In order to distinguish between what we might call different degrees of unrealism, then, we need to return to the question of closure, and the extent to which final couple happy endings present themselves *as* endings.

Looking for comparatively unrealistic happy endings in these terms, we might return to one with which we are already familiar: *Sleepless*'. In the previous chapter I discussed the many ways in which we are encouraged to regard this film's final couple as a conclusive end-point. Regardless of the fact that the characters still currently live on opposite sides of the United States, by its end the film has successfully implied that this meeting constitutes the end of Sam and Annie's story, and we are given no suggestion that the future beyond the fiction should bring the couple anything but undifferentiated happiness. The final pull-out to the cartoon map perhaps makes this point most strongly: as well as conveying a sense of artificiality, the device also suggests that, the story having been resolved by the final couple, the world of *Sleepless* has served its entire purpose. In contrast to Perkins' claim that 'the world does not end with the story's finish. It has a future and the future cannot be closed' (1999: 71), it almost seems here as if time itself – which can of course only pass *within* a world – stops altogether.

Likewise, despite its similarly self-conscious nature, the ending of *Pretty Woman* is also indicative of the 'timeless, formless' (Altman 1981: 197) manner in which a final couple can treat its implied future. When Edward asks, 'So, what happened *after* he climbed up the tower and rescued her?' Vivian answers, 'She rescues him right back.' Other than adding a pointedly post-feminist twist to the fairy tale, what Vivian's answer also tacitly conveys is that it is only the moment of union itself, not anything that may follow it, that is important to this final couple. As with *Sleepless*, the film ends poised at a moment when a great deal is yet to be settled for the couple: living arrangements, marital status, how the characters' huge class differences may impact on their new life together. Minutes earlier, for example, Vivian had predicted, following an attempted rape by Edward's colleague, Stuckey (Jason Alexander), that 'There'll always be some guy, even some friend of yours, thinking he can treat me like Stuckey, thinking that it's allowed'. It would be hypothetically possible for Edward's reference to what happens *after* the final kiss to serve as an invitation to address precisely this question of the future left unspoken by the imagined fairy tale's happy ending. Instead, such issues are brushed aside by Vivian's response, which places the focus firmly back upon what is realistically fleeting, but is rhetorically able to be treated as an 'eternal moment' – the 'rescuing' final kiss – at the expense of such temporal concerns.

Despite finishing only at moments of initial union or reunion, both these endings manage to effectively close down any suggestion of future change for their couples, and thus demonstrate one means by which a happy ending can imply the sense of immutable 'forever' stated more baldly by the phrase 'happily ever after'. Another way to achieve a similar effect, however, is to provide a *little* detail about the future, from which the viewer may extrapolate. This strategy, touched upon in the previous chapter, involves an epilogue that shows us, as Bordwell puts it, 'the final stability achieved by the narrative,' wherein, 'the characters' futures are settled' (1982: 4). As mentioned, such an epilogue may jump forward in time to present us with new information that allows us to imagine the shape of characters' future lives: for instance, letting us know that the couple marry (e.g. *Born Yesterday* [1950], *When Harry Met Sally* [1989], *Leap Year* [2010]), that they have children (e.g. *I Married a Witch* [1942], *Sweet Home Alabama* [2002], *50 First Dates* [2004]), or simply what their new life together looks like (e.g. *Mannequin* [1987], *Serving Sara* [2002], *Rumor Has It* [2005]). This common kind of happy ending does in a sense suggest that 'change is forever banished from [the couple's] life together', yet does so by leaving us *with* a change: a new status quo. In doing so, this approach discourages speculation about anything that might upset the resolution by granting us a glimpse of what the moment of resolution leads to. The fact that it *is* just a glimpse is important, though: attempting too exhaustive a depiction of the future could result in an epilogue like that of the aforementioned *College*, with its montage showing the final couple growing old and dying. I have suggested that one reason that this ending appears somewhat uneasy is that it marks a closing down of any possibility for continuation. We are now in a position to add that this effect is in turn permitted by the fact that the epilogue conveys openly something others often only imply: the ineluctable passage of time. It is far more usual for a romantic epilogue to take us only a *short* distance into the future, as opposed to actually showing (for instance) its coupling ageing. The possibly troubling temporality of an 'ever after' appears to work far more effectively in an epilogue when it is employed somewhat coyly rather than addressed head-on.

This is perhaps because the notion of a romantic couple experiencing an 'illusory eternity' is one about which many films themselves – like film critics – cannot help but appear justifiably suspicious. This much is suggested by a few contemporary movies that find themselves required to engage with the conventional ending of the fairy tale: 'They lived happily ever after,' we are told at the end of *Penelope* (2008), 'or at least – until now . . .'; 'We wound up going to Princeton together,' the teenage heroine of *A Cinderella Story* (2004) says in voiceover at the end of her film, 'and we lived happily ever after. At least for *now* – hey: I'm only a freshman!'; in *Sex and the City* (2008), which begins after its central couple have already settled down, Carrie (Sarah Jessica Parker) comments, 'We were perfectly happy before we decided to live happily ever after.' Again, this suspicion of the silent future implied by 'happily ever after' is by no means only a contemporary phenomenon. 'The prince and Cinderella always lived happily ever afterwards,' a young Kitty says to her father (Ernest Cossart) in *Kitty Foyle*; 'Yes, and that's where these writing fellas are smart,' he responds: 'they always end before the story really begins'. 'All our troubles are over,' says Jennifer (Veronica Lake) just prior to the epilogue of *I Married a Witch*: 'at least, for the *present* . . .'

In fact, while the kinds of securing epilogues mentioned above are certainly common, Hollywood also has a long history of producing final couple happy endings it would be impossible to describe in the atemporal terms suggested by Altman and Shumway. This has been seen in some of the endings we have looked at previously. For instance: in its stressing of a final moment of privacy for the couple, the ending of *The Enchanted Cottage* conveys overtly the fact that its couple's hallucination-induced happiness will be constantly under siege by reality from without, while the couples in *The Clock*, *Remember the Night*, and *I'll Be Seeing You* are happy, but their futures are on hold – in the former because of the war, in the latter two because of prison terms. These endings thus convey not only that life will indeed continue for their characters, but also that circumstances will – must – change, and that these couples' emotional states must themselves necessarily adapt accordingly. Likewise, in the previous chapter I demonstrated ways in which *Best Years* and *The Graduate* adapt their points of view to the effect that their final couples can no longer hope to be conclusive endings to their narratives, and are thus unable to imply anything like a post-narrative 'illusory eternity'.

Moving beyond previous examples, there are a great many romantic comedy final couple happy endings which are famous precisely *for* their precariousness. The comedies of remarriage examined by Cavell, for instance, will regularly offer a clear 'ambivalence or instability' (1981: 124). We might think of David (Cary Grant) embracing Susan (Katharine Hepburn) atop a crumbled dinosaur skeleton in *Bringing Up Baby* (1938); Hopsy (Henry Fonda) in the final moments of *The Lady Eve* still being ignorant of the fact that Jean (Barbara Stanwyck) has been pretending to be two different people; *The Awful Truth*'s couple vowing to create a future that is 'the same, but different'; the reunited lovers of *His Girl Friday* leaving to cover a news story whilst taking their second honeymoon (the thing that caused them to separate in the first place); or *Adam's Rib*, which ends in mid-argument (then implied make-up sex). All these conclusions contain elements which make it difficult to imagine that their couples' futures will be serene for all time, and in this sense produce, as Cavell later put it, 'endings that are not endings' (2005: 52). This, furthermore, is before we acknowledge the broader fact that, as Dana Polan points out, 'the very insistence on *re*marriage' means that 'there can always be a fall from perfection that requires the whole process to start all over again' (1991: 137). Any list of romantic comedies renowned for their ambiguous final couples would also have to include *The Palm Beach Story*, whose final intertitle, following a rushed double-wedding, reads 'They Lived Happily Ever After . . . Or Did They?' – perhaps the quintessential repudiation of the notion that a final couple need suggest that 'time stops' for its lovers following the film's end.

However, it is by no means only in such critically lauded conclusions that we discover happy endings striving to throw open the question of couples' futures. Indeed, it is extremely common for romantic comedy final couples to be left at moments of overt ambivalence or precariousness – say, Irene (Carole Lombard) practically bullying Godfrey (William Powell) into marrying her (without a license) in *My Man Godfrey* ('Stand still, Godfrey: it'll all be over in a minute . . .'); Margit (Myrna Loy) and Charles (William Powell) lying knocked out on the floor after a brawl at a misfired wedding in *Double Wedding*, a wreath reading 'Good Luck!' strewn over their unconscious bodies; *Bluebeard's Eighth Wife*, which ends following Nicole (Claudette Colbert) having driven her husband (Gary Cooper) literally insane, the final scene featuring him still in a straightjacket and rendered virtually mute by rage and sexual frustration; *A Foreign Affair*, with John (John Lund) backing off warily from Phoebe (Jean Arthur) as she is proposing marriage; *Four's a Crowd* (1938), with Bob (Errol Flynn) accidentally kissing the wrong new bride (Olivia de Havilland) before switching to his actual wife (Rosalind Russell) while their car is being pursued by angry dogs; or Paul (Robert Redford) and Corie (Jane Fonda) poised precariously on the roof of their building at the end of *Barefoot in the Park* (1967).

Equally, the ending may leave unresolved the question of to what extent one half of the couple actually knows the identity of the other, as in *Charade* (last line: 'I love you, Adam, Alex, Peter, Brian – whatever your name is . . .'),

Bachelor Mother ('You still think I'm the mother of that baby?' / 'Of course' / 'Haha.'), or *Housesitter* ('I love you, Gwen.' / 'Actually, it's Jessica . . .'). By the same token, at many endings the dialogue is careful to sow seeds of uncertainty about the future: 'We're taking things step by step,' Reuben (Ben Stiller) says of his relationship with Polly (Jennifer Aniston) at the end of *Along Came Polly*, 'seeing how they work out . . .'; 'So how is this going to work?' Kate (Emma Thompson) asks Harvey (Dustin Hoffman) at the end of *Last Chance Harvey*, to which he answers 'I have absolutely no idea'; 'Where are you going?' the couple in *America's Sweethearts* is asked, prompting them to reply 'We don't know!' / 'Isn't that great?!'; at the end of *Maid in Manhattan* the couple is grilled by the press: 'What do you think: the two of you got a chance?', to which Christopher (Ralph Fiennes) merely responds with a smile and a happy shrug. We could equally think of *Down to You* ('How will this work?' / 'I don't know . . .'), *What Happens in Vegas* ('I have absolutely no clue what I'm going to do . . .'), or *Forget Paris* (1995): 'Why's it gonna work *this* time?' / 'It'll be a piece of cake . . .' – this latter line being a phrase that the film has trained us to associate with things being about to go spectacularly wrong. Or, perhaps my favourite for its mixing of optimism, rationalism, and generality: 'So, it might not last,' Rosie (Michelle Pfeiffer) says of her relationship with Adam (Paul Rudd) in the final scene of *I Could Never Be Your Woman* (2007): 'you can say that about anyone . . .'

It is also worth briefly drawing attention to a common feature of romantic comedy that is too little commented upon. We have repeatedly encountered assumptions to the effect that Hollywood films create closure by ensuring 'a resolution is reached, whereupon the film ends' (Armes 1994: 65). This is often not the case in romantic comedies, however. Almost as common as epilogues which shore-up closure are endings that immediately follow their final couple with a gag or comic epilogue that in fact marks the true end of the movie. This may happen by bringing back a secondary figure of fun (e.g. *Ninotchka*'s [1939] protesting Russian envoy), by referring back to an earlier conflict between the couple (e.g. *The Ugly Truth*'s [2009] final faked-orgasm gag), or by showing the comic punishment of a 'villain' (e.g. the ex-boyfriend in *What Happens in Vegas* being punched in the crotch). *Pillow Talk* (1959), for example, concludes with the culmination of a running joke whereby a doctor has mistakenly diagnosed Brad (Rock Hudson) as either pregnant and insane, the film's final image seeing him being dragged away and shouting for help; a similar gag also closes *That Touch of Mink* when the character of Roger (Gig Young) is looking after the final couple's new baby and encounters his psychiatrist, who has previously assumed Roger to be gay and now thinks him both in a homosexual marriage and a father. This long-running convention of final jokes (see also: *Sylvia Scarlett* [1935], *Nothing Sacred* [1937], *Failure to Launch* [2006]) inserts a comic conflict at the moment that should, according to conventional wisdom, see the 'effective resolution of conflicts and the satisfactory settlement of problems and disruptions' (Strinati 2000: 34). Furthermore, such gags also ensure that it is not in fact true that 'the ending leaves the couple isolated in their own bliss', since they insert moments of disorder between the two events seen by Altman as inseparable: 'the couple is united, the film ends'. In this way, as Glitre points out, 'far from reinforcing the return of the status quo, [. . .] the Hollywood romantic comedy epilogue tends to destabilise the final union by the return of a source of conflict' (2006: 16). In doing so, this strategy serves a comparable function to others I have been highlighting, complicating our ability to imagine that romantic union necessarily banishes time, change or discord from the world of the film or the couple's future.

Of course, given that all these examples come from romantic comedies, their intimations of uncertainty are to an extent contained within the safety of a comedic mode. Yet my point is not that we are necessarily encouraged to make *pessimistic* predictions for couples, but only that their futures are not implied to be stable or unchanging. In this sense, all the above films, and many more, find ways to create what amounts to a similar effect, which we might describe as an explicit denial *of* Shumway's 'explicit denial of the temporality of satisfaction'. Thus, despite its potential for treating a beginning as an ending – and despite the proclamations of many critics – the final couple by no means always makes its future appear so 'timeless' as has frequently been imagined. This may be partly due to the very nature of the final couple itself, destined as it is has been to hold the contradictory position of being at once the most familiar of endings and also manifestly an image of beginning. The tensions such films as those discussed above display can, I think, be considered indicative of this fact.

To expand on this, I now wish to look at a recent film that finds a particularly interesting strategy for dealing with this essential paradox at the heart of the final couple: *Eternal Sunshine of the Spotless Mind* (hereafter *Eternal Sunshine*), a film which demonstrates especially clearly that there is nothing inherent in the convention of the final couple that means it must automatically imply anything approaching an 'ever after'.

THE CHALLENGE OF THE FUTURE: *ETERNAL SUNSHINE OF THE SPOTLESS MIND*

The ending of *Eternal Sunshine* needs to be seen in the context of romance narratives as they can frequently be handled by films from 'Indiewood', the deeply blurred economic and aesthetic intersection of independent and Hollywood cinema that has developed since the mid 1990s. Geoff King has suggested that endings which see 'no unqualified "happily-ever-after" for the couple,

but more than a hint that it remains a distinct possibility in the near-future'
represent 'a typically Indiewood limbo' (2009: 55) – perhaps constituting, we
might infer, a desire to create romantic endings that can be differentiated from
what are commonly seen as Hollywood's norms. Overlooking for now the fact
that 'Indiewood' films are themselves by definition a part of the broader contemporary 'Hollywood' landscape, we need to acknowledge that such movies
do regularly navigate the convention of the final couple in interesting ways.
One strategy, for instance, is to end with the central couple dissolved (or
unconsummated) but the lovers still nominally happy (e.g. *Lost in Translation*
[2003], *Waitress* [2007], *The Wackness* [2008]). Equally, the romantic status of
the couple may be left unresolved (e.g. *Adaptation* [2002], *Sideways* [2005],
Lars and the Real Girl [2007], *Greenberg* [2010]), thus allowing for the *possibility* of a happy ending taking place after the end rather than providing it within
the film itself. Or there may be a particularly strong indication that the first
flush of love does indeed only represent a *beginning* rather than an ending (e.g.
Magnolia [1999], *Me and You and Everyone we Know* [2005], *Adventureland*
[2009]). All these strategies represent attempts to complicate (what we have
learned to view as) a quite possibly non-existent, but nevertheless very tenacious, paradigmatic image of what a happy ending is. This is a process in which
Eternal Sunshine can be seen to be taking part.

In the final moments of *Eternal Sunshine*, Joel (Jim Carrey) and Clementine
(Kate Winslet), who are on the verge of beginning a romantic relationship,
learn they have already previously fallen in and out of love, but that this
two-year relationship was wiped from their memories, at their request, by an
organisation called Lacuna. Both receive cassettes in the post on which they
can be heard separately listing the reasons for the failure of the relationship
and the aspects of each other's personalities that they have grown to dislike.
After being offended by listening to Joel's tape in his apartment, Clementine
leaves. Joel, however, rushes to stop her in the hallway, begging her to wait.
The film's final exchange is as follows:

Clementine:	I'm not a concept, Joel. I'm just a fucked-up girl who's looking for my own peace of mind. I'm not perfect.
Joel:	I can't see anything that I don't like about you right now – I *can't*.
Clementine:	But you *will*, you know – you *will* think of things, and *I'll* get bored with you and feel trapped, because that's what happens with *me*.
(Pause)	
Joel:	*(Shrugging and smiling sadly)* Okay.
Clementine:	Okay . . . *(Laughs)* Okay . . .!
Joel:	Okay . . .

We then cut to an image of Joel and Clementine running and playing on a snowy beach, an image previously seen through Joel's mind's-eye during his memory-wiping procedure, as it was being erased from his mind. This epilogue is thus temporally complex. We can understand the first time this image was shown to have been a mixture of memory and imagination, since it ostensibly depicts actions we later learn took place on the day of the couple's first meeting (finding the abandoned house on the beach), but changed slightly (it is now snowing, the two seem already to be a couple). It follows, then, that this final image is not an epilogue showing us the couple's future, but rather an image of a (probably imagined) past. As we watch them cavort on the beach, the image becomes whiter and whiter until it finally disappears and we are left with only a white screen.

Iconographically, the 'happy ending' – as commonly defined – is certainly present: the final couple has been reunited and is framed in a moment of shared bliss in the film's final frames; it is also preceded by that familiar romantic comedy trope, the 'Dark Moment' (Mernit 2000: 115), when it seems that Clementine is about to walk out of Joel's life. However, the list of things that will likely go wrong for the couple means that we are permitted to make rather particular predictions for the future of the relationship, the significance of which lies in our necessary re-examination of what we have seen of Joel and Clementine's relationship throughout the film.

In terms of its narrative structure, *Eternal Sunshine* ostensibly shares some similarities with Cavell's aforementioned comedies of remarriage (as noted by Walters [2009: 87]). However when a divorced or separated couple decide eventually to give their romance a second chance in a remarriage comedy, the antagonistic trials the lovers have undergone are usually implied to have strengthened their romantic bond (perhaps promising that the future relationship will be, as expressed in *The Awful Truth*, 'the same, but different'). What we have seen of Joel and Clementine's romance, by contrast, might seem to confirm the doubts Clementine voices in the final scene. Through fragments of the relationship presented to us via Joel's eroding memory, we have learned that he and Clementine have fundamentally very conflicting personalities, and that their largest problems stem from the ways in which this affects how they communicate. In a comedy of remarriage even the arguments the lovers engage in often tend to reveal the compatibility of the couple through their shared love of combative game-playing; the resulting mutual dialogue is what Cavell has called a 'meet and cheerful conversation' (1981: 151). The past arguments between Joel and Clementine in *Eternal Sunshine*, by contrast, are bitter and humourless, and reveal the extent of the pair's incompatibility. This is made especially clear in a scene in which Clementine accuses Joel of never opening up emotionally to her – a conversation that concludes with Clementine leaving it unceremoniously. The couple have fought over whether or not to have a child (Joel doesn't think Clementine responsible enough), over the fact that Joel is 'boring' (Clementine's view), over Clementine's drinking (Joel calls her an irresponsible 'wino'), and over issues of trust (Joel assumes Clementine has cheated on him because, he says, it is 'how you get people to like you'). It seems significant that at no point in all of Joel's memories do we see them resolving a disagreement civilly: instead one or the other always storms off, or the scene simply ends, the issue at stake no closer to being laid to rest.

Thus, as Clementine predicts, at some point after the film ends, after a period of time, it is likely that this pair's incompatibility will almost certainly rear its head once again, causing them to re-discover the faults with each other that we have heard them itemise – eventually leading, we could well presume, to a second break-up. That Clementine gives the same 'I'm not a concept' speech as she did when they first got together further reinforces the sense of inevitable repetition. We should also remember that the film has been arranged in such a way that we have experienced most of Joel and Clementine's relationship *backwards* via Joel's memories, meaning that all the arguments and recriminations have given way to the sense of promise offered by the initial moments of their relationship (the day on the beach evoked in the final image) – or, in other words, the moments which usually constitute a happy ending. The fact that we have already seen the pain which followed this 'ending' (which, as always, was *not* an ending) the first time round thus ensures that this final couple, poised on the threshold of the relationship being rekindled, most certainly incorporates more than a possibility of Shumway's '*post coitum triste*'.

And yet, despite this, I would nonetheless argue that this film 'could be said to end happily' (Bordwell 1986: 159). If this conclusion is a happy ending, however, then it is clearly of a very different order to the paradigmatic model of the convention offered by Shumway et al. above. What this conclusion suggests for the future of its couple is certainly not an 'undifferentiated "happily ever after"', nor an 'illusory eternity'; indeed, the film's final lines more or less explicitly state that the ensuing romance probably carries an expiration date, even briefly sketching the precise events that may lead to its demise. This seems almost a conscious reaction against the effacing of temporality that numerous critics have associated with the 'happy ending'. However, that this ending *does* feel uplifting in a rather profound sense (to me) is perhaps because of the film's handling of a feature I have earlier suggested may be important to happy endings in general: the reaffirmation of a central value or set of values.

Joel and Clementine's shared acceptance of their past and future mistakes with 'Okay'/ 'Okay', and particularly their subsequent bemused, sad, relieved laughs, help create what Lang calls an '*affirmative* ending' (1948: 29) because of what they imply about the nature of the relationship that is about to develop after this narrative has ended. The moment acknowledges a truth – that the great majority of romantic relationships will *not* last for life – whilst simultaneously reaffirming a belief in the worth of embarking upon each new (or, indeed, old) romance regardless. In other words, in its final moments *Eternal Sunshine* expresses a faith in the value of romantic love (as do, say, *Casablanca* or *Portrait of Jennie*); yet, importantly, the implied conceptions of both that faith and that love are of particular kinds.

The film as a whole appears to place little emphasis on the notion of romantic love as everlasting, and includes alongside its central couple an unusually high number of failed relationships: Dr Mierzwiak (Tom Wilkinson) and Mary (Kirsten Dunst), Dr Mierzwiak and his wife (Deirdre O'Connell), Patrick (Elijah Wood) and Clementine, Mary and Stan (Mark Ruffalo), Joel and his ex-girlfriend, Naomi (unseen) – even the one surviving relationship we see in the film (Joel's friends Carrie [Jane Adams] and Rob [David Cross]) are seen constantly bickering. However, that Joel and Clementine decide to re-begin their romance despite Clementine's list of the ways in which their relationship may itself fail is affirmative precisely because it demonstrates the couple's acceptance that romantic love may indeed be 'an intense, all-consuming passion that is by its very nature short-lived' (Wexman 1993: 8), and – rather than attempting to elide this fact – shows them embracing it. As Lesley Harbridge suggests, 'if Gondry's film posits the central question – would we, knowing that a relationship is ultimately doomed, repeat that relationship in order to experience the good times we shared? – *Eternal Sunshine* reticently but absolutely replies in the positive' (2009: 184). In this sense, we might say that – despite the fact that the majority of the narrative has been concerned with the process of *forgetting* – the couple have eventually acquired knowledge of something very valuable, a fact that relates the film back to the tenets of the comedies of remarriage.

Cavell has said that the comic resolutions of remarriage films 'depend upon an acquisition in time of self-knowledge; say this is a matter of learning who you are' (1981: 56). When they relearn about their forgotten pasts, Joel and Clementine gain self-knowledge in a very literal sense. In his account of *Eternal Sunshine* James Walters suggests that the couple's decision to rekindle their relationship despite having heard a record of their past heartache involves 'rejecting knowledge in favour of each other', and 'disowning the adult commodities of wisdom and judgment' in order to return to 'a childlike state of innocence' (2008: 99). I would suggest, though, that this interpretation downplays the great importance of Clementine's predictions for the relationship, and the mixture of sadness, resolve, and hope conveyed by the couple's ultimate acceptance of them ('Okay' / 'Okay'). The characters' decision to begin this relationship again is made resolutely in knowledge of the fact that they may very well repeat their past mistakes, and thus with a corresponding awareness of the essential fragility of romantic love. Indeed, the power of the ending rests in the fact that Joel and Clementine, while perhaps in some sense behaving quixotically, are precisely *not* 'innocent'. In this sense, their burgeoning romance might recall far less the sorts of eternal and transcendent romantic love established in *Sleepless* and many films in Chapter 1, coming far closer instead to the picture of marriage painted by the more experienced Al and Milly in *Best Years* – one which allows for changes, problems, interruptions, accommodating the ability both to say that they hate each other and to 'fall in love all over again'; in short: a relationship built in conscious awareness of the time which inevitably *follows* a final couple, whatever it may contain – even if that turns out to be another ending.

Looked at in this way, the final shot of the couple playing on the snowy beach can be understood rhetorically as communicating why Joel and Clementine still desire to pursue their relationship despite knowing it may eventually end. As a reference back to their first meeting, it conveys the happiness that they know love can provide them with – its sense of playfulness echoing, for instance, the games we have seen them enjoy earlier in their past relation-ship (for example, their play-acting dead for one another). At the same time, though, rather than implying unending or stasis, the picture of love presented here is also suggested to be both fulfilling *and* fleeting. The bleached-out nature of the image (especially the fact that it slowly grows whiter and whiter, before eventually fading entirely) suggests fragility, the fade-out here offer-ing a sense of ephemerality rather than finality. That the couple are framed by snow also contributes to this sense of the ephemeral, since one of the main characteristics of snow is that it is destined to melt and eventually disappear. Finally, the music accompanying this image, Beck's rendition of 'Everybody's Gotta Learn Sometime', is decidedly melancholy in tone, and was in fact first heard towards the beginning of the film over images of Joel crying following his break-up with Clementine; this moment of joy at the resumption of a rela-tionship is thus performed to the strains of music that has previously accom-panied images of despair at its earlier dissolution.

Yet the previous scene in the hallway confers an important qualifying effect on these gestures. Rather than straightforwardly undercutting or making mel-ancholy the image of the final couple, all the strategies that suggest the relation-ship's potential precariousness are also to a significant extent consonant with Joel and Clementine's current perspective on their relationship's future. Instead of puncturing a naïve view of romantic love, then, the epilogue aligns itself with the awareness that the lovers have developed and demonstrated in their preced-ing exchange. Whether this awareness will ultimately allow them to avoid the pitfalls of their earlier relationship is another question; in many ways, though, it is also no longer the point. The conception of love presented at this ending combines both a belief in it as a value and a belief that it need not last forever in order to *be* valuable. Unlike, say, *Sleepless*, the ending of *Eternal Sunshine* thus does not affirm the value of romantic love as a transcendent bliss on which lifelong happiness, monogamous marriage and a family might be built, but rather a different view of the concept – one which incorporates both its desirability *and* its transitory nature. This is a happy ending that appears both optimistic in its depiction of romantic love as something that may bring happiness and, in keeping with our current formulation, avoids unrealism via its suggestion that this happiness cannot, by its very nature, be unchanging – or eternal.

In a recent article on the film, Michael J. Meyer dubs the ending of *Eternal Sunshine* an 'anxious happy ending' (2008: 77) – a term for a kind of comic conclusion which conveys that 'happy endings are obviously just beginnings' (ibid.: 82). He contrasts this type of ending with the 'more static comic *resolution*' (ibid.: 85; original emphasis), continuing: 'while static happy endings are often a kind of straightjacket for comic characters, anxious happy endings tend to ease this predicament by allowing comic characters and their stories to breathe with some of the reality and uncertainty of the human condition' (ibid.: 85). While I agree with the general logic underpinning Meyer's thesis ('reality' and 'uncertainty' here being aligned with intimations of beginning), I would argue that he overlooks the extent to which happy endings *in general* – even those he might dub static comic resolutions – can often be 'anxious' in this sense. Operating under similar assumptions about the Hollywood 'happy ending' as a whole, Troy Jollimore too argues that *Eternal Sunshine*'s ending stands in stark contrast to 'other movies [that] cheapen love by regarding it as nothing more than the gateway to pleasure and success' (2009: 58). It thus seems that *Eternal Sunshine* may be accruing a similar reputation as *The Graduate* – that is: as offering a 'subversive' final couple where conventional Hollywood romance conclusions provide only closure, and possibly unrealism. It seems to me, by contrast, that Gondry's film in fact makes especially plain a contradiction that final couples in general may have at their heart, and which they can routinely explore to greater or lesser extents.

In the last chapter I suggested that Altman's description of the final couple as 'that beyond which there is no more' misses one of the convention's most distinctive elements: its promise of continuation. Certainly this promise can be made either more or less overt, and more or less stable. It will, however, always be present. Unlike the generic endings of, say, the adventure film in which a quest is completed, the very structure of the final couple as a convention cannot help but contain specific provisions for the future in its very makeup. Given this, it is unsurprising that, in the same way as conclusions in general proved notoriously troublesome for novelists such as Forster and Eliot, so should final couples repeatedly prove troublesome for romantic narratives. As such, the basic problem inherent in the notion of 'happily ever after' is quite clearly not only felt by film critics, but also frequently by the very films which find themselves required to navigate this convention.

We might be tempted to view *Eternal Sunshine* as exceptional – perhaps because of its position as a product of 'Indiewood', or because of its highly idiosyncratic central conceit of memory-erasure. However, as shown by the examples cited prior to my analysis, it is in fact far from uncommon for Hollywood movies to find various ways to inscribe anxiety, discord, or precariousness either alongside or just following the formation of their final couples. Indeed, the same tensions that *Eternal Sunshine* makes so explicit, which result from the basic closural paradox of the final couple, can be detected in the most mainstream of films. *Bridget Jones: The Edge of Reason* (2004) begins with Bridget (Renée Zellweger) telling us in voiceover that 'You always wonder how it's going to work out at the end of the story: Maria and Captain Von Trapp, Snow White and the Seven Dwarfs, Mark Darcy and Bridget Jones. The question is,' she goes on, 'what happens *after* you walk off into the sunset?' – a question that, being thus raised, necessarily lingers after this film's own final couple happy ending. Likewise, in *Enchanted* (2007), Giselle (Amy Adams) tries to explain to her 'unsuitable' prince that she feels the need to plan not only for her wedding to her 'true love', but also for what follows: 'I was thinking about the day *after* happily-ever-after . . .' she tells him. Similarly, in another contemporary treatment of the fairy tale, *Happily N'Ever After* (2007), it is explained to the heroine, Ella (Sarah Michelle Gellar), that her fate is simply to marry the prince:

Mambo:	It's your happy ending. You get wedding bells, roses, you ride off into the sunset . . .
Ella:	And then what?
Mambo:	Nothing. That's the end of your tale.
Ella:	That's all? That's my whole life? I just marry the prince?
Mambo:	What else did you expect?
Ella:	I don't know, I guess just – *more* . . .

What each of these films expresses, then, is a suspicion that the 'happy ending' may be problematic not only because of its excessively conventional nature (as explored in the first half of this chapter), but also because of its potential to be unrealistic in *temporal* terms. Given the dates of these examples, it might again be tempting to suggest that such suspicions are a 'postmodern' phenomenon; yet I hope I have by this point illustrated that this is far from the case.

To reinforce this point, I shall conclude here with two earlier films that navigate in comparable ways the temporal problems posed by the final couple. The first is *Breezy* (1971) – a film about a romance between Breezy (Kay Lenz), a seventeen-year-old hippie, and Frank (William Holden), a man in late-middle age. This movie ends with its couple deciding to give their relationship another try after a previous parting. 'I don't know,' says Frank with a rueful smile as the two reunite, 'if we're lucky we might last a year . . .' 'A *year*?' Breezy replies excitedly, 'Just *think* of it, Frank! A whole *year*!' The two then walk hand-in-hand, away from the camera, across a beautiful park into the late afternoon sun; 'The End'. The second, *The Marrying Kind*, is (like *Eternal Sunshine*) told using a flashback structure, and is bookended by scenes that see its couple (Florrie [Judy Holliday] and Chet [Aldo Ray]) in divorce court. The intervening action is dedicated to documenting the tumultuous marriage that brought them to this point. In the final scene, having told their story to the judge, the couple find themselves on the verge of giving their marriage a second chance:

Chet: See, the only trouble is: I can't promise it'd be no different. The way I am, that's how I am.

Florrie: Me too.

Chet: I know everything wrong with me – too ambitious, disillusions [sic] of grandeur and all that.

Florrie: And what about me getting nervous?

Chet: I get nervous too, don't I? [. . .]

Florrie: I'm too scared. I mean, when we got together finally the first time, I never imagined it could ever be different, and we could bust up or anything. Now I'd always be thinking about it. [. . .] I mean, at least I'd know it's possible.

Chet: Maybe it's a good thing to know it's possible . . .

Florrie: Maybe.

Chet: I'd like to make a promise everything's going to be different, but how could I promise that? I tell you what I can do. I can tell you that I'd certainly *try*.

Florrie: I would too. From the bottom of my heart.

Chet: So what's wrong with that? So: okay?

These endings both relate instructively to the unrealism of the final couple as we have been discussing it, and both find clear echoes in *Eternal Sunshine*.

Breezy suggests more strongly than most films that its final couple's romance is likely to end sooner rather than later. Yet it also simultaneously embraces this fact, Breezy's perpetual positivity turning Frank's prediction of one year from pessimism into optimism – or rather, we might say, from one kind of realism into another. To return momentarily to our abandoned definition of unrealism as wish-fulfillment: we have heard Maltby describe realism as a representation of what 'we pessimistically assume [occurs] in the world outside the cinema' (2003: 29). Perhaps, in accordance with the 'new romances' encountered earlier, we might be tempted to associate this pessimism with the failure of romantic relationships. Yet *Breezy*'s ending, like *Eternal Sunshine*'s, implies that the possibility of a relationship ending need not be something about which it is necessary to *be* pessimistic – that it should instead simply be acknowledged as one of the many possible results of passing time, and should not prevent an appreciation of the value of a relationship *while it lasts*. Like the aforementioned *I Could Never be Your Woman*, then, *Breezy* effectively says of its relationship 'So, it might not last: you could say that about anyone', and finds in this assertion a realism that is by no means synonymous with pessimism – indeed, a realism that allows this sentiment to exist hand-in-hand with a convention too-routinely associated with wishful thinking: a happy ending.

The Marrying Kind similarly incorporates the possibility of a relationship's dissolution, yet places it in a slightly different context. 'When we got together finally the first time,' Florrie says, 'I never imagined it could ever be different, and we could bust up or anything.' This is in fact a perfect description of the unchanging, undifferentiated future seemingly implied by the end of a film such as *Sleepless* – the word 'finally' even hinting at the processes whereby such a future comes to be inferred due to a concluding union's deferral. This couple go on to lay out, however, like *Eternal Sunshine*'s, potential reasons why their relationship may not be able to go the distance – 'disillusions of grandeur', nervousness. They also ultimately suggest that it may be able to *benefit* from this potential for finitude: 'maybe it's a good thing to know it's possible . . .' What takes place in the discussion that closes this film is thus a process of learning, whereby Chet and Florrie cast off an atemporal view of romantic love in favour of a reenergised image of the concept that is capable of accepting the challenges inherent in a happy ending's promise of a future. This new image is also conveyed by the final images of the film itself. Their conversation finished, the couple leave the offices in which their divorce hearing took place, passing a janitor on the way out who is removing their names from tomorrow's schedule; smiling to each other, they move on and through some glass doors to wait for the elevator in long-shot. As the door closes between us and them we see them kiss, this conventionally closural gesture of tenderness now placed in a context which guarantees we can mistake it neither for a conclusive ending, nor for the kind of self-conscious play upon endings evoked by *Pretty Woman*. Instead, it appears to be a convention – certainly – yet at once a fictional and a human convention: one which both regularly closes films, *and* one which we would not be surprised to find a couple in the real world engaging in at such a moment, when agreeing to try to begin again.

*

It seems likely that the final couple happy ending will always be haunted by the spectre of apparent unrealism, whether because of its supposed wish-fulfillment, its perceived excessive conventionality, or its problematic closural position as both putative ending and apparent beginning. As with the association of the final couple with closure, the appearance of the second type of unrealism will likely never fade entirely. So entrenched is the connection between the final couple and fiction that even endings like those of *Eternal Sunshine*, *Breezy* or *The Marrying Kind* cannot help but remind us that they are indeed enacting something we have seen countless times in countless movies – the deployment of familiarly closural images (doors shutting, characters departing from the camera, kisses) only reinforcing this fact. One way of dealing with this situation is for a film to acknowledge it, and in the process to imply that it is taking something like a 'realistic' attitude *towards* its unrealism: this is the strategy of *Pretty Woman*. Yet if a film can manage to suggest that, while its final couple may come at the end of a movie, this does not signify the end of change for the couple's relationship – if it acknowledges something of the 'temporality of satisfaction' – then it can temper significantly the appearance of unrealism with which the convention is so frequently associated.

This approach, practised by the films discussed in the second half of this chapter, may also, finally, allow us to propose a more nuanced assessment of the common accusation that the final couple is wishful. Wishful thinking implies desiring an unrealisable perfection – essentially, a lack of complicating problems, and it is only in a world in which time continues advancing that problems and complications become possible. As such, we might say that, if the final couple happy ending is wishful, it is so in proportion to the extent to which its degree of closure promises to banish time and change from its image of a romantic future. But the opposite of the wishful need not necessarily be the pessimistic, as films such as *Eternal Sunshine* demonstrate. If impermanence and change can be both incorporated and affirmed, if a final couple can seem to say 'okay' to an inevitably uncertain future, then an ending can both elude unrealism and remain 'happy'.

NOTES

1. Similar uses also crop up in *Libelled Lady* (1936), *Network* (1976), *Batman Returns* (1992), *Se7en* (1995), *The Blair Witch Project* (1999), etc.
2. For similar uses of the term, see also *My Man Godfrey*, *It's Love I'm After* (1937), *Kitty Foyle*, *The Best Years of Our Lives*, *People Will Talk* (1951), *The Happy Ending* (1969), *Bed of Roses* (1996), *Made of Honor* (2008), etc.
3. Other examples of this tendency would include Altman (1987: 51), Mellencamp (1995: 36), Lapsley/Westlake (1992: 43), etc.
4. Other instances of 'happily ever after' being used in relation to diegetic fictions include *Stage Door* (1937), *The Adventures of Baron Munchausen*

(1988), *Lord of the Rings: The Fellowship of the Ring* (2001), *Stranger Than Fiction* (2006), etc.

5. For other particularly self-conscious 'new romance' happy endings, see: *The Wedding Planner*, *Alex and Emma*, *13 Going On 30* (2004), etc.

6. This is in keeping with accounts such as Krutink's (1998) concerning the respective ideological implications of 'new romance' and the cycle with which *Annie Hall* is usually associated, 1970s 'nervous romance' – the latter being said to mourn the loss of 'old-fashioned' certainties regarding romantic love in the wake of second-wave feminism and the 'sexual revolution', while the former attempts to resurrect those certainties – albeit with accompanying postmodern irony – for a post-feminist climate (see also Garrett 2007).

CHAPTER 4

Happy endings and ideology

'Girls are taught a lot of stuff growing up,' says Gigi, the narrator of *He's Just Not That Into You*: 'If a guy punches you he likes you. Never trim your own bangs. And some day you will meet a wonderful guy and get your very own happy ending'. A seven-year-old Mary (Cortney Shounia) in *The Wedding Planner* tells her Barbie doll 'You'll live happily ever after,' as she marries her off to a Ken. In *French Kiss* Kate (Meg Ryan) tearfully says of her ex-fiancé: 'I'm going to get him *back*, and make him *love* me, and we are going to live *happily ever after*!'

As I have suggested, most spoken references to 'happy endings' or 'happily-ever-afters' uttered in Hollywood cinema invoke these concepts only to qualify them in some way. The examples above are no exception: Gigi goes on to explain that 'sometimes we're so focused on finding our happy ending that we don't learn how to [. . .] tell the ones who'll stay from the ones who'll leave'; *The Wedding Planner* dissolves from a close-up of Barbie's face to a real-life bride who is apparently petrified by the prospect of marriage ('I'm marrying the wrong guy!' she wails); Kate is at this moment talking about her film's 'unsuitable' partner. Yet – as we saw in the last chapter – Hollywood films *do* nonetheless often invoke these concepts, and not only in order to accuse them of unrealism, but frequently also in a manner suggesting that they are highly relevant to how characters live their lives. Forced upon children, infiltrating childhood games, providing a language through which to discuss relationships: the implication is that real life conceptions of love are intimately bound up – in however ambivalent a fashion – with the convention of the final couple. In short: it forms a central plank of the contemporary ideology of romantic love.

The constant recurrence of the terms in contemporary Western popular discourses of romance would seem to bear these films out: popular songs, self-help books, advice columns, dating sites – it is far from uncommon for all to use the concepts of 'happy ending' and 'happily ever after' as virtual metonyms for a successful romantic relationship.[1] However over-simplified or qualified, what the terms are essentially intended to stand for in most such cases is clear: marriage and/or long-term monogamy. While there are innumerable ways in which we might profitably approach the ideological dimension of the Hollywood 'happy ending' (and I look forward eagerly to such approaches being taken in the future), it is the close association of the notion of the 'happy ending' with long-term, monogamous – usually heterosexual – romantic love and marriage which will be the predominant focus of this chapter.

Of course, none of these phenomena – heterosexuality, romance, marriage, nor monogamy – is simply 'natural', which is to say nothing more surprising than that all are plainly historically and ideologically specific in character.[2] Popular romantic fictions of page and screen are intimately associated with all of the above, and a great deal of scholarship on them is thus characterised by 'a critical discourse that emphasises the genre's overall ideological tendency to endorse and validate the ideal of marriage and monogamy' (Garrett 2007: 99).[3] Many feminist critics have demonstrated ways in which the narrative structures typical of romance fiction might be said to express and potentially reinforce aspects of patriarchal ideology, a context that is clearly key to understanding the ideological dimension of the reputation of the 'happy ending'.[4] What is often granted particular importance in such discussions is the proposition that 'by using courtship rituals [. . .] the romance launches the reader toward the ideologically correct end: marriage and reproduction' (Silbergleid 1997: 156). More specifically, alongside that other generic narrative conclusion of romance – death – marriage has been seen as forming one half of what Alison Booth pithily calls 'the sense of few endings' that have been traditionally available to female fictional characters: 'bad' girls are punished by death, 'good' girls rewarded by marriage (1993: 1). While the romance which ends in death is largely beyond the remit of this study, it is obviously a matter of great ideological significance that the other most common means of bringing a sense of appropriate cessation to a narrative focussed upon a man, a woman, and romantic love, should be the final couple.

The precise *nature* of this ideological significance in practice is a far from simple matter, though, and prompts the two main questions with which this chapter will be concerned. Firstly, a highly contentious one: what potential might the final couple have for structuring ideological beliefs, and thus behaviours? Secondly, a no-less complex issue: what ideological meanings do or can final couples themselves convey? Tackling the first question requires us to address the final couple 'happy ending' in abstract terms – broadly, the clichéd, Platonic terms in which the concept is employed by the films that opened this chapter – before we return to specific final couples later on. It will similarly mean initially approaching the general issue of how films might be said to exert ideological influence, before we can move on to discussing particular aspects *of* their ideological precepts – and relating these to the above critical discourses – later on.

Turning to the first task: any discussion of ideology and film necessarily presupposes, either tacitly or openly, a set of assumptions about how cinema can enact an ideological influence upon audiences. Let us begin by confronting this issue head-on via some familiar theoretical debates concerning the ideological relationship between films and spectators.

IDEOLOGY, AUDIENCES, AND THE FINAL COUPLE

By far the most influential approaches to the ideology of Hollywood cinema to have emerged during Anglophone film studies' formative years have since been given the overarching name of 'subject-position' theory (see Bordwell 1996) – a broad but useful category for a loose yet related set of theoretical approaches that tended to share 'the assumption that the cinematic apparatus "situates", "positions", or otherwise assigns a position of coherence to the implied spectator' (Mayne 2002: 30). Despite great individual variation, a presumption underlying much such theorising was that popular films have, perhaps by their nature, at least the potential to 'allow the ideology a free, unhampered passage, transmit it with crystal clarity,' (Comolli/Narboni 1971: 29), and thus an ability to help form their audiences into acquiescent ideological subjects via variously-conceived processes of 'interpellation' (Althusser's term [1971: 177]). I will return later to some approaches to cinematic endings encouraged by these traditions; for now, let us focus on the assumptions such theories imply about audiences' possible relationships to those endings.

A great deal of writing has since attacked 'subject-position' theories on a number of grounds, with their various pronouncements of the homogeneity and passivity of the cinematic spectator coming in for especially sustained critique (more on this in a moment). Yet despite this, and beyond the influence of the 'continental' philosophy which inspired most 'subject-position' models, comparable assumptions about the relationship between text and reader can also be seen to characterise significant strains of later writing on the ideological functions of media – particularly, for our purposes, that which concerns itself with the ideological influence of popular romantic texts.

One recent media theorist who has taken romantic narratives as her object of study is Mary-Lou Galcian, the author of *Sex, Love & Romance in the Mass Media* (2004). Galcian argues that frequent exposure to mainstream romantic fictions not only affects viewers' own beliefs about romantic love, but that 'higher usage of certain mass media is related to unrealistic expectations about coupleship' (2004: 5). Concerned to 'resist [the] seductive and hazardous influence' (ibid.: 5) of popular romantic narratives, Galcian identifies twelve 'myths' propagated by romance media – one being the 'happily-ever-after' myth, which encourages viewers to feel 'incomplete without a mate, longing for someone to [. . .] ensure that they live happily-ever-after' (ibid.: 203). Other writers in a similar tradition tell us that, for example, *Moulin Rouge* (2001) offers 'a how-to instructional model of romance and love that viewers can use to measure their own relationships' (Hutchins 2007: 241), or that *Maid in Manhattan*'s narrative of 'waiting for a superior Prince Charming to mistake you as a member of [a royal family] because you are wearing borrowed designer clothing [. . .] is not practical, reasonable, or smart' as a plan for one's love life (Rios/Reyes 2007: 110). Similarly, a recent study of contemporary romantic comedy which received significant coverage in UK news media argues that audiences are 'using films [. . .] as a means to obtain information' on how best to conduct their own relationships (Holmes/Johnson 2009: 368). Not necessarily concerned to engage with the feminist critiques of popular romance raised above (to which we shall return), the essential assumption of much such research might rather be summed up by the more general proposition that, 'if we live by the wisdom of these films, we are setting ourselves up for failure' (Asena 2007: 298).

Whilst growing out of an entirely different intellectual tradition than the most significant strands of 'subject-position' theory, this kind of approach to the potential ideological effects of popular film is strikingly similar in one respect: its conception of audiences as having little choice other than to internalise a text's 'seductive and hazardous' ideological precepts wholesale. Equally, in another link between the two disparate traditions, assumptions about the de facto ideological influence of romance narratives in general – and happy endings in particular – are often predicated on the assumption that audiences are 'interpreting media representations [. . .] as being an accurate reflection of reality' (Holmes/Johnson 2009: 352) – an echo of a key 'subject-position' tenet regarding 'realism' (see MacCabe 1974). Applied to our subject, such assumptions can prompt problematic claims: for instance, that, since 'the viewer's perception of the cinematic world as real is a condition for his or her ability to accept its ideology as valid and unquestionable truth', it follows that the 'happy ending [offers] an illusionary world to be viewed uncritically' (Preis 1990: 19). Yet, after our discussions of perceived unrealism in the previous chapter, it seems unlikely that such descriptions can do justice to the probable ideological relationship between happy endings and audiences.

Many of the most influential challenges to 'subject-position' theories resulted, of course, from a shift in emphasis from texts to the potential variety of spectators' interpretations – one outcome of which was the useful and influential concept of 'negotiation' (Hall 1980), which holds that the ideological relationship between text and audience members is never guaranteed to be one of simple submission, and that audiences' acceptance or otherwise of a text's 'encoded' ideological precepts depends on how that text is 'decoded', which may take forms ranging from 'dominant', through 'negotiated', to entirely 'oppositional' (ibid.: 128–38). As Judith Mayne writes, such work 'assumes the necessity for understanding [popular culture] as ideologically influenced, but not necessarily monolithically so' (ibid.: 29).

Regarding the ideological operations of popular romance in particular, Janice Radway's previously-mentioned ethnographic research into the responses of self-professedly avid female readers of romance fiction, *Reading the Romance*, would suggest that those who consume and enjoy such narratives should by no means be understood as necessarily taking them, or their happy endings, as 'valid and unquestionable truth'. Perhaps unsurprisingly – given our examination of romantic cliché in the previous chapter – it emerges that the appeal of romance literature for Radway's interviewees is that it depicts a 'world that they willingly admit bears little resemblance to the one they actually inhabit' (1991: 60). As such, these readers consistently speak of romance fiction portraying the world 'not as it really is' (1991: 98), since these narratives 'usually turn out the way you wish life really was' (ibid.: 88). Echoing Northrop Frye's formulation (and that of the 'new romances' encountered in the previous chapter) whereby 'happy endings do not impress us as true but as desirable' (2002: 152), these readers rank the 'unhappy ending' low on their list of preferred conventions, precisely because, says Radway, 'its presence would negate the romance's difference and distance from day-to-day existence' (ibid.: 73). Furthermore, it seems that the readers tend to 'believe in the mimetic accuracy of the extenuating circumstances that always intervene to thwart [the heroine's] intended actions', thus demonstrating that they 'recognize the inevitability and reality of male power and the force of social convention to circumscribe a woman's ability to act in her own interests' (ibid.: 78). While clearly only based on a very small cross-section of romance fiction consumers, Radway's research nonetheless proves, at least, that extensive exposure to final couple happy endings *need* not make one any more likely to take them as 'accurate representations of reality', nor entirely blind one to the ideological biases of patriarchy.

Anne Swidler's valuable and ambitious sociological study *Talk of Love: How Culture Matters* (2003) discovers similar public attitudes towards popular romances – albeit with certain vital caveats, as we shall see. The starting point for Swidler's research was a series of interviews with numerous heterosexual, middle-class, middle-Americans of various ages on the subject of their beliefs about romantic relationships and how these beliefs relate to their romantic lives. During the course of these interviews it became clear to Swidler that her subjects' relationships to popular discourses of romantic love typically existed in a state of constant navigation, oscillation and equivocation – particularly where Hollywood cinema is concerned. As she puts it, 'almost all my interviewees [. . .]

usually invoke the "Hollywood" image of love (associated especially with "the movies") only to condemn it' (ibid.: 14). Far from being wholly indoctrinated by popular culture (and 'the movies' in particular), Swidler's interviewees thus place themselves in explicit opposition to what they take to be its teachings. One interviewee, for example, speaks of 'that Hollywood image, [. . .] that magical love – dancing through the stage and stuff', another of being 'born and raised on this concept of this movie-star love. A romantic ideal,' and another of a 'Doris Day image' – all these models being used as examples of naïve beliefs which they no longer consciously hold, if they ever did (ibid.: 14–15).

Seemingly combining for these interviewees images of the kinds of transcendent romantic love occasionally touched upon in Chapters 1 and 2, and viewed through the lens of its status as cultural cliché encountered in Chapter 3, the concept of the 'happy ending' – unsurprisingly – earns particular disdain. Swidler too thus identifies 'Happily Ever After' as a key component of what she calls the 'mythic' model of romantic love disowned by her subjects, defining it primarily as 'the ideal that love lasts forever' (ibid.: 123). Very keen to distance themselves from this belief, her interviewees tend to suggest that, 'rather than guaranteeing that one will live "happily ever after", love requires continuing hard work, compromise, and change' (ibid.: 114) (an echo, we might say, of Al and Milly's expressed conception of marriage in *Best Years*). These subjects thus express their support for a 'prosaic-realistic' model (ibid.: 114), wherein romantic love tends to be 'ambiguous, open-ended, [. . .] and fragile' (ibid.: 129). '"Movie" love is intense, overwhelming, and sure,' Swidler says of her subjects' attitudes, 'but real love is often ambiguous, gradual, and uncertain' (ibid.: 114). This contrasting conception of coupledom bears a relation to what has elsewhere been called the discourse of intimacy (see: Giddens [1992], Shumway [2003]) – a development in conceptions of romantic relationships predicated on communication, mutual growth over the duration of an ongoing relationship, and acknowledgment of the potential for love's dissolution. While Swidler rightly acknowledges that 'the prosaic-realistic ideal of [. . .] love is every bit as cultural as the romantic myth', its language similarly 'stereotyped' (ibid.: 117–18), what is important about the discourse for our current purposes is the fact that, as Giddens puts it, it 'jars with the "for-ever" and "one-and-only" qualities of the romantic love complex' (1992: 61).

Another sociological study in a similar tradition to Swidler's, Eva Illouz's *Consuming the Romantic Utopia: Love and the Cultural Contradictions of Capitalism* (1997), discovered similarly sceptical attitudes towards comparable 'mythic' romantic discourses. Particularly interesting in this case are Illouz's interviewees' responses to a story depicting the romantic narrative convention of love-at-first-sight leading to marriage, which was described as a 'Hollywood fantasy', its final couple viewed as representing 'merely the *beginning* of a story with dubious chances of lasting the lifetime of its protagonists' (ibid.: 158;

emphasis mine). While far from anything like proof that all audiences might contrast what they perceive as Hollywood's 'mythic' romantic conventions to their own lives in these ways,[5] such pictures of a 'negotiated' relationship towards popular romantic culture do seem more convincing than one which imagines viewers to be watching so self-consciously fantastical a movie as *Moulin Rouge* as if it were a 'how-to' guide, or which can assume that spectators could believe *Maid in Manhattan*'s high-concept narrative might offer 'practical, reasonable, or smart' relationship advice.

Of course, however, the communication of ideological precepts is not only a matter of influencing consciously-held beliefs, but also a question of encouraging unconsidered assumptions that underlie sense-making procedures and behaviour. As such, it may be significant that Swidler's investigation into her interviewees' relationship to romantic popular culture does not stop simply with the discovery of widespread distrust. Throughout her research Swidler finds that, paradoxically, 'the same interviewees who reject the "movie image" of love use it repeatedly in their own thinking' about their actual romantic relationships (ibid.: 111). It seems that the interviewees' approaches to their own love-lives is defined by a continual 'lurching back and forth between mythic and prosaic views of love' (ibid.: 116), first using one discourse and then the other to conceptualise relationships and justify romantic and sexual beliefs and actions. Such vacillation between condemnation and assent in attitudes towards the assumed tenets of popular romance is a widely noted phenomenon in scholarship on the subject. As Janet McCabe puts it, although we may have 'learnt how to critique [. . .] romance, to know that it is restricted (and restricting),' we nevertheless 'remain at the same time absolutely beguiled, incapable of ever quite relinquishing the belief that being loved will somehow complete us' (2009: 164). Similarly, Lynne Pearce writes of popular romantic narrative: 'here is a story and/or set of conventions [. . .] that none of us can escape, no matter how well we interrogate the manner of our entrapment' (2004: 522).

If indeed true, why might this be? For either 'subject-position' theories or certain aforementioned strands of romance-focused media theory, the continued appeal of the precepts of a 'mythic' romantic discourse might first and foremost offer plain evidence of the inescapable ideological influence of popular culture itself. Swidler, however, suggests an alternative interpretation – one that privileges instead 'the *institutional* encounters that lead people to reproduce even discredited parts of their worldviews' (ibid.: 129; emphasis mine). Her subjects' continual movements between 'mythic' and 'prosaic-realistic' conceptions of romantic love, she suggests, 'are not delusions or mistakes' (ibid.: 117); instead, she provocatively argues,

The 'mythic' view of love is grounded, I believe, in a structural reality. [. . .] That structural reality is marriage. [. . .] As an emotional state love

may not be all-or-nothing, unique, heroic, and enduring. But despite
the prevalence of divorce, marriage still has this structure: One is either
married or not (however ambivalent the underlying feelings may be);
one cannot be married to more than one person at a time; marrying
someone is a fateful, sometimes life-transforming choice; and despite
divorce, marriages are still meant to last. (ibid.: 117–18)

Like many theorists of the subject, Swidler regards culture as 'a system of
inherited conceptions expressed in symbolic forms by means of which [we]
communicate, perpetuate, and develop [our] knowledge about and attitudes
towards life' (Geertz 1973: 89). In this way, a surrounding culture assists us in
'constructing lines of action' (ibid.: 6), yet – crucially – 'culture is elaborated
around the lines of action institutions structure' (ibid.: 131) – a notion that
is infrequently privilege in film studies' discussion of ideology. In the case
of romantic discourses, Swidler argues, 'the love myth accurately describes
the structural constraints of the institution of marriage' – a fact resulting in a
situation whereby 'two cultures of love persist, neither driving out the other,
because people employ their understandings of love in two very different
contexts', to help in the construction of two different lines of action (ibid.:
128–9). Specifically, the 'prosaic-realistic' view of love and intimacy is useful
for conceptualising '*being* married (or "coupled"), offering suggestions about
how to manage an ongoing relationship' (ibid.: 118; original emphasis). A
'mythic' romantic model, by contrast, speaks to a different line of action, its
usefulness lying in its capacity to help people make what are essentially 'yes-
or-no decisions' about their futures (ibid.: 119); for instance: whether or not
one should marry, or divorce, a partner – momentous choices that in practice
seem, Swidler argues, to require a belief, however naïve or consciously dis-
avowed, in the existence of something like a 'one right person' with whom
a romantic relationship can be lifelong (ibid.: 129). Swidler therefore argues
that, in order for the 'mythic' model of romance to be perpetuated, 'neither
hidden ideological hegemony nor brainwashing by mass culture is necessary'
(ibid.: 129); instead, 'the structural constraints of the institution of marriage'
make it entirely unsurprising that the model should have survived.

   Given that this proposition informs much of the early portion of this
chapter, it is worth making clear that we need not understand 'marriage', at
present, purely in terms of the legal category. The salient property of 'marriage' here is the institution's provision of an influential conceptual *structure*, formed according to specific ideological limits, and the 'basic schema
– life-long commitment, exclusivity, an all-or-nothing bond – that is "read"
from the structure' (ibid.: 257).[6] Viewed in this way, the structural features
of marriage provide the predominant model for love relationships in the
contemporary United States, and are thus discernable far beyond the legal

institution itself.[7] Incidentally, this conceptual understanding also governs, I would suggest, ways in which Hollywood films have usually encouraged us to register the significance of marriage. At the end of *Sleepless*, for instance, we are unlikely to be concerned with what will happen to Sam and Annie's finances or visitation rights, or even with whether they will utter vows before witnesses (let alone religious representatives), so much as we are with the fact that they are beginning an exclusive, long-term, romantic relationship. This is not, moreover, simply because *Sleepless* was made long after the fall of the Production Code and that, as Glitre puts it, 'the "union" used to mean marriage; now it implies monogamy' (2006: 12). At the end of *Bluebeard's Eighth Wife* Michael may have been *legally* wed numerous times, but Nicole is still finally able to tell him that 'You've never been married before – not *my* kind of marriage: for keeps, forever.' It is thus a marriage's potential for longevity and monogamy (and/or sanctioning sex, on which more shortly) that are, as far as Hollywood films are concerned, its most pertinent features.

The significance of all this for our discussion of happy endings is the possibility that, through its current institutional and structural status as the dominant social and conceptual model for romantic relationships, 'marriage makes plausible [. . .] arguably the most implausible element of the traditional love myth: the ideal that love lasts forever' (ibid.: 123). This ideal, linked earlier by Swidler (and Galcian) to the concept of 'happily ever after', is of course one key ideological 'message' that the final couple is commonly taken to convey via a 'denial of the temporality of satisfaction' (Shumway 1991: 16/17).

It should now go without saying that the terms in which Swidler's interviewees speak of 'movie' romance (e.g. 'love lasts forever') clearly bespeak at least an extremely generalised understanding of what takes place in real popular romance films (something to which I will return). Indeed, it is precisely in its form as a *cliché* that the 'happy ending' has ideological importance here, with the concept of cliché now assuming an additional social significance (see Zijderveld 1979: 58). Swidler's subjects are not film critics – they are participants in the contemporary West's culture of romantic love, navigating its conceptual structures and weighing its social codes. The structural ideal indissolubly tied to the clichéd concept of 'happily ever after' is currently a central feature of that culture and those codes, and, as such, absolutely demands to be addressed in any ideological account of the final couple.

Before moving on to discuss actual happy endings, then, I first wish to probe further the above account of one possible relationship that may be struck towards 'mythic' romantic discourses. To do so I will be examining a contemporary film which I think we can see as engaging with – and *in* – precisely the kinds of ideological equivocation towards the cultural cliché of 'happily ever after' that several researchers have proposed as typical: *Before Sunrise*. Unlike my previous discussions of 'case study' films, this exploration of Richard Linklater's movie is first and foremost concerned to illuminate less the film's particular handling of its ending, and more its depiction of two characters' ideological negotiation of the line of action with which *the* 'happy ending' is so frequently associated: the life-long, monogamous romantic relationship. While *Before Sunrise* itself very pointedly does *not* end with a final couple, the structural ideal associated with this concept as a cultural cliché exerts a pervasive influence on both this film's characters and the film itself – although the partial and ambivalent nature of that influence is what makes the movie of interest for our present discussion.

Before Sunrise

Before Sunrise takes place over a period of less than twenty-four hours. The bulk of the film consists of a series of conversations between Jesse (Ethan Hawke) and Céline (Julie Delpy), twentysomethings from America and France respectively, who meet on a cross-Europe train and decide to explore Vienna before Jesse has to return to the US the next morning. At nightfall they share their first kiss, suspended in a ferris wheel in the Prater; in the small hours they make love in a secluded corner of a park. Aware of the near-impossibility of a successful long-term relationship, they make a pact to treat this night as the totality of their romance, agreeing not to keep in touch afterwards. This proposal ultimately proves difficult to live up to, however. At the moment Céline is about to board her train to Paris, the pain of the imminent parting proves too great, and the couple make a hastily-concocted plan to meet again in Vienna in six months' time. They then depart their separate ways; 'The End'.

Barely beyond university age and sporting conventional signifiers of Grunge (she with her baggy flannel shirt, he with ripped jumper, Converse trainers and lank hair), Jesse and Céline – like many Linklater protagonists – wish to present themselves as far from passive consumers of dominant Western culture and its attendant ideological assumptions. At one moment early in the day, when the couple are still trying to define themselves in one another's eyes, Céline declares that 'the medias [sic] are trying to control our minds [. . .] It's very subtle, but it's a new form of Fascism, really'; later the pair agree that 'it's a healthy process to rebel against everything that came before.' The couple's burgeoning critical consciousness also extends to their professed attitudes towards romantic love, and towards the line of action often associated with 'happily ever after'. 'Do you know anyone who's in a "happy" relationship?' Céline asks Jesse at one point, her inflection lending the word 'happy' invisible quotation marks; 'Yeah, sure,' Jesse replies, 'but I think they lie to each other though.' The pair often refer to the inevitability of romantic love dwindling over time; in addition to detailing failed relationships of their own, Jesse also speaks of his parents' divorce as something 'they should have done [. . .] a lot sooner'. When Céline tells Jesse of her grandmother's confession of having spent her life pining for a man other than her husband, Jesse responds, 'If she'd ever got to know him I'm sure he would have disappointed her eventually,' since 'people have these romantic projections they put on everything that aren't based in any kind of reality.' They often speak of love in pointedly disillusioned terms, describing it variously as 'an escape for two people who don't know how to be alone', arguing that, contrary to popular belief, 'there's really nothing more selfish'.

Céline and Jesse also apply what we might call this 'prosaic-realistic' attitude to their own budding relationship, wondering aloud on many occasions what they would inevitably come to find aggravating about one another if they had the opportunity to experience 'the temporality of satisfaction' (Shumway 1991: 16/17) – if, as they put it, they 'were together all the time.' Their acknowledgment of the fact that romantic love tends to be, as Wexman puts it, 'by its very nature short-lived' (1993: 8) – particularly in circumstances like theirs – is partly what leads them to do something rather radical for protagonists in a popular American film: intentionally forego the possibility of a long-term relationship. Two thirds of the way into the film the question is raised of what will happen following this night. Sitting at an outdoor café, drawing on past experiences of exchanging addresses and phone numbers with holiday flings only for contact to 'fizzle out', the couple conclude that 'the long-distance thing never works'. Instead, they improvise an alternative model. 'Maybe we should try something different,' Céline says: 'I mean, it's not so bad if tonight is our only night, right?' After some thought, Jesse agrees. 'Why do you think everybody thinks relationships are supposed to last forever anyway?' he asks. 'Yeah, *why?*' Céline concurs, 'it's stupid'. They thus make a pact, sealed by a symbolic holding of hands, to have 'no delusions, no projections', and that tonight will be their only night.

However, Jesse and Céline simultaneously exhibit a second set of attitudes towards romantic love. Céline, for instance, at one point confides that, 'I always feel this pressure to [. . .] not make it look like my whole life is revolving round some guy. But loving someone and being loved means so much to me.' Thus, while Céline here voices a stance that bespeaks her position as a child of the second-wave (her parents were, as she puts it, 'angry May '68 types') – demonstrating that she has, as McCabe put it, 'learnt how to critique [. . .] romance' – she nonetheless seems to 'remain at the same time absolutely beguiled' (2009: 164). Similar equivocations characterise the couple's attitudes towards the concept of clichéd 'romantic projections', to which Jesse disparagingly referred in relation to Céline's grandmother. 'Romantic projections?' Céline asks after Jesse utters this line: "Oh, Mr. Romantic up there in the ferris wheel?! "Oh, *kiss* me, the *sunset*, it's so *beautiful* . . .!"' The reference is to an earlier scene in which the couple first kissed in the Prater, when Jesse seemed far from unmoved by the seductions of popular romantic fantasy:

Jesse: So, we got a sunset here . . .? [. . .] We got the ferris wheel . . .
          [. . .] Feels like this would be a good time to . . . *You* know . . .
Céline: Are you trying to say you want to kiss me?

'Yes,' Jesse mouths, making an ironic but chastened show of his embarrassment. And of course that is what he is trying to say: he wants to kiss her now because it is 'a good time' to do so, because he is in sway – however consciously or awkwardly – to a highly clichéd image of a 'romantic moment', which includes sunsets and picturesque views. Similarly, towards the end of the night, as the couple are discussing their time together, Céline says:

Céline: . . . But then morning comes and we turn into pumpkins,
          right?
Jesse: God . . .
Céline: Well, I think at this moment you are supposed to produce the
          glass slipper and see if it fits.
Jesse: Yeah? It'll fit . . .

Here the lovers are employing an object from a shared culture of popular romance – in this case (as in *Pretty Woman*) Cinderella – to communicate about their relationship. Again, however playful these uses of traditional romantic conventions, they nonetheless demonstrate the persistence for these characters of 'mythic' romantic frameworks alongside their 'prosaic-realistic' counterparts.

The tension resulting from the characters' continual oscillation between these frameworks culminates in the second, revised plan for the future of their relationship: the arrangement to meet again in six months' time. So much of Céline and Jesse's discussion has been dedicated to critiquing the idea of lifelong romantic love, stressing their acknowledgment of its fragility and finitude. They ultimately, however, choose not to behave in a manner that accords with those critiques – that is: give up on the chance of a future together. 'All this bullshit we're talking about not seeing each other again?' Jesse breathlessly blurts as they stand on the platform: 'I don't want to do that.' 'I don't want to do it either!' Céline replies with huge relief. Thus, despite their pact to have 'no delusions, no projections', the couple end their time together, and the film, with what amounts to a very clear 'projection' indeed. And what does this projection involve? Although they have described the notion that 'relationships are supposed to last forever' as 'stupid', when they reach the agreed end of their relationship, they feel that they must leave open the possibility for precisely such an outcome. In this way, although the film's ending itself is extremely hermeneutically 'open' (indulging more fully than any previously-examined film the realistic impulse to '[leave] the reader free to imagine that the characters go on living – as if they were real people' after the narrative's end [Thickstun 1988: 7]), the couple's promised six-months-ahead date represents nothing so much as the potential for a final couple happy ending after the film's close.

The plan, in fact, strongly recalls Annie's scheme in *Sleepless* – inspired by *An Affair to Remember* – to meet Sam on Valentine's Day. Most banally, both Annie's plan and that of Jesse and Céline clearly reflect a desire to enter into the category of the long-term monogamous couple, the dominant ideological model by which their society organises romantic love. Equally though, both are influenced by 'mythic' cultural models regarding how this category can be achieved. Céline and Jesse are scarcely so in thrall to the 'magic' of popular romance as Annie, who hatches her plan whilst watching *An Affair to Remember* on video: she sees the scene in which Nickie (Cary Grant) and Terry (Deborah Kerr) arrange to meet on the Empire State Building, and (at the suggestion of her friend) inserts this idea directly into the letter she is writing to Sam. Nonetheless, *Before Sunrise*'s lovers do arrange a date for a romantic reunion and – significantly – take the highly clichéd romantic step of not exchanging addresses or telephone numbers. To do so would be, Jesse says, 'depressing', a word likely representing banality, or perhaps dull rationality – as opposed, that is, to a conventionally romantic *ir*rationality (true romance being, as Shumway says, 'by definition irresponsible' [2003: 126]). By foregoing the chance to keep in touch, the couple clearly intend to avoid the possibility that their romance will, as they put it, 'fizzle out', perhaps hoping instead that it may grow in each other's absence, ultimately achieving culmination in the moment of their proposed reunion. This allows for the kind of postponed idealised desire that conventionally drives both romantic love *and* romantic narrative (Belsey 1994), and indeed is indicative in part of the general process whereby 'romantic love [introduces] the idea of a narrative into an individual's life' (Giddens 1993: 39). This is not to say that Céline and Jesse actually imagine their own meeting will magically result in anything like an 'ever after'; however, the nature of their plan means that it nevertheless has this *structure* – a structure that is indebted to both narrative and ideological convention.

These conventions are, in turn, likely to be equally significant for the relationship between *Before Sunrise*'s ending and its audience. Speaking of the experiences fostered by endings of different modes of narrative filmmaking, Neupert notes that, while we are never in any doubt as to how a romantic comedy such as *The Awful Truth* will end, 'it would be nearly impossible to guess that Antoine Doinel will eventually run to the ocean at the end of *The 400 Blows*'; moreover, 'simply knowing the ending [of this film] does not seem to provide us with the same sort of satisfaction' (1995: 11). It is instructive to consider that the ending of *Before Sunrise* is not quite like those of either *The Awful Truth* or *The 400 Blows* (1959), yet it contains elements of both. Like

The 400 Blows, *Before Sunrise*'s ending is explicitly 'open'; however, while we may ponder Antoine's (Jean-Pierre Léaud) future after the end of his narrative, we are unlikely to feel anything like the same *need* for answers about it as *Before Sunrise*'s ending seems to require of us. This is because, as Neupert rightly notes, 'there is no single goal or quest in sight [for Antoine]' about which we are able to speculate (ibid.: 88). By contrast, the moment a narrative introduces the possibility of a romantic couple – be it in *The Awful Truth* or *Before Sunrise* – we know that we are being invited to infer a potential 'goal', i.e. we feel encouraged to wonder whether these characters will become and remain united by the end of the film. In one sense simply reflecting a desire for conventional narrative closure, it must be acknowledged that this desire is also related to matters of ideology.

Jesse and Céline's aim of a long-term monogamous relationship is at once the traditional 'goal' of romantic narrative and, very schematically put, the 'goal' by which their society ideologically organises intimate relations: marriage, viewed as a conceptual structure. Being conscious of this fact, however, may not suppress investment in the line of action to which it refers – neither for characters nor audiences. Robin Wood's book *Sexual Politics and Narrative Film* is dedicated to critiquing aspects of patriarchal ideology through analyses of cinematic representations of love and sexuality. In a chapter concerning *Before Sunrise* (written prior to *Before Sunset* [2004], on which more in a moment), Wood effectively confirms the difference between this film and one like *The 400 Blows* when he reports that 'everyone with whom I have watched [the film] immediately raises the question of whether or not Jesse and Céline will keep their six-months-ahead date' (1998: 323). He then suggests they probably will not; yet, he continues,

> the verdict is always reached with great reluctance, testifying to the continuing pull, despite the battering it has received, of the romantic ideal as a powerful and seductive component of our ideology of love and sexuality. [. . .] The tug of the longing for permanence is so powerful that one would love to see a sequel [. . .] in which they *did* keep the appointment and returned together to . . . France? America? . . . and tried to work out ways in which 'commitment' is still feasible. (ibid.: 325)

Later, raising the question of whether romantic love's patriarchal and heterosexist history means that it is so ideologically tainted a concept as to require denouncing entirely, Wood suggests that 'the question of "Will they or won't they?" may be a simple (and sentimental) evasion of the real question posed by the film's ending, which is far more radical and disturbing: Would it be better if they did or if they didn't?' (ibid.: 325). By remaining so pointedly unresolved, the film opens up the possibility of asking such a question. Clearly (as with *Eternal Sunshine*), *Before Sunrise* needs to be seen partly in terms of an 'Indiewood' context which remains ostentatiously uneasy about the 'traditional' final couple; yet its ending similarly does not seem to wholly relinquish a belief in its possibility. Comparably, although Wood may raise that radical question about the conclusion, he nonetheless remains beguiled by a far more sentimental one: 'Will they or won't they?' This is surely because the line of action associated with a clichéd image of the final couple has become, by this point in Western history, the dominant structural framework in terms of which romantic love continues to be conceptualised – whether one consciously endorses this ideological state of affairs or otherwise.

Thus, while they may not organise their entire romantic and sexual lives according to the dictates of romance narrative, as *Sleepless'* Annie does, at least one aspect of romantic convention – the final couple – still retains its socially symbolic appeal and usefulness for Céline and Jesse. Whereas Annie seems to want to 'be in love in a movie', and applies the logic of movies to construct an imaginary bond with a man she has never met, the lovers of *Before Sunrise* can be said to apply something like the logic of 'the movies' to organise their responses to a relationship which is based not solely upon such logic. Whilst Annie appears to have wrested her ideals of romantic love, marriage and long-term monogamy wholesale from popular culture, Céline and Jesse's conception of these ideals and culture is more critical, though not immune to their influence. Relatedly, while the film presents us with an 'open' ending that in theory allows its audience to relinquish the hope that this couple will have the chance at a long-term relationship, it seems unlikely that we will finally do so (or, if we *do*, then perhaps 'the verdict is [. . .] reached with great reluctance'). That is to say, no matter how much Céline and Jesse question it, 'the tug of the longing for permanence' – which is represented here by the potential for a final couple – seemingly pervades *Before Sunrise* (and perhaps our responses to it) almost as strongly as it does *Sleepless*. Similarly, even the film's creators themselves apparently felt this longing, since they *did* in fact make a sequel, and in a 'making-of' documentary on the *Before Sunset* DVD, Julie Delpy explains that this project was attractive because 'it felt like something was unfinished – because they never meet again, and because [*Before Sunrise*] ends on this kind of open ending . . .'[8]

The crucial question, though, asked by Jesse, is: 'Why do you think everybody thinks relationships are supposed to last forever anyway?' Rephrasing this question in terms appropriate to our present discussion, we might ask: what function might the convention of the final couple serve in inculcating in 'everybody' an ideological ideal wherein romantic relationships are intended to be lifelong and monogamous? The answer 'none' would plainly be incorrect;

yet so too would its opposite. This latter answer, however, seems effectively to be the one proposed by a film like *Sleepless*. Annie appears to be ideologically affected by popular romantic culture in essentially the same manner as the hypothetical viewers watching *Moulin Rouge* or *Maid in Manhattan* as if they were instructional guides. By contrast, in *Before Sunrise* Jesse and Céline instead make use of structures that are recognisably related to clichéd images of popular romantic narrative when they are faced with an example of 'the lines of action institutions structure' (Swidler 2003: 131). Presented with someone with whom they feel they *could* potentially have a long-term relationship – that is: someone with whom they would happily attempt to enact the conceptual structure of a marriage – Céline and Jesse find themselves required to construct a plan that allows them a chance at achieving that 'goal'. To help them in this, they employ the conceptual model of a kind of 'happy ending' – perhaps because, we might speculate, 'the love myth accurately describes the structural constraints of the institution of marriage' (ibid.: 128).

This, then, is a matter of whether the cultural cliché of the final couple should be viewed either as *dictating* or *informing* attitudes and approaches to romantic relationships. Clearly, both our films' couples broadly adhere to the dominant ideological model of romantic love offered by their society and its culture: marriage and/or long-term monogamy. Yet, while *Sleepless* presents a world in which such adherence appears guaranteed due to the influence of romantic narratives, in the world of *Before Sunrise* romantic narrative seems to have the comparatively ambiguous relationship with ideological beliefs and actions that Swidler suggests is more typical of the world we live in. By no means free, but nonetheless *freer*, Jesse and Céline emerge as characters who seem to be 'ideologically influenced, but not necessarily monolithically so' (Mayne 2003: 29).

Towards the end of *Talk of Love*, Swidler suggests that 'criticism of a dominant ideal will not eliminate it as long as it still provides a useful guide to action', leading her to the hypothesis that 'marriage may explain why dramas of love retain their popular appeal' (ibid.: 129). This suggestion is rather more convincing, at least, than one which might represent the causal relationship as running in precisely the opposite direction. As Britton puts it,

> [H]uman beings are the only animals who are capable of formulating social projects independent, and often in defiance, of their instinctual drives. It is scarcely astonishing, in the light of this fact [. . .] that these same human beings are possessed of an insatiable impulse to construct symbolic dramas in which such projects are conceived, impeded, thwarted and accomplished, and in which feelings about the nature, conditions, limits and consequences of human action are worked through. (2009: 435)

Marriage and lifelong monogamy seem to be examples of just such social projects which defy our instinctual drives (see Barah/Lipton 2001). Romance narratives and final couples are, in turn, forms of symbolic drama which allow many societies to work through and evaluate feelings towards these projects. As suggested by Swidler's interviewees, attitudes towards romantic love that are drawn – in however clichéd a form – from places such as Hollywood cinema can certainly help to organise lines of action. Yet this is unlikely to be a matter of popular culture wholly interpellating us into pre-established social roles, but rather a question of social actors using pertinent aspects of a culture as and when they facilitate the navigation of already-existing institutions and social structures at hand. In short: it is not clear that marriage and long-term monogamy currently persist as the dominant social structures by which we conceptualise romantic love because of the ideological influence of final couples; it is very likely, however, that final couples currently persist because they offer us a way to conceptualise our encounters with the dominant social structures of marriage and long-term monogamy. Though hardly the last word on the subject, this shift in emphasis may permit us to begin rethinking the ideological significance of the final couple in terms of the convention being not simply a cause of, but also a response to a need created by, these structures' maintenance.

*

We have so far been focusing on the potential ideological significance of, not actual Hollywood happy endings, but rather the clichéd *concept* of the Hollywood 'happy ending'. Before moving on to consider the former, and following my reservations about imagining cinematic spectators' utter passivity in the face of an all-powerful text, it is important to offer a caveat or two concerning the potential for happy endings to be 'negotiated'.

Ideology and the text

> The question of whether value is in the poem or in the reader is radically and permanently ambiguous, requiring two answers. Of course the value is not there, *actually*, until it is actualized by the reader. But of course it could not be actualized if it were not there, *in potential*, in the poem. (Booth 1988: 89)

Wayne Booth's warning here is salutary, and applies just as readily to questions of a text's ideological inducements as to its value. It is thus worth acknowledging some familiar objections to approaches concerning themselves solely with reception. I earlier referred to the useful research into the reception of popular culture that emerged in the 1980s. Other scholarship has questioned some of the potential for excess within such work's methodologies – the proposition, for example, that 'cultural artifacts are *not* containers with immanent meanings' (Staiger 1992: xi; emphasis mine). Judith Mayne, for instance, has perceptively noted that, in some work on reception 'the activity / passivity of the ['subject-position'] model appears to be reversed in favour of an active reader / viewer and a relatively stable, if not completely passive, text' (ibid.: 40). We must remember that texts are not so passive and spectators so active that a given text can be made to mean simply *anything*. It is therefore one valid function of criticism to attempt to determine what ideological meanings or precepts a text contains 'in potential' – in other words, to try to identify a film's 'preferred reading, with which most audience members enter into some kind of negotiation' (Brunsdon/Morley 1999: 15). While certainly not itself the cause of, say, marriage or monogamy's persistence, then, the convention of the final couple is nonetheless certainly capable of endorsing certain ideological premises, and it is necessary to explore further what those premises are, or can be.

We have previously seen that the final couple is a far more flexible convention than is regularly assumed, capable of offering greatly varying kinds of – for instance – happiness, closure and unrealism (something that has remained unacknowledged in our earlier discussion of popular romance's 'mythic' clichés). Even while acknowledging this, however, the convention does of course have the ability to convey ideological premises, and these require analysis. Most fundamentally and obviously, there is a basic premise we might call 'the primary importance of the couple' (Jeffers 2007: 13) – however defined. Though we should always remain open to discussing (for example) the degree of enthusiasm with which a particular film actually presents its final couple, the very fact of the convention's prevalence has the capacity to habituate this most broad of ideological premises. I will be arguing later that to be tied to such a very general premise is, at least in theory, a relatively loose ideological constraint for the convention, but it is assuredly a constraint nonetheless. At certain points in the final couple's history, however, the constraints have been tighter and more unambiguously reactionary. Most obviously, for decades the Production Code – an ostentatiously conservative document – guaranteed, firstly, the exclusion of romantic fulfilment for (and indeed the virtual wholesale absence of) same-sex couples, meaning that the final couple unavoidably had 'a heterosexist bias since its codification' (Benshoff/Griffin 2004b: 61). Equally, the Code included an explicitly racist clause, bluntly stating that 'miscegenation is forbidden' (Maltby 2003: 595). Finally, it decreed the delaying of sex until after marriage (that is: films were prohibited to 'infer that low forms of sex relationships are the accepted or common thing' [Maltby 2003: 595]). Of course, we know that what films themselves affirmed need by no means always be equal to what the PCA affirmed. Nonetheless, each of these requirements is unambiguously ideologically reactionary in intent, and – moreover – all ensured the final couple as a convention could not help but lend legitimacy to significant aspects of this ideology.[9]

This is merely to raise forcefully the uncontroversial point that, although it is important to acknowledge audiences' latitude in how texts' meanings are ideologically navigated, the ideological meanings of texts themselves also plainly demand our attention. Thus, having suggested something of the ideological relationship between audiences and the 'happy ending' as conceived in the clichéd abstract, we must now turn to the ideological implications of actual final couple happy endings.

IDEOLOGY, CLOSURE AND THE 'HAPPY ENDING'

As I suggested in the introduction, perhaps the most central reason for film studies' hostility towards the 'happy ending' is its perceived links with narrative closure. As for the Production Code Administration so for film scholars, the ability of endings to have 'the last word' on their narratives has meant that they have been assumed to hold great potential ideological importance. In a particularly concise condensation of many critical trends, Harry M. Benshoff and Sean Griffin tell us that,

> Hollywood's use of the happy ending, a specific form of closure, ties up all the story's loose ends and frequently includes the protagonist and the love interest uniting as a romantic/sexual couple. [. . .] Any actual ideological issues or social strife that may have been raised by the film are allegedly solved by narrative closure [. . .]. Closure in Hollywood tends to reaffirm the status quo of American society. (Benshoff/Griffin 2004a: 28)

Such characterisations of closure are extremely common within film studies, and their roots lie fundamentally in one approach to *texts* fostered by the 'subject-position' model, among others. Since it is so central to the critical reputation of the 'happy ending', even today, we must sketch some of this tradition's contours.

It is a common tendency of 'subject-position' theory to automatically align narrative closure (or resolution, coherence, unity, wholeness, boundedness, etc.) with conservatism, and 'openness' (including loose ends, fissures, contradictions, paradoxes, etc.) with the potential for ideological resistance. Claude Lévi-Strauss laid effective foundations for the reputation that the concept of closure would endure throughout the latter half of the twentieth century when he wrote that 'mythical thought always progresses from the awareness of oppositions toward their resolution' (1955: 440), mythic narrative's purpose being 'to provide a logical model capable of overcoming contradiction' (ibid.: 443). The structuralist emphasis placed here on binaries and the resolution of contradictions – which might be interpreted in ideological as well as narrative terms – has found many echoes in innumerable theories of both literature and film that went on to regard narrative closure per se as a simultaneously salving and authoritarian narrative device.

Indeed, since the 1960s various theoretical approaches to film and literature have managed to draw parallels between narrative closure and virtually every 'conservative' impulse in Western culture, for example: the 'repressive order of the nineteenth-century bourgeoisie' (Miller 1981: 281); capitalism (Hayward 2006: 194); patriarchy (Kuhn 1994: 16); male sexuality (Gallop 1982: 27); heterosexual normativity (Roof 1996: xxix); the 'misrecognition' of the self as a coherent social subject (Kristeva 1980: 55); dominant versions of history (Mulvey 1989: 159), 'family values' (Kolker 2006: 212); the military industrial complex (Slocum 2005: 40), and so on. Thus, via various metaphors, 'ideological "solutions" to social contradictions become [. . .] the "resolutions" offered in traditional fiction' (Boone 1987: 8). In short, according to a great deal of both literary and film theory, 'narrative closure reaffirms [. . .] cultural norms with little variation' (Carson et al. 1994: 250). In keeping with so numerous and damning a set of assumptions about the innately conservative character of closure, such claims may often be accompanied by the advancement of contrasting claims for ideologically progressive texts which are 'relatively disabused of teleological illusions' (Miller 1981: 281), since 'an open ending doesn't confirm or reassure existing ideology; it questions ideology and demystifies it' (Preis 1990: 18). Whether it be the 'writerly text' (Barthes [1970]), modernism (Wollen 1985), postmodernism (Nash 2001: 16), intertextuality (Kristeva 1980: 38), the epistolary form (Macarthur 1990), the feminist avant-garde (Mulvey 1989: 159), counter-cinema (Hayward 2006: 76), new-wave films (Russell [1995]), female-focused films (Kuhn 1994: 132), films by black female filmmakers (Springer 1984), soap operas (Modleski 1979), or otherwise, the prevailing attitude towards closure ensures that one overarching critical claim can afford to be largely the same: since X complicates closure, X has progressive potential.[10]

But what, in this context, of Hollywood movies – which, as we have already seen, are routinely deemed to possess a 'heavily "closed" discourse' (MacCabe 1974: 16), fundamentally 'aimed at containment' (Heath 1975: 49)? For the film theorist committed to something like the above view of closure, yet wishing to make positive claims for a classical film, the answer has often been to suggest that a film in question only *appears* 'closed', and that analysis can uncover ways in which it tacitly leaves 'open' contradictions which more straightforwardly conservative films would contain. As Charlotte Brunsdon puts it, 'Hollywood cinema [. . .] could be retrieved if its textual (here standing for ideological) coherence could be demonstrated to be only apparent' (1989: 122). Hollywood films seen as tacitly complicating closure contributed immeasurably to 'one of the most influential critical categories of the 1970s, the formally subversive 'progressive' text' (Klinger 1984a: 17). Numerous theoretical models, such as Comolli and Narboni's 'category (e)' film (1971), MacCabe's 'classic realist text' (1974), and many approaches to melodrama (see: Gledhill 1987), have presented the covert or accidental 'opening' of an otherwise 'closed' form – via style, 'excess', irony, etc. – as the primary if not only means by which a classical Hollywood film might convey anything other than a staid ideological conservatism. We may, with Klinger, call this broad approach to the textual politics of Hollywood movies the 'rupture thesis' (1984b: 42).

While 'closure' in many such accounts was taken to refer to far more than simply narrative endings, it is nonetheless unsurprising that in this climate the 'happy ending' became considered intrinsically ideologically pernicious. It is equally unsurprising, however, that happy endings should have become particularly important as potential sites for tensions which 'exceed the conventions of closure' (Klinger 1984a: 22). If wishing to argue that a film with a seemingly 'closed' happy ending is valuable, such a context makes it vital that this ending be in some way discredited. Perhaps the most common means of arguing that this has happened is to invoke a critical category we have already encountered: the implausible happy ending. This approach to the convention is here taken to be significant not only for its strategy of deliberate unrealism (see Chapter 3), but because of its ability to ironically undermine a 'closed' conclusion that would otherwise necessarily serve conservative functions. This, indeed, is by far the most frequently used model by which positive ideological arguments for individual happy endings have ever been made by film studies, regardless of period.[11] Given the great importance of this model to the convention's reputation, then, let us turn to a director whose work has been central to its development: Douglas Sirk.

Sirk, the 'happy ending' and closure

The theoretical climate I have outlined virtually necessitated the development of a 'rupture thesis'. As Peter Wollen puts it: 'While Hollywood is an implacable foe, it is not monolithic. It contains contradictions within itself, different kinds of conflicts and fissures' (1998: 118). If Hollywood cinema is first and foremost assumed to be a 'foe', then it is hardly surprising that covert *subversion* should be treated as the only means by which a text can ever hope to avoid our enmity. In other words: in this context no 'progressive' ideological meanings can ever be made *overtly* by a Hollywood movie, but can emerge only via either smuggling or fortunate mistake, and are observable only when viewing a film 'obliquely, looking for symptoms' (Comolli/Narboni 1971: 7).

While approaches to 'symptomatic reading' (Althusser 1970: 28) by no means always assume that a film's 'fissures' are intentional, Sirk has gained a reputation as a director who deliberately subverted Hollywood's ideological operations by subtly rupturing the coherence of his films' narratives. A series of interviews that John Halliday conducted with Sirk in the late 1960s helped grow both this reputation and the notion of the progressive implausible happy ending. Sirk explained to Halliday, 'I had to go by the rules, [. . .] have "happy endings" and so on' (ibid.: 97); however, he went on, in his films, 'there is no real solution to the predicament the people in the play are in' (ibid.: 152); instead, there is 'only one way out, the irony of the "happy end"' (ibid.: 136). Thus, he claimed, in his films, 'you don't believe the happy end, and you're not really supposed to' (ibid.: 68). Even when Sirk's films' subversive elements became considered a general feature of melodrama rather than evidence of an auteur's vision (e.g. Nowell-Smith 1977), an emphasis on the disruption of closure still remains central. Accordingly, a great many writers have claimed that Sirk made films with only 'pseudo-happy endings' (Affron 1980: 51), which seem both 'tacked on' (Smith 1977) and 'forced' (Pollock 1977: 109), and which 'expose the stylization of cinematic discourse' (Henke 1994: 37); ultimately, conventional wisdom dictates, his happy endings should be considered merely 'an ironic appurtenance' (Rodowick 1987: 276).[12] It is important to stress that the impact of this model is by no means restricted to this director, genre, period or theoretical tradition. For instance, *The Classical Hollywood Cinema*, which is explicitly sceptical of most '*Screen* theory', tells us that an 'unmotivated happy ending' can 'break down the ideological unity of the classical Hollywood film' (Bordwell et al. 1985: 83). Indeed, as seen in the introduction, it is a common tendency in virtually all periods and theoretical traditions to refer to the subversive implications of Hollywood happy endings which guarantee 'we cannot rest secure' (Modleski 1988: 54). As recently as 2009, for instance, we can see Sirk still being invoked to bolster a reading of *Groundhog Day*'s ending as tacitly ironic, and therefore ideologically progressive (Sutton 2009: 40).

I wish to make three main points about the assumptions underlying this approach to the 'happy ending'. The first, already made in Chapter 2, is that 'closure' is not a fixed commodity: happy endings very frequently offer different degrees of closure and, indeed, the creation of one kind of 'openness' – pointing towards the future – seems rather fundamental to the convention. Secondly, though, we should certainly not let this blind us to the fact that there *do* exist endings which, by virtue of being presented in an ironic fashion, act to undermine what could otherwise serve as a comparatively 'closed' and ideologically conservative conclusion. Finally, however, the assumption that a happy ending *requires* ironic treatment in order to avoid conservatism is a damaging one. I will now expand on these points with reference to two

Sirk films: *There's Always Tomorrow* (1956) and *All That Heaven Allows* (1955).

There's Always Tomorrow

There's Always Tomorrow seems to me to be a film for which the notion of the subversive, implausible happy ending is absolutely appropriate – if 'implausible' here means something like unconvincing-as-'happy', and 'subversive' means the tacit conveying of oppositional ideological meanings. At the end of this film, as in many Code-era melodramas, an affair (or almost-affair) is forced to end – in this case so that a married man may return to his wife and family. Toy-designer Cliff Grove (Fred MacMurray) and fashion designer Norma Miller Vale (Barbara Stanwyck) knew each other some twenty years ago when Norma worked for Cliff's company. During the film we learn that they enjoyed something of a flirtation in this earlier life, though it came to an abrupt end when Norma suddenly resigned. This, however, emerges some time into the narrative. Our introduction to Norma comes when she shows up unexpectedly at Cliff's family home one night – a night when he has been left alone in the house, resignedly frustrated that his plans to celebrate his wife Marion's (Joan Bennett) birthday have been cancelled because each family member has made other arrangements. Over the next few days Cliff and Norma spend a number of happy times together, eventually declare their renewed love for each other, and long for a shared life. Yet, following pressure from two of Cliff's scandalised and uncomprehending teenage children, Vinnie (William Reynolds) and Ellen (Gigi Perreau), Norma decides to end the burgeoning relationship. Thus, although Cliff eventually reaches the point at which he feels prepared to abandon his family in favour of Norma, and tells her so, Norma puts a stop to this dream when she announces that she will fly back to New York that evening; they part ways.

In the film's final scene Cliff returns home, depressed and interacting only distractedly with his children, who buzz around him as he passes through the living room. He goes to an open window and sees what we take to be Norma's plane flying across the evening sky, upon which we cut to Norma onboard the plane, who is also distraught, glancing out of the window as she chokes back tears. Marion, who has never suspected anything, now approaches Cliff as he closes the window shutters, telling him that she has been concerned by his recent behaviour: 'It's not like you to be irritable and depressed,' she says. 'I know,' answers Cliff as the two move arm-in-arm away from the window, 'but I'm all right now.' 'Good,' she replies, smiling. 'You know me better than I know myself,' he tells her. Smiling at one another – she sweetly, he hesitantly – they move out of shot as the camera pans to reveal their three children, who watch them happily. The youngest child, Frankie (Judy Nugent), sighs contentedly: 'They make a handsome couple, don't they?' We fade to black; 'The End'.

It has been said that Sirk often 'imbues [a] conclusion with unmistakable irony' (Klinger 1984a: 38–9). Yet the presence of irony as a rhetorical strategy can in fact often be a very difficult thing to point to with certainty. Because hinging on a disparity between 'seeming' and 'actual' meanings, it is often 'hard to say what is the overt and what the covert meaning' (Booth 1974: 27). I nevertheless think that we may describe the ending of *There's Always Tomorrow* in terms of its irony, since (1) it contains numerous invitations to infer implicit rhetorical meanings which run directly counter to other ostensible meanings, and (2) it contrasts our perspective on events against those of various characters.

The ironies begin with the attitudes we are encouraged to take to the very sense of closure offered by the film – for this is indeed a remarkably 'closed' conclusion. At the hermeneutic level, the film's overarching narrative question (whether Cliff will or will not forsake his family) is answered by Norma's departure and Cliff's return home; in terms of rhetoric, too, there is significant 'bracketing' through the final scene's repetition of actions we remember from towards the film's opening: the children talking on the telephone while sitting on floor, Cliff arriving from work via the front door, and so on. For such a conclusion – one that appears 'closed' – to also appear 'happy', it must affirm its means of resolution. In *There's Always Tomorrow*, however, closure is instead made to appear as a kind of suffocation rather than stability – an act of *en*closing.

Cliff's desire for Norma is shown throughout the film to have merely heightened feelings that already simmered in him before her reappearance: specifically, the sense that his home life is constricting and unsatisfying.[13] At one moment Cliff describes to Norma how he felt when returning home after one of their meetings – a scene we witnessed a few minutes previously: 'All of a sudden I felt desperate sitting in my own living room. I felt as though I were trapped in a tomb of my own making, and all the years until today were stones closing up the tomb.' The final scene takes place in this very living room and is careful to stress precisely this sense of enclosure. This starts with a visual call-back to the moment to which Cliff is referring in the above dialogue: we begin the final scene with a shot that places a framed family portrait in the foreground – the same portrait which, when Cliff felt so entombed earlier, he had looked at with an exasperated sigh and then purposely blocked from his vision with a newspaper. Secondly, after Cliff has watched Norma's receding plane, and after a shot from outside that has visually trapped him behind the window frame, he closes the window shutters with a noticeable bang. Finally, the last shot uses the imagery of, not quite a tomb, but (like *The Reckless Moment* [1949]) a prison – banisters creating vertical bars that entrap the smiling children. In this way, the family life to which Cliff has returned is itself figured as offering a kind of closure, and while this state of resolution may leave his children, Marion, and (he is currently outwardly professing) him happy, it is something that we are instead invited to understand as an ideologically-sanctioned form of repression aimed at upholding certain values. In other words, the narrative is absolutely 'closed', but this is a closure by which we are likely to feel prevented from being satisfied.

The ending also contains literal ironies. Firstly, Cliff claims to be 'all right now,' just a few seconds after we have seen him looking far from it whilst staring longingly from the window. He then tells Marion that she knows him better than he knows himself, which the preceding film has shown to be entirely untrue: Marion has not only failed to notice her husband's near-affair – which would certainly be necessary for a full understanding of him and his current mental and emotional state – but she has also consistently failed to intuit the causes of his more general frustrations. In a scene following an uncomfortable family dinner with Norma, for example, Marion has misunderstood Cliff's complaints about the stifling nature of their existence as being merely a matter of money (her: 'I know it's expensive . . ' / him: 'I'm not talking about expenses, I'm talking about *life*.'), finally prompting Cliff to exclaim, 'You *know* that isn't what I mean!' While Marion may respond with 'Well, I wish I knew what you *did* mean, dear, then maybe I could help you,' she soon leaves the conversation none the wiser, and – importantly – remains so until the end of the film. Similarly, Frankie's last question, 'They make a handsome couple, don't they?' is likely to encourage us to mentally respond 'no,' for precisely this reason. Forever talking at cross-purposes, seldom communicating openly, Cliff and Marion are by no means a handsome couple if by handsome we mean appealing. Simply put: because of all that has gone before, it is not Marion but *Norma* with whom we are likely to have desired Cliff to form a final couple. The pair may be handsome if we take the word to mean 'good-looking', but this is exactly the (ironic) point this ending is concerned to make: while the Groves family may *look* the ideologically 'perfect' part, it is in fact both constricting and dangerously close to coming apart at the seams. It is highly significant in this respect that the film's final, platitudinous line is spoken by the young Frankie, who is literally a naïve spectator – her ability to correctly interpret what she is seeing being compromised both by her age and by the fact that (unlike her siblings) she knows nothing of her father's relationship with Norma.

This ending thus takes narrative and iconographic materials that are certainly capable of serving a 'closed', conservative happy ending (a 'home-wrecker' sent packing, a return home, a family reunited) and treats them in precisely the manner described by Klinger, wherein various rhetorical strategies 'undercut the affirmative ending, [conspiring] to disturb the harmonising tendencies of closure' (ibid.: 39). This, then, truly is a happy ending that we would seem justified in calling ironic. A brief comparison with two films we have already looked at might help to define more precisely what this means.

Both *Intermezzo* and *September Affair* solve their similar narrative problems in comparably Code-approved ways to *There's Always Tomorrow*, separating adulterous final couples so that husbands may (it is at least implied) return to their families. Yet we saw in Chapter 1 that each film treats this convention rather differently. In *September Affair* we leave the adulterous couple at the moment of their painful separation and, while Manina is offered some hope for the future, there is no suggestion that David will be happy if he returns home. This film, then, offers one possible approach to the end-of-the-affair trope: attempt no especially strong closural sense that, as Bordwell would say, 'the characters' futures are settled' (1982: 4), end before the moment of home-coming, and do not imply that this homecoming itself would necessarily prove 'happy'. *Intermezzo*, on the other hand, takes great pains to shift the value of family to its centre in its final ten minutes, thus placing far more positive rhetorical emphasis on Holger's return. This represents another option: try to convince us that the closure offered by the homecoming is something about which we should feel 'happy'. (Of course, in keeping with the concept of audience 'negotiation', we as viewers may *not* in fact be convinced by this ending, and this is most certainly one ending that would benefit from being looked at 'obliquely, looking for symptoms' [Comolli/Narboni 1971: 7].) These contrasting strategies also have contrasting ideological significance: *September Affair* makes barely any attempt to paper over the cracks that have appeared in the façade of the central nuclear family, while *Intermezzo* strains to recuperate this important ideological unit by downplaying any challenges to its security or authority.

If described cursorily, the ending of *There's Always Tomorrow* might seem more like *Intermezzo*'s than *September Affair*'s; in foregoing the chance to conclude at the moment of separation itself, it opens up the possibility of presenting the return home as a comparatively 'happy' moment of closure by affirming the value of reconstituting the family. Yet, as we have seen, while this film may play similar notes to *Intermezzo*, the result is very different music. Firstly, instead of banishing Norma from the screen early enough to place more importance upon Cliff's homecoming, Sirk rather makes Norma's presence poignantly and emphatically felt in the final scene itself via the cut to her on the plane – a measure that, indeed, makes the scene revolve in large part around her absence and distance from Cliff. (In *Intermezzo* an equivalent rhetorical strategy would have to involve the earlier shot of Anita looking miserable on the train, or something similar, being inserted into the home-coming scene.) Secondly, instead of attempting to convince us that Cliff may be made happy by family life in the future, the film has established that he already felt trapped within it even *before* Norma's return. Finally, instead of finishing with an affirmation of future domesticity made to feel both sincere and significant by all that has built up to it ('Welcome home'), Sirk's film concludes with dialogue whose context has prepared us to register it as naïve and untrue. If, during these moments, we remember the 'tomorrow' invoked by the film's title, the sense of future promise the term implies can only seem hopeless.

It is interesting in this respect that, according to Sirk, this film was in fact originally intended to conclude in a manner more similar to *September Affair*, ending with Cliff watching Norma's plane, not from the family living room, but from his office window, prior to any return home. By denying the possibility of creating even a tenuous sense of the consolations of a secure domestic life, this conclusion would have stressed, as Sirk puts it, 'complete hopelessness' (Stern 1979: 125) – and quite unambiguously. Rather than achieving this 'hopelessness' so overtly, the film we have nonetheless communicates something like it through what we can justifiably call irony – taking similar feelings and meanings to those made *explicit* in *September Affair* and conveying them comparatively *implicitly* within an ending that it would be possible to describe, superficially, as if it resembled *Intermezzo*'s. This irony is in turn what makes the 'rupture thesis' applicable in this case: the film conveys something akin to the ideologically ambivalent 'openness' of *September Affair* within an ending that might initially appear to resemble the far more 'closed' (and more straight-forwardly ideologically affirmative) treatment offered by *Intermezzo*. It is in this sense that *There's Always Tomorrow* truly does possess what Christopher Sharrett calls a 'remarkably subversive conclusion' (2010: 1).

These are not, however, the strategies employed by the more famous *All That Heaven Allows*.

All That Heaven Allows

All That Heaven Allows tells the story of Cary (Jane Wyman), a middle-aged widow of good social standing in the town of Stoningham, and her relationship with Ron (Rock Hudson), a (younger) gardener. Their romance encounters strong opposition, both from Cary's grown son and daughter, Ned (William Reynolds) and Kay (Gloria Talbott), and from their town's gossiping social set, headed by Cary's 'friend', Mona (Jacqueline de Wit). The primary cause of the scandal is class anxiety – the ideological narrowness of Stoningham encouraging many to infer that Ron is merely interested in Cary for her wealth, and presume that such a man would simply not 'fit' within the echelons of society in which Cary moves. Eventually succumbing to pressure from those around her (particularly her children), Cary breaks off her relationship with Ron. This, however, fails to bring her closer to the children, and she feels the weight of her loss both emotionally and physiologically (via chronic headaches). Following a period of separation, Cary discovers from a mutual friend (Alida – Virginia Grey) that Ron is still single, and is spurred on by advice from her friend and doctor, Dan (Hayden Rorke), to visit him. She sets off in her car to do so; yet, when she arrives at his converted mill-house, she thinks better of the idea, turns, and drives away. Ron sees this and tries to hail her from a nearby snowy ridge, but slips in his excitement and tumbles down the cliff face, severely injuring himself. Cary receives news of his accident from Alida and rushes to see him at the mill, where he is convalescing. Dan, the doctor, tells her that Ron will heal, but that it will take time; he asks whether Cary intends to stay with him. 'Yes,' she replies, smiling, 'no more running away.' Ron now awakens and sees Cary sitting by him. 'You've come home,' he manages; 'Yes,' responds Cary, 'I – I've come home.' She rests her head lovingly on his chest as the camera moves to a view of the window, through which we see a deer standing just outside; 'The End'.

All That Heaven Allows has often been used as a key example of its director's predilection for implausible happy endings. Barry Keith Grant, for instance, argues that,

> [rather] than the denial of closure, *All That Heaven Allows* provides it so completely, so 'picture perfect', that it seems artificial and teeters on the edge of ringing hollow – a final ironic comment on the values of a society that, after all, is the audience for whom the film was made. (2007: 79)

Similarly, Roger D. McNiven claims that the film '[culminates] in the final image of Carrie [sic] and Ron pitted against an utterly "false" view of the natural world through the picture window, [which] amounts to a devastating indictment of the entire society's world-view as essentially artificial' (1985: 55). We will encounter other such arguments shortly, and it is easy to understand why so many critics would wish to treat this ending as ironic. Iconographically, it is a relatively 'closed' ending depicting a final couple in their new home; thus, according to the views about both closure and happy endings I have outlined (not to mention those regarding Sirk), it *must* be ironic in order for it to be read positively within the terms of the 'rupture thesis'. It seems to me, however, that this conclusion does not employ irony in anything like the same manner as *There's Always Tomorrow* and, furthermore, that it would make little sense for it to do so – from either a narrative and or an ideological perspective.

Regarding narrative: it seems rather strange that the ending of *All That Heaven Allows* has come to be viewed as something of an exemplar of the implausible happy ending. It is a measure of how ill-fitting this reputation might be that at least one critic should have attempted to use the conclusion to illustrate both sides of a single argument. In Chapter 1 of *The End*, Neupert argues that *All That Heaven Allows* exhibits classically motivated story resolution:

Story resolution demands the termination of the large action codes that propel and dominate narrative events and characters. In a melodrama like *All That Heaven Allows*, the story's resolution involves the final decision by Cary whether to follow her heart and stay with gardener Ron Kirby; this decision marks the culmination of many other related action codes involving her family and friends. (1995: 18)

In Chapter 2, however, Neupert references the film again, yet this time as an example of Bordwell's category of the 'unmotivated happy end', arguing that Sirk's 'ironic addition of an unwarranted happy ending foregrounds the rules and restrictions of both the classical melodrama and audience expectations' (ibid.: 72). What allows this unfortunate contradiction is, I would argue, the occasional disparity between Sirk's reputation and what actually takes place in his films. Cary's return to Ron does indeed mark the logical 'culmination' of the narrative – having been set up, for example, by the various traumas she endures following their separation: her tension headaches, further estrangement from her children (their missing an arranged weekend visit, Kay getting engaged, Ned's plans abroad, their gift of a television), and so on. If anything – given that in the two scenes preceding her drive to the mill Cary has (1) received friendly encouragement to rekindle the relationship, and (2) learned that Ron is not (as feared) in a relationship – the more narratively 'unmotivated' action is actually Cary's last-minute decision *not* to call on Ron. Thus, neither Cary's getting back into her car, nor Ron's fall constitutes an 'unwarranted addition' necessary for a happy ending, since the narrative path was already open for such an ending. It appears that Neupert recognises this on page 18, yet disregards it on page 72, and the only possible explanation for such confusion would seem to be the influence of received ideas concerning Sirk, closure, implausible happy endings, and happy endings in general.

That Ron's fall quite plainly serves to make the ending nowhere near as 'happy' as it could be is important, and worth pausing on. Firstly, this obviously casts significant doubt upon one claim sometimes confusingly made about this conclusion: that it is somehow *too* happy, and thus necessitates being ironised for that reason. The fact that this ending could have been characterised by some as 'so "picture perfect" [. . .] that it seems artificial' (Grant 2007: 79) tells us something about the trouble critics often have discussing happy endings in anything other than binary terms: either as unproblematically celebratory or seditiously subversive. George Toles has perceptively noted that there is often assumed to be 'something deeply suspect about closing a serious film with images of comfort and repose. [. . .] Tranquillity by fiat automatically sets us on edge and encourages ironic dismissal' (2001: 290). This does indeed seem to be the case, and is doubtless thanks to the kinds of widespread assumptions about both closure and 'happy ending' explored in this book. What, though, when we are faced with an ending that certainly provides an image of at least partial success, hope, or 'repose', yet hardly total 'comfort' nor complete 'tranquillity'?

It would appear that the most readily available critical impulse is to treat any 'negative' elements included in such an ending as if they were surreptitiously spoiling an imagined, 'perfect' cliché 'happy ending', rather than simply acknowledging them as constituent features of the quite openly ambiguous happy ending in front of us. An example of this tendency can be found in Laura Mulvey's otherwise excellent 'Notes on Sirk and Melodrama' (1978). Firstly describing the conclusion in a way that rightly refutes the notion that the happy ending is 'unwarranted' (Neupert 1995: 72), Mulvey neatly refers to Ron's fall as a *'deus ex machina* in reverse', and points to the obvious fact that the couple's 'gratification is postponed by Ron's accident' (ibid.: 56). However, she then goes on to claim that, due to the accident, 'a hidden shadow is cast implicitly over their perfect, joyful acceptance of love' (ibid.: 56). Given the aforementioned postponed gratification, the fact that the figure of the convalescing Ron dominates the space of the film's final scene, and that he is barely able to smile upon Cary's return, I would question the appropriateness of describing the 'shadow' cast here as either 'hidden' or 'implicit'. In fact, we might say that the main function of the accident – other than to provide an opportunity for a final act of commitment from Cary – is to reinforce symbolically the hardships that this couple will necessarily face in the future. 'It's going to take time for him to recover,' Dan has told Cary, 'He'll need rest and care'; likewise, the film ends with the promise of a romance that has been extremely hard-won, and will require continued efforts from its members in the future. Far from attempting to convince us that it is 'perfect, joyful' (ibid.: 56), then, this is an openly tentative romantic ending and, as such, not one which seems to necessitate clandestine ironic puncturing. The desire to read it as otherwise reflects (1) the lack of a ready critical vocabulary for describing the complications that routinely attend happy endings without recourse to notions of irony or subversion, (2) the contrastingly easy seductions of the 'rupture thesis', and (3), most pervasively, a critical context that has resolved to distrust the very concept of the 'happy ending' as a matter of principle.

One possible challenge to the interpretation I have so far set forth is the aforementioned deer, to which the camera directs us in the film's very last shot, and which comes closest to offering a final image characterised by Toles' 'tranquillity' (2001: 290). One could choose to take the presence of this animal as 'excruciatingly twee' (Richardson 2006: 1), or otherwise somehow 'too much', to invoke Sontag's definition of camp (1969: 284). However, moving from its mere presence to the nature of its presentation, it is worth admitting that this single deer (not, say, a graceful *herd* of deer) is not in fact presented in a manner that seems especially 'too much': Sirk has not chosen to shoot it particularly beautifully – say, exploiting the full possibilities of Technicolor by grandly posing the creature against a dazzling sunrise or stunning natural vista in the manner of Landseer's *Monarch of the Glen* (1851); instead the deer is presented in a matter-of-fact medium shot, sniffing around the largely colourless garden for a few seconds before sidling out of frame. Given this relative modesty of rhetoric, does it make sense to assume that this must be a parodic treatment of a 'clichéd image', as some have claimed (Willemen 1971: 66)? Furthermore, while to the trained (or, alternatively, modern) eye it may be clear that the deer is standing not in a real snowy garden but rather on a soundstage, is there evidence to support the proposition that this material fact is being stressed here to a greater extent than in other studio-set Hollywood films? That is: should we feel invited to view this image as in any meaningful sense pointedly artificial – let alone 'utterly "false"' (McNiven 1985: 55)? I would argue rather that the primary function of this final shot is instead to leave us with an image of the deeply un-Stoningham lifestyle that Cary and Ron will from now on be living.

This points to further problems with claims for the shot's ironic intentions. Given that the deer represents the world of Ron (we have seen him feeding a deer earlier in the film), and that this world has been placed in structural opposition to the repressive bourgeois society of Stoningham, to present it as 'false' would hardly constitute an effective 'final ironic comment on the values of a society that, after all, is the audience for whom the film was made' (Grant 2007: 79), since this is not the stratum of society whose values the film has been concerned to indict (nor, we can presume, the kind of society inhabited by the majority of the film's original audience). As such, that the deer is seen through the window from inside stresses not enclosure (as in *There's Always Tomorrow*), but rather a comparatively liberating image of the interconnectedness of this house with the outside world. This leads us to a consideration of the shortcomings of the 'implausibility' argument on ideological grounds.

I can suggest two hypothetical scenarios in which it would make ideological sense for this ending to be made, or read as, ironic. One is if the film had strongly encouraged us to regard the lifestyle embodied by Ron negatively – in a similar manner to *There's Always Tomorrow*'s perspective on Cliff's family life. Yet throughout the film it has been the parochial town of Stoningham that has been the object of the film's critique, while Ron's Thoreau-inspired life of nature has been consistently presented as a more desirable alternative mode of social organisation. Where Stoningham is characterised by class stratification, prejudice and repression, the life of Ron and his friends is shown to promote community, sharing, and comparatively free expression. This has been demonstrated in scenes such as the paralleled parties at the house of Ron's friends Mick (Charles Drake) and Alida, and at Stoningham's country club (Mulvey 1978) – the latter allowed to seem all the worse for taking place after we have

seen the alternative possible life represented by the former. The Stoningham
party is typified by clusters of guests prying through windows ('Just *look* at
that car . . .'), cruel gossiping ('It's always the quiet ones, isn't it?'), and misog-
ynist sexual threat (Howard [Donald Curtis] forcing himself upon Cary).
Mick/Alida's, meanwhile, is characterised by communal sharing of food and
drink (with guests contributing to the spread), a bustling mix of different social
groups (artists, fishermen, Cary), spontaneous physicality (Ron extracting a
wine cork with his teeth), joyful dancing and music (with guests improvising
percussion instruments from crockery), and comparatively liberated attitudes
towards sexuality (Ron's jokey song about 'the flirty eye'). The way the movie
pointedly contrasts these lifestyles bears out a comment made by Sirk, that
'the film is about the antithesis of Thoreau's qualified Rousseauism and established American society' (Halliday 1971: 113–14). Given all this, when in the
final scene Ron gratefully says 'Cary, you've come home', the concept of home
cannot here carry the same constricting connotations attached to it in *There's
Always Tomorrow* precisely because this home does not belong to Stoningham
and its repressive values, but constitutes a *new* home, suggestive of a more
hopeful future.

On this point, some critics have suggested that Cary's new life with Ron is in
fact 'scarcely a radical departure from the one Cary has known' (Schatz 1981:
251) – either because Ron deals with Cary in an authoritarian and paternalistic
fashion (he requires she change her life rather than offering to compromise his;
see Mercer/Shingler 2004: 67); because their new home in some ways reflects
her old one (Ron has finished redecorating the mill in a manner that might be
called more 'bourgeois': comfortably furnished, fireplace, etc.; Massie 1980:
272; Camper 1971: 1); or because Ron's dependent state means Cary is once
again placed in the maternal role of care-giver rather than lover (Mulvey 1978:
56; Schatz 1981: 252; Grant 2007: 79). We might note that the second of
these arguments effectively disqualifies the first: an important moment in the
final sequence comes when Cary notices the further alterations made to the
mill ('The *beauty* that Ron's put into it! And the love.'), which demonstrate
that, despite Ron's earlier expressed fears about 'how easy it would be to let
[himself] be changed', he *has* indeed made changes for her. Meanwhile, the
suggestion that these alterations convey continuity with Stoningham would
be more convincing if the new house contained any remnants of Cary's former
lifestyle that had been explicitly criticised (a television set, for example), or if
the film didn't end on something which would *never* be found in Stoningham:
the deer. Finally, while the role of 'nurse' that Cary takes on may have some
symbolic connections with motherhood, it is equally important that it is not
actual motherhood: a real, specific social role from which Cary has by this
point had to openly distance herself. Also vital is that this new care-giver
role will only be temporary: as the doctor says, Ron *will* recover, and thus

will once again become Cary's lover (see Babbington/Evans 1990) – a fact that helps offer the kind of promise for the future so common to happy endings.

It is true that Ron's milieu is not presented as entirely immune from questionable ideological strictures: for instance, Mick at one point says of Cary – 'boorishly' indeed (Babbington/Evans 1990: 54) – that 'she doesn't want to make up her own mind: no girl does; she wants you to make it up *for* her'; equally, his wife Alida is shown undertaking the traditional domestic role of cook prior to the party thrown by the couple. These, however, are drops in the ocean when compared with the sexual politics and values of Stoningham, which encompass sexual repression (the denial of Cary's right to sexual fulfilment), comforting but limiting sexual calcification (Harvey's [Conrad Nagel] offer of marital 'companionship'), and explicit sexual threat (Howard's advances). A telling contrast between the spheres comes at a moment when Cary is momentarily disturbed by noticing Ron and Mick laughing jocularly and gesturing towards her; rather than the secretive and vaguely sinister implications of this moment being allowed to linger, Cary soon asks Ron what the men were laughing about, and Ron unembarrassedly answers her plainly: 'I told him you had the prettiest legs I'd ever seen!' – clearing the air with an honesty and an affirmation of Cary's sexuality that seem quite alien to Stoningham. By the end of the film Cary has turned her back on her old world and, as Mary Beth Haralovich rightly says, 'Cary's friends are represented as so bound within social conventions that their influence on her life *deserves* to be repudiated' (1990: 60). Despite some minor similarities, the two social spheres have indeed been generally presented, as Sirk says, as one another's 'antithesis', and our heroine's rejection of one for the other contributes crucially to the 'moral satisfaction' that can assist in any conclusion becoming a happy ending (Chatman 1980: 85). Given this, it would make little sense for Sirk finally to ironise the putative triumph of a mode of living and set of values which he has in general rhetorically affirmed throughout the preceding film.

Having said this, the other plausible ideological reason for imbuing the ending with irony would be if this triumph were *too* total or came too easily: that is to say, if it appeared to be at all in the mould of *Pretty Woman*, in which class division is finally elided and overcome with little-to-no difficulty – ideological contradictions being glossed over rather than acknowledged as significant forces. Yet this is clearly not true of *All That Heaven Allows* either. Cary's decision has required her to sacrifice entirely the social sphere she has called home, and possibly even close relationships with her children: while Kay sympathises with her mother when she realises the pain caused her by the separation, crying with her in the television scene, Ned has not yet waivered from his view that, if Cary moves in with Ron, 'Don't expect *me* to visit. How could I bring my friends? I'd be *ashamed*'. An exaggeratedly neat resolution to the narrative might have involved the children and the society of Stoningham repenting and welcoming Ron with open arms: this would truly exploit possibilities of closure in a manner recalling Lévi-Strauss' mythic progression 'from the awareness of oppositions toward their resolution', and might indeed warrant ironic treatment. Yet the ending we have makes little effort finally to resolve all the ideological contradictions the film has exposed: Cary has had to *move out* of Stoningham in order to offer herself a chance of happiness. Thus, again, we can admit with confidence that the ending is far from uncomplicated: Cary's slight hesitation on 'Yes, I – I've come home . . .' might encourage us to reflect on the enormity of her decision to commit to using that word of this new space. Yet we badly need a critical language that is able to accommodate the presence of such complexity in a happy ending without the automatic recourse to the concepts of subversion or irony. Neither subversion nor irony is ideologically necessary here, because the ending dramatises the difficult rejection of, rather than a resigned submission to, ideological values which the film has presented as pernicious.

While *There's Always Tomorrow* demonstrates that the 'rupture thesis' can certainly have its uses, then, *All That Heaven Allows* exposes its limitations. The process I have followed in analysing these films is similar to that proposed by Booth's work on the rhetoric of irony, in which he argues that identifying irony involves 'judging parts according to function', that is: placing hypotheses about a work's individual strategies in the context of its broader strategies in order to demonstrate that 'a given ironic effect is appropriate or necessary at a given spot' (1974: 197). The 'rupture thesis' discourages such a process, firstly, by constructing an image of closure, and thus the 'happy ending', wherein both are cast as *innately* conservative. This in turn requires it to assume that a happy ending must '"contradict" or subvert [its] manifest moral intent or ideological bias' (Elsaesser 1972: 6) in order to avoid accusations of conservatism. Our analysis of *All That Heaven Allows*, meanwhile, has allowed us to see that its ending's 'moral intent' is already so far removed from that of *There's Always Tomorrow* that irony is made inappropriate to the task to which a 'rupture thesis' critic would put it. The problem with the thesis is the wholesale ideological power it grants to abstracted categories of narrative over the ideological meanings of specific narratives – an approach whose shortcomings are easily diagnosed. Robin Wood, while acknowledging both Hollywood's tendency towards closure and the patriarchal bias of many of its films, has insisted that 'where the line of argument becomes very dubious is in its tendency to collapse the two premises together, so that [. . .] closure [is] seen as indissolubly linked with the reaffirmation of patriarchy' (1988/89: 16). To illustrate his point, he goes on to imagine a narrative that it would be entirely impossible to describe as affirming patriarchy, but which is nonetheless classically 'closed':

At the beginning of the film a housewife arrives home from the daily shopping; during the ensuing 90 minutes of screen time she comes to learn that she is oppressed, subordinated, trapped in her domestic role; at the end of the film she packs her suitcase and leaves. There you have a very precise example of symmetry (arriving home/leaving home, opening the door/closing the door, carrying shopping bags/carrying suitcases) and a permissible type of closure (the end of a marriage which also marks 'a new beginning'). One need not be surprised that such a scenario has not formed the basis for a great many Hollywood films [. . .] but its possibility surely challenges any notion of a necessary and indissoluble link between symmetry/closure and the restoration of patriarchy. (ibid.: 16)

All That Heaven Allows may not be so radical as this, but it nevertheless has its similarities: Cary comes to recognise Stoningham's harmful and patriarchal ideology, which believes, as Kay unwittingly puts it, in 'walling up the widow alive in the funeral chamber of her dead husband along with all his other possessions'; by the end of the film she has rejected her role as a beholden, widowed 'possession' and bullied mother, and escaped into what promises to be a rather different (even if not *perfect*) kind of society, in which she can play a different kind of role – and whose homes contain 'walls' with windows that permit continuity with the outside world. That this 'closed' ending can convey such different ideological meanings to, say, *Intermezzo*'s is for the simple reason that the convention of closure, in-and-of-itself, guarantees the affirmation of no single ideological premise.

To assume an inherent link between closure and ideological conservatism or patriarchy, then, inevitably leads to distortions because it leaves us unable to distinguish between the wildly divergent *means* by which closure can be achieved: in the case of *All That Heaven Allows* and *There's Always Tomorrow*, between a final couple that *is* 'reaffirmed' by its film and one which is not. As Douglas Kellner and Michael Ryan point out, if one adheres to 'a preordained category of ideological closure that operates the same way everywhere without differentiation' one 'overlooks the distinctive and multiple rhetorical and representational strategies and effects of films' (1990: 1–2). This question of rhetoric does seem key, since I am broadly in agreement with Noël Carroll's view that 'ideological beliefs are propagated by films through their specific rhetorical organization' – rhetoric being 'a matter of influencing thought – a matter of persuasion' (1996: 280). It is undeniable that endings possess particular power for rhetorical persuasion, and thus assume ideological importance, simply by virtue of their position as the final stage in the process of sense-making so fundamental to narrative. That is simply to say, as Peter Brooks writes of the novel, that endings, by 'terminating the dynamic process of reading,

[. . .] bestow meaning and significance on the beginning and the middle' (1984: 19). In discussing closure it is necessary, however, to attend to the particular meanings that an ending bestows, rather than assuming there is something ideologically pernicious in the mere act *of* an ending bestowing meaning.

While the innate critical distrust of closure might sometimes seem to be behind us, the fact that the category of the implausible happy ending is still regularly invoked to rescue conclusions from accusations of ideological conservatism would suggest that the tenets of such theorising have become deeply rooted in film studies' approaches to Hollywood narrative (see Rushton 2011). For instance, later in the same book that provided us above with a welcome argument in favour of discussing rhetoric rather than making de facto ideological assumptions about closure, Kellner and Ryan still nonetheless refer to 'traditional "patriarchal" forms such as meaningful resolution, narrative closure' (1990: 145). Though it clearly has its uses, the model of the ideologically necessary implausible happy ending will need to be rethought if we are to find a productive way of discussing our subject. Doing so will require that we abandon the view that the 'happy ending' fundamentally requires 'subversion', and attend instead to the ideological meanings rhetorically offered by specific instances of the convention.

*

All That Heaven Allows thus demonstrates that a final couple happy ending need not be in some way *discredited* in order to avoid affirming the worst impulses of patriarchal ideology. Yet – while the idea of an unironic final couple conveying anything more ideologically worthwhile than telltale contradictions is already beyond the scope of much scholarly engagement with the convention – it could still seem unsurprising to find less conservative impulses at play in a film such as *All That Heaven Allows*, given what Klinger calls 'the progressive status of the family melodrama' in general (1984a: 32). Before moving into this chapter's final section – in which I will argue that the meaning of happy endings need not *necessarily* be more rigid even within that supposedly most conservative of genres, the romantic comedy – it is worth taking a moment to consider the relative statuses of these genres in relation to the final couple's reputation.

HAPPY ENDINGS, IDEOLOGY AND ROMANTIC COMEDY

There isn't *one* of you who can look me straight in the eye and tell me you're happily married!

– Clemson (Cary Grant), *Dream Wife*

It has often been noted that a Hollywood narrative about courtship will usually be a comedy, while one about marriage will tend to be a melodrama. Speaking of these two approaches to romance narratives, Britton suggests,

> Normative romanticism can be sustained only by the suppression of marriage and family altogether – or rather, by their projection into a certain but undramatised future beyond the close of the narrative. [Following marriage], romanticism appears as transgression, as a rebellion against bourgeois norms which is tragically doomed by the necessity of upholding them. (2003: 179)

To an extent, this broad pattern – romantic comedy's 'normative' romanticism and its 'transgression' in melodrama – might in fact be explained by the nature of plot itself, which is only made possible, as thinkers as far back as Aristotle have noted, by conflict (or *agon*). If a narrative addresses the question of what follows marriage, the stability of that marriage will almost necessarily have to be threatened in order to sustain the conflict essential for narrative – a process often (though not *necessarily*) leading to melodrama. Indeed, in Hollywood cinema sometimes what begins as a comedy can threaten to transform into a melodrama simply because, seemingly, a marriage takes place. The aptly-titled *No Time for Comedy* (1940) is particularly striking in this respect: following its couple's wedding (at about the 40-minute mark) the film immediately begins to display melodramatic tendencies, with Gaylord (James Stewart) being suddenly revealed to have developed a drinking problem, and a potential affair looming on the horizon (see also, for instance, *Made for Each Other* [1939] or *Penny Serenade* [1941]). Equally, in order for a *comedy* to tell a story focused on an existing marriage, the relationship will tend either to have to fall apart temporarily, only to be eventually reformed (as in many remarriage comedies), or it will be required to form the backdrop to a more prominent narrative strand (in *The Thin Man* [1934] and its sequels, for instance, a detective plot).[14]

Thus faced with the basic necessity of generating narrative conflict, post-marital melodramas repeatedly draw upon those features of marriage which regularly encourage social conflict in the institution itself – which might be, for instance, challenges to monogamy (e.g. *There's Always Tomorrow*, *Intermezzo*, *September Affair*, etc.), the strains of motherhood (e.g. 'maternal melodramas' [Williams 1984] such as *Stella Dallas* [1937], *Mildred Pierce* [1945], *Imitation of Life* [1959], etc.), power imbalances within the couple (e.g. 'persecuted wife' melodramas [Britton 2009: 14] such as *Suspicion*, *Gaslight* [1944], *Caught*, etc.), and so on. We might therefore say that a post-marital melodrama has the potential for an ideological critique of the value of monogamous marriage built in at its ground floor, as it were. Its ability to tell 'the story of what *follows* the happy ending' (Rowe 1995a: 51; original emphasis) seems to allow for the values embodied by marriage and family life to be demystified, and often, in the process, 'presents a recognizable picture of woman's ambivalent position under patriarchy' (Williams 1984: 23).

By extension and contrast, the final couple – so frequent a feature of romantic comedy – has often been criticised not only because it seems to reflect the 'sense of few endings' offered to women, but also because to *end* in this way necessarily consigns marriage to a narrative afterlife. We have previously addressed this matter in relation to closure and unrealism, but it is now time to confront the possibility that another outcome of leaving a couple's future life unrepresented is that it might allow marriage's validity as an ideological value to go unchallenged (see Haskell 1987: 2). As Rick Altman argues, the final couple could seem simply to ensure the process by which marriage comes to '[represent] a timeless, formless state in American mythology, precisely so that it will not be open to question' (1981: 198). Given this, it is unsurprising that critics frequently suggest or imply that romantic comedy, because usually ending with a final couple, has 'a firmly ingrained conservatism, for it pushes toward and seeks to relegitimise a *sanctioned* heterosexual union – marriage' (Krutnik 1998: 62; original emphasis).

Before addressing this, let us first note that the Hollywood romantic comedy in general is by no means incapable of representing similar anxieties about marriage to those found in so many marital melodramas. It is striking, for instance, how frequently characters in the genre express overt hostility towards the institution. Marriage can be described variously as requiring 'giving up a whole way of thinking, behaving – a whole existence' (*Bell, Book and Candle* [1958]), as 'a prison' (*Forces of Nature* [1999]), a 'patriarchal' form of 'ritualised property transfer' (*The Bachelor* [1999]), or 'a form of institutionalised rape' (*Forget Paris*). It can be accused of being based upon 'a bourgeois desire to fulfill an ideal that society embeds in us from an early age to promote a consumer-capitalist agenda' (*Definitely Maybe*), and even the assumed ideological link between marriage and the 'happy ending' can be explicitly called into question: '*Then* what happens?' medical student Paige (Julia Stiles) asks of a burgeoning relationship in *The Prince and Me*, 'We get married and live happily ever after? Then all my hard work goes down the drain because I'm too busy shopping for groceries and picking my kids up at soccer . . .'

This, however, is clearly where the final couple comes in again. Such dissenting voices may be present, but they tend not to have the rhetorical 'last word' that an ending can bestow. This might seem to bear out the received wisdom that genre movies in general tend, as Altman puts it, to '[offer] an increasingly intense counter-cultural genre pleasure experience, only eventually to reverse that pattern and revert to cultural dominance' (1999: 155). It is certainly true that final couple happy endings have often worked in precisely such ways – either by serving as the proverbial 'emergency exit' (Wood

2003: 63) or otherwise (more on this shortly). For instance, we have already acknowledged that, although films of any genre made between the early 1930s and the mid-1960s could present certain Code-riling sexual politics during the course of their narratives, those subjects then *had* to be submitted to particular restraints by the conclusion, however complex a film's navigation of or attitudes towards those constraints may be.[15]

Furthermore, the appeasingly conservative final couple happy ending is, of course, also certainly not a classical-era-specific phenomenon. Krutnik has similarly referred to 'the emergency exit of romantic comedy convention' (1998: 20) in relation to contemporary final couples in the genre, and we would not need to look hard to find myriad modern instances of the convention that could be described in precisely such terms. It is also true that the dissolution of the Production Code has by no means managed to rid the Hollywood final couple of certain aspects of that document's troubling ideological legacy. For instance, although they may certainly be found in films made during the last few decades, final couples featuring lovers of different races, or the same sex, are still noticeably and unforgivably rare. Even if unsurprising given the United States' ignoble history of marriage inequality for interracial (Pascoe 2009) and homosexual (Retter/Williams 2003) couples, this is a highly ideologically significant fact, and a state of affairs demanding of the most astringent critique (see Kirkland 2007; Moddelmog 2009; Bowdre 2009).

Yet the clear necessity of such a critique should still not lead us to presume to know in advance what romantic comedy happy endings will or can mean ideologically in every instance, and it will not be my primary focus for the remainder of this chapter. Instead, in keeping with this book's project of testing the potential flexibility of this convention against its reputation, in what follows I will attempt to answer not what the romantic comedy final couple necessarily usually does (a job for a subsequent study), but rather what it seems to be *capable* of doing.

Tamar Jeffers McDonald writes that 'the basic ideology the romantic comedy genre supports is the primary importance of the couple' (2007: 13). It is surely true that in all genres the final couple will be by nature well-suited to affirming a belief in something we might abstractly call 'the couple'. Historically, it has also been true that a romantic comedy's central couple has usually been race-matched, heterosexual and monogamous. Although we *could* choose to view as monolithically conservative every affirmation of a white, monogamous heterosexual couple, however, this will logically leave us entirely unable to differentiate between what may be the very great differences between any such couples – between, say, Emma/Mr Knightly and Snow White/'The Prince'; or between Beatrice/Benedict and Superman/Lois Lane; or between Harry/Sally and Jane Eyre/Rochester. I suggest that this would not behove us as critics of culture. I ended Chapter 2 by arguing that the very prevalence of the final couple means it will likely be required to serve different closural needs for different kinds of film; the same is true of the relationship between the final couple and ideology. This is simply because, as Britton writes, unlike clichés, 'conventions [. . .] conduce to the most complex particularized modifications and inflections within the general ideological field which they define' (1993: 214). In the case of the romantic comedy final couple, that 'ideological field' – i.e. the 'importance of the couple' – will certainly define limits, but there is also undoubtedly room for manoeuver within those limits; it is to that potential for manoeuver that I now turn.

There are many obvious questions we might productively ask of individual heterosexual romantic comedy final couples if wishing to move beyond a view which assumed that all are rigidly bound to convey the same ideological meanings in every instance. For example: has the woman been represented as desperate to become a wife, as in *Every Girl Should be Married* (1948), or is she finally reluctant to wed and has to be talked into it by a previously-caddish man, as happens in *Indiscreet* (1958)? Is the formation of the final couple predicated on the woman having to give up a career opportunity, as in *How to Lose a Guy in 10 Days* (2003), or is her desire for a professional life in fact one of the foundations upon which the relationship is built, as in a film such as *His Girl Friday* (1940)? Does the significance of the ultimate union lie primarily in allowing the couple to finally have sex, as in *Pillow Talk* – or is it made comparatively chaste due to the preceding virtual absence of sex as a subject, as in *Sleepless in Seattle*? Is the final couple aligned with a sense of freedom via the lovers being united on an ocean liner bound for foreign lands, as happens in *Holiday* (1938), or is it made to seem somewhat threatening, as in *She Done Him Wrong* (1933), which ends with Cary Grant telling Mae West 'you're my prisoner and I'm going to be your jailer for a long time . . .'? If a contrast has been established between one 'wild' woman and another who is more prim and conservative, does the male protagonist choose the former, as in *What's Up Doc?* (1972) or the latter, as in *Forces of Nature*? Equally, if the genders are reversed, does the woman pick the 'bad boy', as in *The Ugly Truth*, or reject him for the safer and more buttoned-down man, as in *Bridget Jones's Diary*?

This is merely to raise a handful of questions whose answers will have a significant bearing on the specific ideological implications of the endings of a handful of disparate films. If my casual juxtaposition above of movies taken from different periods strikes the reader as odd, then that is also to some extent now the point: *of course* we are likely to see significant shifts in the ideological specifics of final couple happy endings over time. This in itself, though, is far from routinely acknowledged. As we have seen, more frequent are accounts that will state (Hayward 2006: 83), or imply (Kuhn 1994: 16) something of the order that the 'ideological point' of the final couple in Hollywood cinema as a whole cannot help *but* amount to a conservative affirmation of the institution of

marriage (Burch 1990: 196), and possibly patriarchy (Lauretis 1984: 139–40)
– unless, of course, the convention is made to seem plausible or ineffectual by
'subversion'. Notable exceptions to this rule can be found, however, within
strands of the criticism on romantic comedy, and I will be drawing on such work
in what follows. Glitre, for instance, provides a helpful start when she notes:

> It is not enough to claim that The End is the meaning – that, simply
> by ending with the union of the heterosexual couple, romantic comedy
> is about the traditional institutions of patriarchal society and must be
> inherently conservative. The context of The End must be taken into
> account. (2006: 17)

There are two important ways in which we might account for the 'context'
of a final couple. Firstly, there is the context provided by the preceding film.
As suggested by some of my questions about endings above (and my earlier
analysis of Sirk), what has taken place between the couple *prior* to their ultimate union will always have a determining effect on the ideological meanings
of that union. Secondly, there is the broader context of societal norms and
social relations at particular historical moments. Referring again to the critical
tendency to use the 'apparent universality of the happy ending' as evidence of
the genre's innate conservatism, Celestino Deleyto argues that this approach
can prevent us from appreciating what is in fact romantic comedy's 'main discursive space': 'the artistic articulation of current discourses on love, sex and
marriage, discourses that [are] multiple and contradictory' (2009: 29). To conceptualise the ideological significance of the genre in this way, he goes on, 'does
not invalidate the importance of the happy ending'; what it does, however, is
liberate it from 'ideological rigidity' by acknowledging that this convention can
hardly be assumed to always express one, monolithic ideological meaning, but
is rather – like, indeed all generic conventions – bound to enter into 'complex
and fluid relationships with the social context' (Deleyto, 2009: 29).

Following Glitre's and Deleyto's leads, I will thus be concluding this
chapter by examining four variations on the final couple happy ending that
express notably distinct relationships to their contexts – both their preceding
narratives, and contemporaneous social discourses concerning love, sex and
marriage. As with the Sirk films above, questions of what values an ending
affirms will clearly assume significance in my accounts of these films. In
addition, since my previous analyses have often centred on the final couple's
provisions for the future, I shall in part now be looking to those promised
futures from an ideological perspective. Finally, it is also necessary to begin
a discussion about ways in which changing historical contexts might permit
happy endings to assume different ideological implications. This is still not to
say, however, that even two conclusions of broadly the same historical moment

need convey anything like the same ideological meanings, as the contrasting qualities of my first two, very famous, final couples should demonstrate.

The Philadelphia Story and Bringing Up Baby

The Philadelphia Story opens with the divorce of wealthy socialite Tracy Lord (Katharine Hepburn) from C. K. Dexter Haven (Cary Grant). Set over the course of a weekend two years later, the rest of the film tells of how Tracy comes to call off her wedding to George Kittredge (John Howard) and remarry Dexter. In the film's final moments, Tracy first receives a marriage proposal from Mike Connor (James Stewart), with whom she has had a brief and tanta-lising flirtation, though she turns him down. Nervously addressing the gath-ered wedding congregation, Tracy looks to Dexter for advice; he obliges by feeding her lines that amount to a second marriage proposal, and she accepts. Dexter and Tracy are re-wed; 'The End'.

Bringing Up Baby begins with David Huxley (Cary Grant), a paleontologist, atop a brontosaurus skeleton in his museum. It is the eve of his marriage to his secretary, Alice Swallow (Virginia Walker) – a marriage Alice makes clear will be 'a dedication to [David's] work', entailing 'no domestic entanglements of any kind'. Playing golf with a prospective museum donor later that day, David encounters the vivacious Susan Vance (Katharine Hepburn) who, during the ensuing day and night, turns David's life upside down via a madcap 'series of misadventures' that include the loss of a vital brontosaurus bone, the pursuit of two escaped leopards, grand theft auto, and the pair's arrest. Back at the museum in the final scene, a disappointed Alice ends the couple's engagement. Susan then arrives to return the missing bone, prompting David to retreat to the top of his brontosaurus skeleton. After Susan has pursued him by climbing a ladder, however, David soon relents, saying, 'I've just discovered that was the best day of my whole life!' and the two excitedly declare their love for one another. Susan's ladder begins to sway, causing her to climb onto the brontosaurus between them, which sends the skeleton crashing to the ground, David hauling her to safety at the last minute. David resigns himself to the destruction of four years' work ('Oh dear; oh well . . .') and to Susan's enthusiastic embrace; 'The End'.

As well as both starring Cary Grant and Katharine Hepburn and being made only two years apart, both these movies also famously belong to Stanley Cavell's category of the comedy of remarriage. This series of films, Cavell argues, emerged at a time when 'a phase of [first-wave] feminism, and requirements of a genre [. . .] met together on the issue of the creation of a woman' (1981: 19–20). Yet, as he goes on, in these movies this 'creation of a woman' is sometimes only made possible by a man: 'in the genre of remarriage the man's lecturing indi-cates that an essential goal of the narrative is the education of the woman' (ibid.: 84). Brian Henderson has expressed dismay at Cavell's characterisation of this process, which he sees as amounting to an *apologia* for the notion that 'woman is an object to be moulded by men' – a paradigm 'inconsistent [. . .] with any version of feminism that one can think of' (1982: 26). While not relevant to all remarriage comedies, it is undeniably true that in *The Philadelphia Story* 'the hero presides over the heroine's [. . .] education' (Britton 2009: 503).

Although Dexter may at one point accuse Tracy of being 'a scold', it is primarily he and Tracy's father, Seth Lord (John Halliday), who 'typically scold, lecture, admonish, or preach' (Shumway 1991: 13) in the film. By the time of the ending both have been repeatedly concerned simultaneously to praise Tracy for having the potential to be 'the finest woman who ever lived', and to hector her for being 'hard', with no 'regard for human frailty'. Elsewhere, Tracy's sister and mother have also expressed similar concerns regarding Tracy's 'very definite opinions', reinforcing the sense of both the movie's world in general and the film's rhetoric endorsing these critiques of her. Furthermore, far from Tracy's 'opinions' being ideologically neutral, both her 'so-called strength' (as Dexter calls it) and the means by which it is criticised have been drawn sharply along gender lines. Although it is not mentioned by name, Tracy's views have appeared unmistakably aligned with feminism, since her principles include denouncing the commodification of the female body ('putting up a hundred thousand dollars to display shapely legs'), and arguing for the right of women to divorce philandering men ('the only stand a woman could take and keep her self-respect'). In turn, Dexter may have told Tracy that she needs to become 'a first-rate human being', but it is the following phrase, 'first-rate *woman*', which caused him to pause for emphasis during the dressing room dressing-down scene. The issue throughout has thus seemed to be not simply that Tracy is too strong a human being, but that she is too strong a *woman* – indeed, a particular kind of 'unruly woman' (see: Rowe 1995b), who is initially unwilling to play for these men the roles they desire of her. This has been reflected in Dexter and her father continually using highly gender-specific language and concepts in support of their drubbings, accusing her of being a 'virgin goddess', a 'married maiden', a 'special-class of the American female', a 'perennial spinster', and of 'talking like a jealous woman'.

It is a condition of the happy ending being achieved that, although Tracy is permitted to reject George and his condescending 'ideals of womanhood', she must nonetheless finally acknowledge Dexter and Seth Lord's critiques, apologise to them both for her failings, and revise her opinions to the point at which she will admit, 'I don't know anything anymore'. By contrast, Dexter's degree of knowledge and calm control throughout the film (which stands in contrast to Tracy and Mike's drunkenness and games)[16] has prompted Cavell to acknowledge that there is 'something of paternal authority' about him (ibid.: 137). Another way of describing that authority would be to say that it is, fundamentally, patriarchal; furthermore, this authority is very much in evidence in the film's final moments. Despite Tracy declaring her independence in the final scene by resolving that she 'won't be got out of anything anymore', when making her announcement to the congregation she nonetheless looks to Dexter for instruction ('Dexter, Dexter – what next?'). In a microcosm of the troubling process of the 'creation of a woman' by a man, Tracy then goes on to repeat Dexter's words more or less precisely and, in so doing, voices *his* wishes for remarriage, with which she subsequently agrees. Thus, while it might appear to her gathered audience that she has come to this decision herself, in reality the decision belongs to Dexter, the man in the wings, who is ensuring that she 'says exactly what [he] tells her to' (Shumway 1991: 15). Although Dexter responds to Tracy's final 'promise to be "yare"' (or, as she earlier defined this word, 'easy to handle') with 'be whatever you like', the truth is that she has had to become what *he* likes, and that we have seen him undergo no such changes on her behalf. It is in this sense that the film is ultimately, despite its many pleasures, vulnerable to the accusation that it is 'a reactionary comedy of remarriage' (Britton 2009: 504).

Citing remarriage comedy's historical context, Shumway has asserted that 'the major cultural work of these films is [. . .] the affirmation of marriage in the face of the threat of a growing divorce rate and liberalized divorce laws' (ibid: 7), going on to argue that these movies in general 'suggest that spunky, strong women are attractive, but that their submission is required for the romance to be consummated' (ibid.: 15). Similarly, Neupert claims that screwball comedy endings typically constitute 'the restriction of woman, and the end of feminine "spunk" and independence, guaranteeing the desiring male's success' (1995: 73). While it might be feasible to make a hypothetical claim for *The Philadelphia Story* responding to its sociohistorical moment in something like this way, *Bringing up Baby* cannot possibly be described in such terms.

For one thing, far from feeling orchestrated by a calm, controlling, 'desiring male' like Dexter, by the time we reach its ending the entirety of *Bringing Up Baby*'s narrative has been driven at least as much by Susan's desire for David as by his for her. She has taken him on a hunt for Mr Peabody (George Irving), she has lied to get him to her apartment, she has brought him to and kept him in Connecticut, and so on – all because, she explains in the final scene, 'I was trying to keep you near me and I just did anything that came into my head!' As for 'spunk': Susan's irrepressibly haphazard behaviour not only survives until the end of the film, but actually reaches a peak in its final moments with the accidental destruction of the brontosaurus; this is an 'unruly' woman who remains unrestrained to the very last (see Rowe 1995b: 147–56).

It is important to ask what this collapse of the brontosaurus skeleton means, and why it is an appropriate climax for a film in which there has been a clear 'need to "educate" [David] before the couple can be formed' (Britton 2003: 180). It may be going too far to assert that the brontosaurus is either an 'image of bourgeois patriarchy' (Britton 2009: 7) or a symbolic representation of capitalism (Glitre 2006: 62), as some have suggested. However, the film certainly has associated the skeleton with values towards which *Bringing up Baby* has been highly irreverent. Firstly, it is representative of the dull job from which David's escapades with Susan provide (a retrospectively welcome) respite; secondly, that job has involved David having to prostrate himself in front of donors in order to obtain funding to finish the dinosaur; finally, the skeleton has been related to a passionless potential marriage with Alice: in the film's first scene Alice rejects 'children and all that sort of thing', instead turning to face the brontosaurus and announcing, '*this* will be our child!' Cavell has said that 'the collapsing of the skeleton poses the obvious discomfort in this conclusion, or shadow on its happiness' (ibid.: 120–1). Yet in fact it seems fundamental to the 'happiness' of this happy ending precisely that the film rhetorically affirms the notion that the energies that fuelled the couple's play should ultimately topple their thematic opposite, and that we are thus encouraged to take both the collapse and its acceptance as joyful.

Another pattern that receives its culmination in this final scene is one whereby David has remained always 'strangely drawn' to Susan despite continually claiming he wants to leave her ('You're following *me*!' / 'Now, don't be absurd: who's always behind whom?'). Although it might seem David has been forever attempting to extricate himself from Susan, twice Susan has attempted to leave only for David to persuade her to stay: first when her dress rips at the club, and again in the forest after she trips over a branch. In this way, the film has exemplified the remarriage structure identified by Cavell whereby 'we are permanently in doubt [as to] who is the active partner, which of them is in quest, who is following whom. A working title for this structure might be "the comedy of equality"' (ibid.: 122). Whereas Dexter and Tracy's relationship in *The Philadelphia Story* entirely lacks both this structure and its resultant sense of 'equality', in *Bringing up Baby* it has been the organising principle, and it reaches its climax in the film's final moments: as Cavell reminds us, David 'instinctively ran up the scaffold – perhaps *in order* to be followed up', meaning that he 'was as much the cause of the collapse [. . .] as she was' (ibid.: 121).

Looking to the future: we are absolutely free to presume David and Susan will marry after the end of the film; quite apart from this assumption accompanying virtually any studio-era final couple, Susan does at one point tell Aunt Elizabeth, 'I know that I'm going to marry him; *he* doesn't know it, but I am!' Nevertheless, the lack of a wedding ceremony – or even a proposal – is entirely appropriate. Not only does *The Philadelphia Story* ultimately present us with the social ritual itself, but its final non-diegetic music is even a jazzed-up version of 'The Wedding March', and its concluding shots are photographs of the bride and groom as published in *Spy* magazine: a very public 'blessing' of the couple indeed (Shumway 2003: 99). By contrast, the ending of *Bringing up Baby* severs its couple almost entirely from the society around them: balanced above the world, they are beyond the reach of authority figures, or even witnesses (Glitre 2006: 62). *The Philadelphia Story*'s final couple are embraced and remain bound by a social world whose values are intimately linked with patriarchal impulses in the culture; as such, their relationship seems destined to perpetuate this world's inequalities, however happily. *Bringing up Baby*, on the other hand, which ultimately leaves us with nothing like a paternalistic relationship, nor a blessing from the film's social world, promises a very different future: one that finally implies, in fact, a 'commitment to the construction of a non-patriarchal heterosexual couple' (Britton 2003: 180).

We have seen Shumway argue that all remarriage comedies amount fundamentally to an 'affirmation of marriage' (ibid.: 7); yet, as Glitre reminds us, 'it would be literally impossible for a [. . .] Hollywood film, made under the moral guardianship of the Production Code, to explicitly reject marriage as the framework for a heterosexual relationship' (2006: 44). As such, we need to ask what a studio-era final couple is nonetheless able to convey within these limits. Writing of the critical tendency to conflate marital final couples with the affirmation of patriarchy, Roberta Garrett suggests that,

> the level of equality within the relationship is, from a feminist
> perspective, a more important indicator of the degree to which the film
> challenges patriarchal assumptions concerning the balance of power
> within heterosexual relationships than its inclusion or rejection of the
> marital denouement. (2007: 101)

The Philadelphia Story and *Bringing up Baby* demonstrate that this approach is wise, especially for films made under the Code. Even if Hawks' final couple does still constitute an affirmation of *a* marriage, the level of equality established between this man and this woman by the time of the film's ending guarantees that the precise nature of the future 'marriage' being promised and affirmed can only appear far different than that implied by Cukor's happy ending. Moreover, by concluding not with the 'taming' of Susan but precisely the culmination of her disruptive energies, *Bringing up Baby*'s ending allows us to see that ideological accounts of the final couple need not restrict themselves only to 'the amount of dust the story raises along the road' (Mulvey 1977: 54), but should remain open to the possibility that a significant amount of 'dust' may also be raised by a final couple itself. Beyond the strictures of the Production Code, the limitations set on the final couple's ability to kick up such dust – in theory – decrease significantly.

Same Time, Next Year

Same Time, Next Year (1978) opens in 1951. Doris (Ellen Burstyn), a twenty-four-year-old housewife, and George (Alan Alda), a twenty-seven-year-old married accountant, meet by chance at a holiday inn on the Northern Californian Coast while both on trips away from their families. We see them share dinner, then rejoin them the next morning to discover that they have slept together. The next morning they express guilt over their infidelity, yet also sense that they may be falling in love with one another. The rest of the film covers a twenty-six-year period, during which the couple continue their affair, but only meeting once every year at this inn for the space of a weekend. The film ends in 1977, when the couple are in their 50s. During this meeting George tells Doris that his wife (Helen) has passed away in the year since their last tryst. He implores Doris to leave her husband (Harry) and marry him; he claims that he cannot bear to live alone and that, if Doris won't marry him, he will likely marry a friend of his wife's, Connie. Doris turns his proposal down, saying that she is not prepared to destroy the life she has built with Harry. Disappointed, George leaves; Doris collapses on the hotel bed in tears. Suddenly, however, George bursts back through the door and exclaims irritably that his threat to remarry someone else was a comically ill-considered bluff (Connie, it turns out, is eighty-seven years old). 'I'm back, and I'm going to keep coming back every year till our bones are too brittle to risk contact!' he announces. The couple embrace in a clinch in close-up.

Clearly, this final couple has extremely different ideological implications than those of either *The Philadelphia Story* or *Bringing Up Baby*. Firstly, there is the fact that here the ending does indeed 'explicitly reject marriage as the framework for [its] heterosexual relationship' (Glitre 2006: 44): though George desires it, the lovers' conversation before his exit establishes unambiguously that they will not marry so long as Harry is still alive. Secondly, this couple have already enjoyed a sexual relationship outside the sanctioning bonds of matrimony for decades (in the final scene George in fact estimates the number of times they have made love: 113!). Finally, almost radical is the fact that the implied future relationship will continue to be both adulterous and non-monogamous. While the most obvious ideological implications of these features in some sense already speak for themselves, it is worth briefly placing them into the context of some arguments we have previously touched upon.

The historical specificity of this final couple has partly, of course, to do with the absence of the Code, which would have allowed none of the things outlined in the paragraph above. We have already examined ways in which the Code's demands necessarily affected the endings of melodramatic adultery narratives, but just as important for the ideological meanings of romantic comedy was the requirement that sex be eschewed until after marriage (at least for couples who would ultimately receive a happy ending). This is one unambiguous way in which the final couple has changed its significance over time: although it has been claimed that contemporary romantic comedy often 'greatly de-emphasises sexuality' (McDonald 2007: 97; see also Kirkland 2007), it is also very common since the fall of the Code for final couples to have sex long before the end, and prior to their marriage.[17] This fact constitutes a major shift in the ideological horizons of the convention, and *Same Time, Next Year* provides an excellent example of further places the convention can go when freed from the PCA's moral strictures on the depiction of intimate relations.

Another historical dimension of this final couple obviously has to do with shifts in social discourses around gender roles in the United States, specifically the rise during the 1960s and 1970s of second-wave feminism, and its attendant reconsideration of male-female sexual relations (see, for instance, Gerhard 2001). This is a historical narrative that *Same Time, Next Year*'s sexual politics are both indebted to and in dialogue with. In keeping with the photographs of significant events in US history that mark the passing years between their meetings (e.g. Kennedy's assassination, Vietnam-era protests, women's rights marches, etc.), between the years 1951 and 1977 both members of the couple go through numerous, sometimes contradictory, changes in what they refer to variously as their 'value systems' and what they 'stand for'. Doris begins the film in the 50s as a suburban housewife who dresses like Jane Wyman in *All That Heaven Allows* and holidays at a Catholic retreat; by 1966 she has enrolled at Berkley, adopting hippy clothing and language, expressing amusement at a newly-conservative-leaning George's prudish consternation that magazines are now 'telling women what sort of orgasms they should have', and threatening to withhold sex because of his support for Barry Goldwater's 1964 presidential bid; in 1972 we discover she has become a successful businesswoman with a company grossing half a million a year (to the chagrin of her less professionally-successful husband, we are told). Equally, her beliefs come to be explicitly defined in feminist terms: 'I take it you *are* for women's liberation?' she asks George at one point. 'Hey, I'm for any kind of liberation,' comes the reply. 'That's a cop-out,' she rebuts; 'women have always been exploited by men and you know it.'

By the very fact that such populist feminist values are made central to this character (who is neither chastised for them, as in *The Philadelphia Story*, nor embodies them in a more metaphorical sense, as we might say does Susan in *Bringing up Baby*), *Same Time, Next Year*'s final couple is itself implicitly imbued with and affirmative of those values. As such, it seems significant that it is Doris who dictates the terms on which the future of the relationship will be conducted, and of the pair it is she who (it is clearer) will be living a non-monogamous, adulterous lifestyle – a far cry indeed from the disproportionately harsh punishment of the female half of the extra-marital couple in a film like *Intermezzo*. This is still a white, heterosexual (and upper-middle class) final couple, then, but one that – in part thanks to its historical context and subject matter – affirms very different ideological possibilities than are usually assumed to be hard-wired into the convention.

There is also, finally, the important fact that by 1978 this narrative can be told as romantic comedy at all, rather than as an adulterous romantic melo-drama – meaning in part that taboo expressions of romantic desire need not '[lock] the romantic couple into a tight and repressive world', but might rather 'in some way liberate them' (Thomas 2000: 99).[18] Thus, topics such as the philanderers' guilt (treated as so oppressive in *Intermezzo* or *There's Always Tomorrow*), for instance, can be handled here with intermittent levity (e.g. Doris calling George's bluff following a particularly self-pitying outburst by teasing, 'I'll bet you've got a scarlet "A" embroidered on your boxer shorts!'). It is in large part this shift in mode and/or genre that allows the film to over-come the comedy/melodrama ideological dualism suggested by Britton above, wherein romanticism *after* marriage can appear only as 'a rebellion against bourgeois norms which is tragically doomed by the necessity of upholding them' (2003: 179). George and Doris' romance is indeed a rebellion against such norms, but – even if it can only be fulfilled in utopian and (as in *Bringing up Baby*) private moments – it need not here be foredoomed. It is in large part this that permits both the final couple and its comparatively progressive ideological character. The potential for the comedic treatment of ideologically 'rebellious' subject matter assumes even greater significance for the happy ending of our final film – one yet further removed from both the period and precepts of the PCA: John Cameron Mitchell's *Shortbus* (2006)

Shortbus

Shortbus is a multi-protagonist film revolving around patrons of the titular 'queer-friendly but not queer-exclusive' sex club-cabaret-salon in contempo-rary New York City (Williams 2008: 289). Despite its unconventional subject-matter (and approach to production – the film features unsimulated sex), the movie could nonetheless also easily be described as a romantic comedy-drama, and is focused primarily on the relationships between two established, long-term couples: one between the Canadian-Chinese couples counsellor Sofia (Sook-Yin Lee) and her husband Rob (Raphael Barker), and another between former hustler James (Paul Dawson) and his boyfriend of five years, Jamie (P. J. DeBoy). It is demonstrated early on that both couples are experienc-ing problems: Sofia is unable to achieve orgasm and has been deceiving Rob about this, eventually leading to bitter arguments, while James is suicidally depressed. Sofia's quest to climax leads her to try new experiences, including striking up a therapeutic (and at one point sexual) friendship with a profes-sional dominatrix, Severin (Lindsay Beamish). James and Jamie, meanwhile, introduce a new man, Ceth (Jay Brannan), into their relationship at James' suggestion – his intention (it emerges later) being to ensure that Jamie is not left alone following his planned suicide. Over the course of the film the central couples grow increasingly apart: Sofia and Rob end up having a major fight at the club; Rob secretly hires Severin for the S&M sex he feels he cannot indulge with Sofia; James fails in his suicide attempt at a swimming pool, then subsequently has sex with the man who saved him, Caleb (Peter Stickles).

The film's final sequence begins with an electrical blackout that descends suddenly on the entire city. One by one our protagonists show up to a gathering at Shortbus, where the club's transgender mistress (Justin Bond) is holding an impromptu concert by candlelight. Feeling a sense of community heightened by the power outage (and the surprise appearance, after a moment, of a marching band wandering into the club), the concert escalates into a group singalong and quasi-orgy involving all present, during which various erotic groupings spontaneously emerge: among many others, James and Jamie make out on the floor; Ceth kisses Caleb and jumps into his lap, before then subsequently sharing his attention with James and Jamie; Rob begins kissing a female (incidentally, black) stranger on the couch next to him; and Sofia is approached by a swinging couple – club regulars whom she has previously admired from afar. As the caresses of this last threesome escalate, we cut into an extreme close-up on Sofia's face as she experiences her first orgasm; at this moment power immediately returns to New York, and the film ends.

Clearly, if it is indeed a final couple happy ending at all, *Shortbus'* is an exceptional one. Furthermore, it must be noted up front that the film is only peripherally definable as a 'Hollywood' movie at all in 'Indiewood' terms at the level of distribution.[19] I have chosen to conclude this chapter with it, however, for precisely these reasons, since it both expresses several ideological impulses that we do not frequently find within Hollywood happy endings, and yet *is* also very much a happy ending. This thus brings us finally back, in a sense, to the question that implicitly informed all my analyses in Chapter 1, now from an ideological perspective: what are the limits of this convention?

Considering that (1) Sofia has by the end shared intimate moments with her husband, the couple at the club, Severin, and the transgendered Justin Bond, (2) that the final scene includes participants of numerous (sometimes indeterminate – that is: queer) sexual and gender identities, and (3) that the film has not rhetorically devalued any of the above, it almost seems fair to suggest, as some have, that this ending indeed 'transgresses any normative heterosexual expectations' (Yeatman 2008: 1). More modestly, we can say without fear of contradiction that *Shortbus* is not a film which is especially concerned to affirm the values of either heterosexuality or monogamy – at least, not over and above other possible 'discourses on love, sex and marriage' (Deleyto 2009: 29). Taking for now the relative unconventionality of much of this ending as read, however, let us also note some ways in which it resembles other happy endings.

In traditional romantic comedy fashion, this ending is 'happy' partly because it brings back together couples following a 'Dark Moment' (Mernit

2000: 115) during which they became estranged: James and Jamie reunite as a final couple following the former's suicide attempt and tryst with Caleb; and for Sofia and Rob too – whom we last saw together in the midst of an angry dispute – this happy ending is to a significant extent *about* a couple, even if they are not *quite* a final couple. When Sofia is approached, and begins to be kissed, by the swinging couple, she looks across the room to her husband, who fixes her with a calm, tender, assenting half-smile in close-up; she indicates her appreciation and understanding with a smile (a level of understanding, indeed, that has previously eluded the pair), then turns to kiss the couple's female member. While one 'goal' for Sofia throughout the film has been to finally achieve orgasm, she has earlier expressed another plainly when she confided to Severin, 'I want to be able to save my marriage'. And indeed, it seems very possible that the new sexual freedom the couple allow themselves here could help facilitate just that. Quite apart from permitting Sofia to over-come her emotionally-debilitating sexual 'clog' (her term for her inability to reach orgasm), her and Rob's encounters with these strangers exist far from the brief guilt-ridden adultery of *Intermezzo*, or even the sustained and more positively-handled infidelity of *Same Time, Next Year* – in fact, this cannot even be appropriately accommodated by the *terms* infidelity or adultery, given its public and mutually agreed nature. Especially considering Sofia's profes-sion, it seems likely that what we are seeing here is the beginning of a new approach to the 'discourse of intimacy' for the couple (Shumway 2003) – an open relationship – and that this development might indeed help 'save' rather than end this marriage. In this sense and others, we are offered an unconven-tional ideological inflection on a very conventional feature of happy endings: a hopeful promise of continuation.

Another way in which this happy ending is rather traditional is how rela-tively 'closed' it nonetheless is. As well as the couples' reunions, the film also borrows a closural convention from a multi-protagonist film such as *Best Years* by ultimately bringing its characters together in the same space, as well as a familiar device from the musical genre by ending with what amounts to a big musical number. Equally, hermeneutically, there is the fact that we leave Sofia precisely at the moment she comes, i.e. when she achieves a primary goal she has been pursuing since the film's first sequence, in which she and Rob were seen having athletic but (for her) finally unclimactic sex.[20] Beginning and ending with sex scenes also constitutes an act of narrative 'bracketing', some-thing achieved at the stylistic level too: following Sofia's ecstatic close-up we cut to an animated long shot of the same colourful, toy model-like rendering of New York to which we were introduced in the film's very first shot, the buildings' lights all now fizzing back on, beginning with Shortbus' window and spreading out from there across the whole city. Already rather recalling *Sleepless*' final recessional image of New York to this extent, Mitchell's film resembles Ephron's even more when the 'camera' cranes back faster and faster from the cityscape until moving into space. This is thus another emphatic use of the 'rhetoric of an ending' to assist in creating a great closural sense of appropriate cessation – an effect that this film, if no other, should teach us to recognise as in no way *automatically* translating to the communication of hegemonic ideological meanings.

Thus in some ways offering certain familiar conventions, it is perhaps unsurprising that a number of contemporaneous reviewers also called this conclusion what it in fact is: a happy ending.[21] Though most of these references to the convention are (unusually) positive, most pertinent for our present purposes is the phenomenon of conservative critics denouncing the film precisely *for* ending happily.[22] Chris Tookey, for instance, writes in the *Daily Mail* that 'Mitchell's idea of a happy ending is to have his leading man finally allow himself to be sodomised, while his leading lady has three-way sex' – a conclusion he considers 'harmful and irresponsible' because ignoring 'the sordid realities and health implications of an orgiastic lifestyle' (2006: 1). Apart from the fact that it misrepresents the ending, this hysterical account also helps make plain that in certain circumstances the ideological implications of a happy ending can in fact be radical – or at the very least can appear so to those opposed to its implied values.

A similar point has been made by Jackie Stacey in relation to the popular lesbian romance film *Desert Hearts* (1985). Due to the fact that cinematic homosexual characters have historically frequently been depicted as 'neurotic, criminal, unnatural, and by the end of the film, often dead' (1995: 97) – in both Hollywood (e.g. *Basic Instinct* [1992]) *and* independent 'New Queer Cinema' (e.g. *Swoon* [1991]) – Stacey argues that gay-focused 'Hollywoodstyle, Happy-ending romances' (ibid.: 93) are in fact something that can be praised, since it is ultimately *Desert Hearts'* final couple that lets it become an 'unapologetic celebration of lesbian love' (1995: 111). Going several steps further in the radicalism of its sexual politics, *Shortbus* nonetheless similarly adopts key aspects of Hollywood's closural conventions to assist in its happy ending. As well as those mentioned, in its final shot, for instance, the film repurposes the sense of the 'transcendental' value of love found in *Sleepless* and many films in Chapter 1. However, instead of a final pull-out into space from a heart-adorned Empire State Building suggesting the transcendent fate associated with predestined heterosexual romantic love, here the final shot is aligned instead with the 'utopian powers of the queer community' (Lippert 2010: 204), which are symbolically suggested (by *Shortbus'* windows being the first to illuminate) to bring back power and light to New York City. Such strategies might tell us something about the progressive ideological possibilities actually created *by* the convention of the happy ending, rather than those that may exist simply in spite of it.

In *There's Always Tomorrow* we saw an example of an ending that achieves subversive meanings via the method that has too often been treated as the *only* means by which a happy ending can avoid ideological conservatism: undercutting the convention to the point that it barely makes sense to define it as 'happy' at all. As well as stemming from a distrust of the authoritarian impulses supposedly inherent in closure, theoretical approaches which tend to value this method above all others also tend to distrust the very 'happiness' of the 'happy ending'. Writing about the model of the paradigmatic 'progressive text' that emerged during the height of 'subject-position' theory, Klinger notes that a key trait argued to have been shared by the majority of films associated with that model was 'a "pessimistic" world view': 'instead of the optimism which characterises the typical celebratory or complacent view of the American way of life in the classic text [. . .] the overall atmosphere of these films is bleak, cynical, apocalyptic and/or highly ironic [. . .] in such a way as to disturb or disable an unproblematic transmission of affirmative ideology' (1984a: 35). It is thus not only a suspicion of the rhetorical power of endings to confer meaning that is rejected by such a model, but also their power rhetorically to *affirm*. And, as we have seen throughout this book – since Fritz Lang's conception of the '*affirmative* ending' (1948: 29) – happy endings do certainly have a tendency to affirm things – more specifically, they are likely to affirm certain values. However, as with closure, I would suggest that for an ending simply to be 'affirmative' is not in-and-of-itself for it to adopt a specific ideological position: what matters is not *that* it affirms values, but *what* values it affirms.

A film such as *Shortbus* demonstrates that it can sometimes be a more radical gesture to affirm than to be 'pessimistic'. Happy endings are thus – however occasionally – capable of making such gestures. Writing of his (ultimately posthumously-published) novel that told a homosexual love story, *Maurice*, E. M. Forster wrote:

A happy ending was imperative. I shouldn't have bothered to write otherwise. I was determined that in fiction anyway two men should fall in love and remain in it for the ever and ever that fiction allows, [. . .] which, by the way, has had an unexpected result: it has made the book more difficult to publish [. . .] If it ended unhappily, with a lad dangling from a noose or with a suicide pact, all would be well' (1971: 236).

As with *Maurice*, *Shortbus*' happy ending is 'imperative' to its progressive ideological character. This can be effectively confirmed by the rabid denunciation of it by voices such as Tookey, who can clearly be seen longing instead for an *un*happy conclusion that depicts, if not a suicide pact, then at least supposed 'sordid realities [. . .] of an orgiastic lifestyle' (ibid.: 1). Also as with Forster, it is by ultimately being rhetorically 'affirmative' (i.e. un-subverted, unironic) that Mitchell's ending becomes radical. Various tendencies common to happy endings help it in this: the overcoming of a 'Dark Moment', the reunion of a couple, intimations of transcendence suggesting the triumph of a certain set of values, and hopeful promises of continuation for characters. We might thus say that, here, far from progressive ideological meanings emerging only via an implicit subversion of the convention of the happy ending, it is the very gesture of allowing itself to end with a wholehearted, celebratory instance of this convention that permits *Shortbus* to be as joyously 'subversive' as it finally is.

*

This book has for the most part been concerned with films featuring white, heterosexual, and (mainly) monogamous final couples for two main reasons. Firstly and most obviously: since I have been seeking to expand our understanding of the flexibility of what tends to be treated as perhaps the most homogeneous 'cliché' in Hollywood cinema, it has made sense to dedicate myself primarily to demonstrating the variation and complexity so frequently elided by sweeping pronouncements such as 'the heterosexual couple is united romantically, signaling a traditional "happy ending"' (Benshoff/Griffin 2004b: 61). Secondly, however, there is also of course the aforementioned fact that, even decades after the fall of the Production Code, white, heterosexual, monogamous (even if now not necessarily married) final couples are *still* disproportionately the norm for happy endings in Hollywood cinema – within romantic comedy and elsewhere. In concluding this chapter on happy endings and ideology, it is necessary to keep the implications of both these facts in mind.

In this chapter we have focused on some of the excesses that routinely attend pronouncements about the *de facto* ideological significance of the final couple happy ending. As with previous chapters, it has been argued that the convention has the potential to be more flexible in this regard than its clichéd reputation would have us assume. Not only should we not presume that the convention necessarily has an iron ideological grip over spectators' beliefs or actions, but we should also acknowledge that closure does not itself *guarantee* patriarchal or conservative meanings (and thus does not automatically demand subversion), as well as the fact that the ideological values affirmed by individual happy endings are clearly able to incorporate multiple and divergent discourses on love, sex and marriage: from, indeed, the effective quelling of an 'unruly' woman prior to marriage, all the way to the pleasures of a three-way gay relationship and the opening-up of a marriage in the midst of a sex-positive, gender-queer community. It has been beholden on the first in-depth book on the 'happy ending' to demonstrate the convention's *potential* to be this ideologically heterogeneous because – while film studies has for most aspects of Hollywood cinema largely moved beyond such schematic doxy – the very presence of a happy ending *itself* is still too often treated as necessarily reinforcing the most conservative ideological values available in US culture.

On the other hand, however, the conclusion of every preceding chapter has featured an acknowledgment of a degree of validity in the convention's traditional reputation, and it would be very misleading to conclude our discussion of ideology and happy endings in any other way. It would be wrong to confuse the convention's *capacity* for great ideological flexibility with a *tendency* towards such flexibility. It goes without saying that *Shortbus* is, of course, very far from a 'typical' final couple happy ending – indeed, the very fact that it introduces new partners into a couple (however much this act is defined in terms *of* the couple) necessarily means that its very status as an instance of the convention is made problematic. Existing thus on the very periphery of something definable as the final couple, this should remind us of the obvious fact that, while the ideological possibilities open to conclusions that 'could be said to end happily' (Bordwell 1986: 159) will surely be far broader (at least in theory) than this book has even begun to explore, the relative limitations of the category of the final couple happy ending may be made clear by the very wording of the term I have assigned it. Furthermore, although it is true (again, in theory) that there are great possibilities for flexibility within these limits (see *Sleepless, The Philadelphia Story, Bringing up Baby, Same Time, Next Year, Shortbus*), in practice – as we have noted – the ideological values actually affirmed by the majority of Hollywood films released, even today, tend to be considerably more circumscribed.[23] It is important to acknowledge that this does not indicate limits of the convention per se but instead expresses ideological limitations of the Hollywood industry and wider culture at specific historical moments (again, *Shortbus*' industrial status as a not-quite-Hollywood movie is certainly significant); but it is equally as vital to acknowledge and critique those limitations as long as they persist.

As it stands, then, *Shortbus*' conclusion will have to serve as a provocation – not only for those who would automatically align the 'happy ending' with a homogeneous ideological conservatism – but also for Hollywood cinema itself: this particular happy ending offers a tantalising glimpse of one direction in which the convention is plausibly capable of evolving if granted the opportunity.

NOTES

1. For instance: the blurb for the self-help book *What Was I Thinking? How Not to Date* describes the author's husband as 'the happy ending to her real-life love story' (Earley 2007: 112); 'There's no need for pretending /

You're my happy ending,' sings Barbra Streisand in 'Just One Lifetime'; 'If you can suss out the areas that you don't agree on now and find a way round them, then there's no reason why you won't live happily ever after,' *Cosmopolitan* tells us (Twomey 2008: 1); '"Love-visualize" your happy ending,' offers a writer for the dating site *Match.com* (Spencer 2011: 1); 'We all want a happy ending,' asserts *The Guardian* (Roiphe 2001: 1).

2. The sciences, for instance, have long acknowledged that 'human beings are not 'naturally' monogamous [. . .] (and it is another question altogether whether we should be)' (Barash/Lipton 2001: 1); see also, for instance, Foucault (1979) for an analysis of the ideological history of human sexuality, Rich (1980) on the ideological dimensions of heterosexuality, and Giddens (1992) and Shumway (2003) on the ideological development of the 'romantic love complex' in the West and its attendant shifting conceptions of marriage.

3. Of course, partly thanks to what Yvonne Tasker calls 'feminism's rediscovery of the popular' (1991: 86), there now certainly exists an intellectual tradition dedicated to complicating the view of popular romance fiction as unquestioningly patriarchal, both from the perspective of its readers (e.g. Radway [1987]) and its texts (e.g. Modleski [1982]), as well as valuable critical work by romance authors themselves (e.g. Krentz [1992], Cruise [1997]). Nevertheless, the negative critical reputation of romance genres still holds significant power.

4. See, for instance: Gilbert/Gubar (1979), Boone (1987), Booth (1993), Dubino (1993), Roof (1996), etc.

5. The possibility that such attitudes may be historically linked with the postmodern climate outlined in the previous chapter, for instance, deserves to be acknowledged (though not assumed), as well as, of course, the particular national, racial and class formations of interviewees. Regardless of how pervasive they are or are not, however, such views nonetheless at least demonstrate that these kinds of relationships between subjects' conscious beliefs and 'mythic' romance *exist*, even if not that they should be taken as representative.

6. This understanding is offered according to sociological theories common to the 'new institutionalism' (e.g. Mayer/Rowan 1977), of which Swidler is a proponent.

7. 'Even,' as Swidler notes, 'for those who do not marry, or those like gays and lesbians who are denied the legal right to marry' (ibid.: 117). On the latter, as well as the campaign for marriage equality (Retter/Williams 2003), we might also point to findings (e.g. Gotta et al. 2011) that suggest great increases in monogamy as a generalised goal for homosexual couples in the United States during the latter half of the twentieth century.

8. Of course, however, this sequel does not simply provide us with the union

that still remained a possibility at the end of *Sunrise*, but rather continues the deferral further. Nevertheless, see MacDowell (2005) and Deleyto (2009) for discussions of ways in which *Sunset* contains significant traces of what we might call 'mythic' discourses of romance. Equally, the fact that the filmmakers have at the time of press just finished still one further film in this series (purportedly titled *Before Midnight*) testifies again to the difficulty they seemingly have with leaving this fictional relationship 'unresolved'.

9. See Benshoff/Griffin (2004a, 2004b, 2006) for discussions of aspects of this history as it relates to the suppression of both interracial and homosexual desire; see also White (1999) on representations of lesbianism in classical Hollywood cinema, as well as Cortes (1991) and Courtney (2005) on miscegenation narratives.

10. There have certainly been some critics who have questioned this logic, particularly in literary studies, arguing that drawing 'easy correspondence between closed endings and conservative politics or open endings and progressive ideology is too facile' (Richardson 2002: 254) – see also: Torgovnick (1981: 204–6), Booth (1997: 9), and DuCille (1993) – but the paradigm has nonetheless been and remains extremely influential.

11. This is not to say that critics have never made approving claims about the ideology of individual happy endings in other ways. Romantic comedy scholarship, for instance, has produced some significant work on the subject (on which more shortly). Elsewhere, however, particularly interesting – because perhaps unique in film studies – is Isabel Cristina Pinedo's argument that the happy ending of the slasher film *The Stepfather* (1987) is progressive precisely *because* of its strong degree of closure, since it is this that allows it to become 'a feminist horror film' (1997: 95).

12. See also: Camper (1971), Neale (1986), Mercer/Shingler (2004: 14), etc.

13. For a detailed and sensitive interpretation of ways in which the film's opening depiction of Cliff's home life demonstrates feelings of dissatisfaction that he is being required to repress, see Klevan (2005: 53–63).

14. Serge Chauvin has written usefully on the matter that happy endings in romantic comedy have meant that 'classical Hollywood [. . .] offers very few chronicles of married life' (2010: 40). Equally, however, see Pillai (2012) for an excellent discussion of classical Hollywood comedies that *do* focus on marriage.

15. See Wexman (1993), for instance, on classical films flirting with but ultimately rejecting homosexual couples and racial miscegenation.

16. See MacDowell (2013) for an argument that Mike is in fact a more attractive potential partner for Tracy than Dexter.

17. A selection of post-Code romantic comedies and the amount of screen time elapsed before the final couple has sex: *Same Time, Next Year* (3 mins), *A Lot Like Love* (4 minutes), *Fools Rush In* (12 mins), *Speechless*

(13 mins), *Housesitter* (15 mins), *What Happens in Vegas* (17 mins), *Down to You* (30 mins), *Splash* (35 mins), *Failure to Launch* (40 mins), *The Back-Up Plan* (42 mins), *Lucky You* (44 mins), *Along Came Polly*, (47 mins), *Shakespeare in Love* (47 mins), *Sliding Doors* (50 mins), *Happy Together* (53 mins) *I Could Never be Your Woman* (55 mins), *Head Over Heels* (56 mins), *Something's Gotta Give* (1 hour), *The American President* (1 hour), *America's Sweethearts* (1.05), *Mannequin* (1.07), *Overboard* (1:16).

18. See also Deleyto (2009) on the 'magic space' of romantic comedy, which can offer a 'special atmosphere' – potentially even an 'erotic utopia' – 'as an antidote against the sexual and affective frustrations of everyday life' (ibid.: 35). Neither inherently conservative nor inherently progressive, this space is 'an empty formal concept, not an ideologically charged one', meaning different films 'may associate it with different discourses on love and desire' (ibid.: 37) – from *The Philadelphia Story* to *Same Time, Next Year*. I would suggest that something similar may be said of happy endings in general, and the final couple in particular.

19. Specifically, the purchase of international distribution rights by Universal Pictures; its domestic theatrical distribution (by Thinkfilm) was effectively stymied by the MPAA NC-17 rating awarded the film – another reminder that, though the Production Code is long gone, some of its proscriptions linger in other forms (Williams 2008: 259).

20. Though we should note, in keeping with the broader point of view permitted by the multi-protagonist film (see *Best Years*), that not all our characters' plotlines have been equally hermeneutically resolved: Severin, for instance, is more integrated into the community around her than we have previously seen her be (her impulse towards emotional isolation has been an issue throughout), but she is not partnered with anyone.

21. And not *always* for the phrase's contemporary resonance as a *double entendre*! e.g. Dargis 2006: 1; Ridley 2006: 1.

22. In addition to Tookey, see Taylor (2006).

23. Though see Deleyto (1998, 2003, 2010), Ruiz Pardos (2010) and Azcona (2010) for discussions of recent romantic comedy which argue that 'different versions of what a happy ending within the sphere of intimate relations may entail [. . .] have started to be possible' (Ruiz Pardos 2010: 111). These versions might range across a woman divorcing her husband (e.g. *Alice* [1990]), a couple moving from a romantic to a platonic relationship (e.g. *The Break-Up*), or a woman not winning back the man she wanted but instead enjoying a friendship with her gay confidante (e.g. *My Best Friend's Wedding*). Though not focused on final couples, all such conclusions are nevertheless happy endings and, as Celestino Deleyto says, could only be considered otherwise 'by those who come to [a] film with preconceived ideas of what a happy ending should consist of' (2010: 111).

Conclusion
Provisions for the future

How does one conclude a book about the complexities of endings? Given my recurring interest in how happy endings tend to contain promises of continuation, it seems inescapable that I should end by hinting at what future scholarly work on this convention might look like. First, though, a few words about what we have learned.

Clearly, the 'happy ending' is not as simple as is commonly assumed. This is unsurprising, however, since most assumptions about how simple the convention is have themselves been notable precisely for their tendency to oversimplify. Indeed, if being uncharitable we could say that the true homogeneous cliché at this point is not the 'happy ending', but the critical orthodoxy surrounding it. Having said this, as we have seen, there certainly has nonetheless been useful work that has delved more deeply into cinematic happy endings than most, and such scholarship will be invaluable for any future researchers on the subject. There is also perhaps, however, something to be learned from more familiar strands of film studies' engagement with the convention.

Surveying critical references to the 'happy ending', it is striking how commonly the words are placed between inverted commas. Rather than indicating that the term itself is problematic, however, the qualification usually seems intended to convey that it may not apply in *this* instance – that is: the critic intends to show that, in the case of whichever conclusion s/he is analysing, the 'supposedly "happy ending" is really anything but' (Schneider 2003: 87). Yet I would suggest that these two possible reasons for qualifying the term could in fact be seen as mutually enriching. Because of the convention's reputation as a standardised cliché, scholars have of course frequently felt the need to demonstrate that an ending for which they wish to make claims manages to avoid being an example of *the* 'happy ending': perhaps by appearing implausible or ironic, by being 'subversive', by not fully erasing the memory of earlier narrative conflicts – essentially, by including any dissonant qualities. I would argue that the fact that there do indeed seem to be so many Hollywood conclusions which are simultaneously 'happy endings', and yet which are somehow also not *the* typical 'happy ending', should suggest that the baseline requires shifting, and that the very notion of *the* typical 'happy ending' stands in need of revision.

One of the few critics to have consistently questioned accepted views of the 'happy ending', Deleyto, is in my view absolutely correct when he argues that 'a closer look at this [. . .] convention proves that ambiguity and variety are relatively frequent'; furthermore, he is virtually revolutionary when he goes on to suggest what no other critic (as far as I know) has ever acknowledged: that such ambiguity and variety are perhaps 'even part of the convention itself' (2009: 127). I believe that this may very well be correct and, furthermore, that the recurrent scholarly attention paid to the many complex happy endings produced by Hollywood implies that film studies has, in a sense, already inadvertently demonstrated this to be so. This book has suggested that, because the convention itself appears to be so relatively flexible, no 'subversion' is necessarily required in order to create 'happy endings' which are complex, ambiguous, or in some other way simply *distinctive*. As such, although we have noted that in some cases the recourse to the notion of the 'ironic' implausible 'happy ending' may be entirely valid, in many other instances, a happy ending containing a degree of 'openness' or a 'bitter taste' (Žižek 1991: 9) may simply indicate that it offers a degree of instability or ambiguity that is entirely *usual* for the convention, if conceptualised appropriately broadly. Furthermore, we could note that even genuinely ironic and subversive happy endings (such as *There's Always Tomorrow*'s) themselves do not exist somehow outside of the convention, but rather constitute one possibility open to it. As Britton put it, speaking of a slightly different context: 'we have here a perfect illustration of that familiar intellectual trick whereby, once an untenable definition has been established, an inordinate and distorted significance is attached [. . .] to instances which show the definition to be incorrect' (2009: 413).

Having hopefully productively complicated some deeply-held critical beliefs regarding the convention, how should we now proceed? At the end of Chapter 1 I introduced my own game with inverted commas, abandoning them when referring to *a* happy ending – that is: a particular use of an evolving convention – yet retaining them when discussing the Platonic cliché of *the* 'happy ending'. It seems to me that future research into happy endings would be wise to maintain this distinction. I also believe, though, that work on both these phenomena might lead in fruitful directions – we simply need to remain cognisant of which we are talking about in any given instance.

As I have argued, while it can mislead us as to the potential uses and meanings of actual happy endings, the concept of the clichéd 'happy ending' is nonetheless important, since it has been so central to how the convention is commonly understood – not only by critics, but also by films, within popular culture, and amongst the public. There are myriad questions left to pursue regarding the cultural significance of this concept. We might try to discover, for instance, when the final couple, and the 'happy ending' more generally, seem to have begun earning their reputations as Hollywood clichés. For example, at what point did reviewers first start commenting upon or objecting to their perceived prevalence and homogeneity, and what precursors did such discourses have in the criticism of drama and literature? How early did spoofs such as *Sherlock, Jr.*'s begin appearing, and what was the nature of their development? It could also be productive to ask what individual implausible happy endings seem to imply about the cliché: while, say, *Sleepless* associates the concept primarily with destiny and Hollywood romance, *Pretty Woman* links it more with childhood fantasies and fairy tales; tracing similar associations in other films (and periods) would help us better understand how the 'happy ending' has been conceptualised and navigated by Hollywood cinema. From a cultural studies perspective, it would also be fascinating to trace the rise of the term 'happy ending' as a virtual byword for success and/or romance in journalism, popular music, advertising, advice columns, and so on. It could also be enlightening from a sociological and reception-studies standpoint to explore in a more focused manner the responses and attitudes of spectators towards individual happy endings, the cliché 'happy ending', and the ways that concepts associated with both may be related to or contrasted by viewers to their own lives.

If discussing happy ending*s*, on the other hand, the most pressing task is to address other aspects of the convention than those relating to romantic narratives. While this book has been concerned primarily with the final couple, it has also noted tendencies that could well be central to happy endings more broadly: the affirmation of (and sometimes choice between) values made central to the film; the promise of continuation for characters' lives beyond the end; a certain sense of closure (depending on multiple determinants), which is nonetheless capable of great degrees of variation; an association with unrealism (for numerous reasons), which may encourage self-conscious acknowledgment or attempts to temper the association; finally, a significant potential for flexibility in the possible ideological tenets ultimately affirmed. It may be that other kinds of happy ending – for instance, say, those centred on 'heroes' defeating 'villains' – usually share all these tendencies, or relatively few of them, and research into the conclusions of Hollywood films in other genres and periods will be essential. At the same time, there is certainly a huge amount of work still to be carried out on the final couple itself. It would be fruitful, for example, to explore the possible functions of the features in films that are less centrally concerned with romantic love: to what uses can the final couple be put when shouldering a lesser burden of expectation regarding narrative closure? Equally, within the realm of romance-focused films too, I look forward eagerly to more work both on the historically-specific sexual politics of final couples of all permutations, as well as on films which focus on intimate relationships, do not end with a final couple, and yet still assuredly offer happy endings.

The extent to which the cases made by this book will prove valid or applicable for the broader domain of Hollywood happy endings is something that careful critical attention to such endings will be able to determine. Indeed, it has been central to my argument that it is only by such attention to examples of this convention, and not by a priori assumptions based on a cliché's reputation, that we can hope meaningfully to discuss any happy ending. That there are so many avenues still left to explore tells us that there are a great many productive questions still waiting to be asked of the convention. Of course, the reputation of the Hollywood 'happy ending' is predicated precisely on discouraging questions – providing a closure that rights all wrongs, resolves all problems, and ties up all loose ends. I would suggest, however, that it has not been happy endings themselves, but rather critics, who have tended to narrow the range of questions that can be posed of such endings. If it has accomplished nothing else, it is my hope that this book has convincingly argued that we should no longer cease asking questions simply because a movie might conclude, say, with a kiss.

Bibliography

Abbott, H. Porter (2008), *The Cambridge Companion to Narrative*, second edition, Cambridge: Cambridge University Press.

Adorno, Theodor and Max Horkheimer (1997), *Dialectic of Enlightenment: Philosophical Fragments*, London: Verso.

Affron, Charles (1980), 'Performing Performing: Irony and Affect', *Cinema Journal* 20:1, 42–52.

Althusser, Louis (1970), *Reading Capital*, London: New Left Books.

Althusser, Louis (1971), *Lenin and Philosophy and Other Essays*, trans. by Ben Brewster, New York: Monthly Review Press.

Altman, Rick (1981), *Genre: The Musical*, London: Routledge.

Altman, Rick (1987), *The American Film Musical*, Bloomington: Indiana University Press.

Altman, Rick (1992), 'Dickens, Griffith and Film Theory Today', in Jane Gaines (ed.), *Classical Hollywood Narrative: The Paradigm Wars*, London: Duke University Press, 9–47.

Altman, Rick (1999), *Film/Genre*, London: BFI.

Altman, Rick (2008), *A Theory of Narrative*, New York: Columbia University Press.

Amossy, Ruth and Terese Lyons (1982), 'The Cliché in the Reading Process', *SubStance* 11:2:35, 34–45.

Aristotle (1962), *On the Art of Poetry*, trans. by Ingram Bywater, Oxford: Clarendon Press.

Armes, Roy (1994), *Action and Image: Dramatic Structure in Cinema*, Manchester: Manchester University Press.

Aumont, Jacques (1980), 'Griffith, le Cadre, la Figure', in Raymond Bellour (ed.), *Le Cinema Americain*, Paris: Flammarion, 51–67.

Azcona, María del Mar (2010a), 'Precarious Teleologies: New Endings for a New Genre', in Armelle Parey, Isabelle Roblin and Dominique

Sipière (eds), *Happy Endings and Films*, Paris: Michel Houdiard, 151–9.

Azcona, María del Mar (2010b), *The Multi-Protagonist Film*, Chichester: Wiley-Blackwell.

Babbington, Bruce and Peter Evans (1990), 'All That Heaven Allowed: Another Look at Sirkian Irony', *Movie*, 34:5, 48–58.

Bakhtin, Mikhail (1984), *Problems of Dostoevsky's Poetics*, ed and trans. by Caryl Emerson, Minneapolis: University of Minnesota Press.

Barash, David P. and Judith Eve Lipton (2001), *The Myth of Monogamy: Fidelity and Infidelity in Animals and People*, New York: Henry Holt & Co.

Barthes, Roland (1977), *S/Z: An Essay*, trans. by Richard Miller, New York: Hill and Wang.

Bazin, André (1997), 'William Wyler, or the Jansenist of Directing', *Bazin at Work: Major Essays & Reviews From the Forties & Fifties*, trans. by Alain Piette and Bert Cardullo, London: Routledge, 1–22.

Belsey, Catherine (1994), *Desire: Love Stories in Western Culture*, Oxford: Blackwell.

Belton, John (1994), *American Cinema/American Culture*, New York: McGraw-Hill.

Bellour, Raymond (1979), 'Alternation, Segmentation, Hypnosis: an Interview with Raymond Bellour. Conducted by Janet Bergstrom', *Camera Obscura*, 3:4, 71–103.

Benshoff, Harry M. and Sean Griffin (2004a), *American Film: Representing Race, Class, Gender and Sexuality at the Movies*, Oxford: Blackwell.

Benshoff, Harry M. and Sean Griffin (2004b), *Queer Cinema: The Film Reader*, London and New York: Routledge.

Benshoff, Harry M. and Sean Griffin (2006), *Queer Images: A History of Gay and Lesbian Film in America*, New York: Rowman & Littlefield.

Best, Steven and Douglas Kellner (1997), *The Postmodern Turn*, New York: Guilford Press.

Blair, Lindsay (1998), *Joseph Cornell's Vision of Spiritual Order*, London: Reaktion Books.

Booker, M. Keith (2007), *Postmodern Hollywood: What's New in Film and Why it Makes us Feel so Strange*, London: Praeger.

Boone, Joseph Allen (1987), *Tradition, Counter-Tradition: Love and the Form of Fiction*, London: University of Chicago Press.

Booth, Alison (1993), 'Introduction: The Sense of Few Endings', in Alison Booth (ed.), *Famous Last Words: Changes in Gender and Narrative Closure*, Charlottesville: University Press of Virginia, 1–32.

Booth, Wayne C. (1974), *A Rhetoric of Irony*, London: University of Chicago Press.

Booth, Wayne (1983), *The Rhetoric of Fiction*, London: University of Chicago Press.

Booth, Wayne (1988), *The Company We Keep: an Ethics of Fiction*, Los Angeles: University of California Press.

Bordwell, David (1982), 'Happily Ever After, Part Two', *Velvet Light Trap*, 19: 2–7.

Bordwell, David, Janet Staiger and Kristin Thompson (1985), *The Classical Hollywood Cinema: Film Style and Mode of Production to 1960*, London: Routledge.

Bordwell, David (1986), *Narration in the Fiction Film*, London: Methuen.

Bordwell, David (1996), 'Contemporary Film Studies and the Vicissitudes of Grand Theory', in David Bordwell and Noël Carroll (eds), *Post-Theory: Reconstructing Film Studies*, Madison: University of Wisconsin Press, 1–36.

Bordwell, David (2006), *The Way Hollywood Tells It: Story and Style in Modern Movies*, Los Angeles: University of California Press.

Bowdre, Karen (2009), 'Romantic Comedies and the Raced Body', in Stacey Abbott, Deborah Jermyn (eds), *Falling in Love Again: Romantic Comedy in Contemporary Cinema*, London: I. B. Tauris, 105–16.

Bratu-Hansen, Miriam (1991), *Babel and Babylon: Spectatorship in American Silent Film*, Cambridge, MA: Harvard University Press.

Bratu-Hansen, Miriam (1997), '*Schindler's List* is not *Shoah*: Second Commandment, Popular Modernism and Public Memory', in Yosefa Loshitzky (ed.), *Spielberg's Holocaust: Critical Perspectives on Schindler's List*, Bloomington: Indiana University Press, 77–103.

Braudy, Leo (1976), *The World in a Frame: What we see in Films*, New York: Anchor Press.

Britton, Andrew (1993), '*The Lady From Shanghai*: Betrayed by Rita Hayworth', in Ian Cameron (ed.), *The Movie Book of Film Noir*, New York: Continuum, 213–21.

Britton, Andrew (2003), *Katharine Hepburn: Star as Feminist*, New York: Columbia University Press.

Britton, Andrew (2009), *Britton on Film: The Complete Film Criticism of Andrew Britton*, Barry Keith Grant (ed.), London: Wayne State University Press.

Brooks, Peter (1976), *The Melodramatic Imagination*, New York: Columbia University Press.

Brooks, Peter (1984), *Reading for the Plot: Design and Intention in Narrative*, London: Harvard University Press.

Brownlow, Kevin (1987), '*Hungry Hearts*: A Hollywood Social Problem Film of the 1920s', *Film History* 1:2, 113–25.

Bruns, John (2008), 'The Polyphonic Film', *New Review of Film and Television Studies*, 6:2, 189–212.

Brunsdon, Charlotte (1989), 'Text and Audience', in Ellen Seiter, Hans Borchers, Gabrielle Kreutzner, Eva-Maria Warth (eds), *Remote Control: Television, Audiences & Cultural Power*, London: Routledge, 116–29.

Brunsdon, Charlotte and David Morley (1999), *The Nationwide Television Studies*, London: Routledge.

Brylla, Catalin (2004), 'How are Film Endings Shaped by their Socio-historical Context? (Part I)', *Image & Narrative* 8, available at <http://www.imageandnarrative.be/inarchive/issue08/catalynbrylla.htm> (last accessed 1 May 2009).

Buckland, Warren (2006), *Directed by Steven Spielberg: the Poetics of the Hollywood Blockbuster*, London: Continuum.

Burch, Noël (1990), *Life to Those Shadows*, Berkley: University of California Press.

'Bureau of Motion Pictures Report: *Casablanca*' (1942), available at <http://www.digitalhistory.uh.edu/learning_history/casablanca/bmp_report_casablanca.cfm> (last accessed 20 February 2007).

Buscombe, Edward (2003), 'The Idea of Genre in the American Cinema', in Barry Keith Grant (ed.), *Film Genre Reader III*, Austin: University of Texas Press, 12–26.

Butler, Alison (2002), *Women's Cinema: The Contested Screen*, London: Wallflower.

Byars, Jackie (1991), *All That Hollywood Allows: Re-Reading Gender in 1950s Melodrama*, University of North Carolina Press.

Byron, George (1831), *The Complete Works of Lord Byron*, Paris: J. Smith.

Cagle, Chris (2007), 'Two Modes of Prestige Film', *Screen*, 48:3, 291–31.

Camper, Fred (1971), 'The Films of Douglas Sirk: The Epistemologist of Despair', available at <http://www.fredcamper.com/Film/Sirk.html> (last accessed 8 March 2008).

Carroll, Noël (1980), 'The Moral Ecology of Melodrama: The Family Plot and *Magnificent Obsession*', *New York Literary Forum* 7, 183–91.

Carroll, Noël (1982) 'The Future of Allusion: Hollywood in the Seventies (and Beyond),' *October* 20, 51–81.

Carroll, Noël (1988), *Mystifying Movies: Fads and Fallacies in Contemporary Film Theory*, New York: Columbia University Press.

Carroll, Noël (1994), 'The Paradox of Junk Fiction', *Philosophy and Literature*, 18:1, 225–41.

Carroll, Noël (1996), *Theorizing the Moving Image*, Cambridge: Cambridge University Press.

Carroll, Noël (2007), 'Narrative Closure', *Philosophical Studies*, 135:1, 1–15.

Cavell, Stanley (1981), *Pursuits of Happiness: The Hollywood Comedy of Remarriage*, Cambridge, MA: Harvard University Press.

Cavell, Stanley (1996), *Contesting Tears: The Hollywood Melodrama of the Unknown Woman*, Chicago: University of Chicago Press.

Cavell, Stanley (2005), 'Falling in Love Again', *Film Comment*, 41:5, 50–54.

Cawelti, John G. (1991), 'The Evolution of Social Melodrama', in Marcia Landy (ed.), *Imitations of Life: a Reader on Film & Television Melodrama*, Detroit: Wayne State University Press, 33–49.

Chatman, Seymour (1980), *Story and Discourse: Narrative Structure in Fiction and Film*, New York: Cornell University Press.

Chauvin, Serge (2010), '"And They Lived Happily Ever After . . . Or Did They?": Matrimony as False Ending in (Post-) Classical Hollywood Fictions of Re/Marriage', in Armelle Parey, Isabelle Roblin and Dominque Sipière (eds), *Happy Endings and Films*, Paris: Michel Houdiard, 40–54.

Colwell, C. Carter (1981), 'Where is Happiness? A Study in Film Closure', *Journal of the University Film Association*, 33:1, 39–48.

Comolli, Jean-Louis and Jean Narboni (1971), 'Cinema/Ideology/Criticism', *Screen*, 12:1, 27–36.

Cook, Pam (1999), *The Cinema Book*, second edition, London: BFI .

Cortés, Carlos E. (1991), 'Hollywood Interracial Love: Social Taboo as Screen Titillation', in Paul Loukides and Linda K. Fuller (eds), *Beyond the Stars 2: Plot Conventions in American Popular Film*, Bowling Green: Bowling Green State University Press, 21–34.

Courtney, Susan (2005), *Hollywood Fantasies of Miscegenation: Spectacular Narratives of Gender and Race, 1903–1967*, Princeton: Princeton University Press.

Couvares, Francis G. (1996), *Movie Censorship and American Culture*, London: Smithsonian Institution Press.

Cowie, Elizabeth (1976), 'Fantasia', *M/f* 9, 71–105.

Creed, Barbara (1995), 'Horror and the Carnivalesque', in Leslie Devereaux and Roger Hillman (eds), *Fields of Vision: Essays in Film Studies, Visual Anthropology, and Photography*, Los Angeles: University of California Press, 127–59.

Cruise, Jennifer (1997), 'Romancing Reality: The Power of Romance Fiction to Reinforce and Re-Vision the Real', *Paradoxa: Studies in World Literary Genres*, 1:2, 81–93.

Dargis, Manohla (2006), '*Shortbus:* Naughty and Nice in a Carnal Carnival', *The Village Voice*, available at <http://movies.nytimes.com/2006/10/04/movies/04shor.html?_r=0> (last accessed 20 January 2011).

Deleyto, Celestino (1992), 'The Dupes Strike Back: Comedy, Melodrama and Point of View in *The Apartment*', *Atlantis* 14:1/2, 37–61.

Deleyto, Celestino (1998), 'They Lived Happily Ever After: Ending

Contemporary Romantic Comedy', *Misceleana: A Journal of English and American Studies* 19, 39–55.

Deleyto, Celestino (2003), 'Between Friends: Love and Friendship in Contemporary Hollywood Romantic Comedy', *Screen*, 44:2, 167–82.

Deleyto, Celestino (2009), *The Secret Life of Romantic Comedy*, Manchester: Manchester University Press.

Deleyto, Celestino (2010), 'Tales of the Millennium (Park): The Happy Ending and the Magic Cityscape of Contemporary Romantic Comedy', in Armelle Parey, Isabelle Roblin and Dominique Sipière (eds), *Happy Endings and Films*, Paris: Michel Houdiard, 103–12.

Deleyto, Celestino and Peter Williams Evans (1998), 'Introduction: Surviving Love', in Celestino Deleyto and Peter Williams Evans (eds), *Terms of Endearment: Hollywood Romantic Comedy of the 1980s and 1990s*, Edinburgh: Edinburgh University Press, 1–14.

Denisoff, Serge and William D. Romanowski (1991), *Risky Business: Rock in Film, Volume 1990*, New Brunswick, NJ: Transaction Publishers.

Doane, Mary Ann (1987), *The Desire to Desire: The Woman's Film of the 1940s*, London: Macmillan Press.

Dolar, Mladen (1991), 'Hitchcock's Objects', in Slavoj Žižek (ed.), *Everything You Always Wanted to Know About Lacan but Were Afraid to Ask Hitchcock*, New York: Verso, 31–46.

Dowd, James J. and Nicole R. Pallotta (2000), 'The Demystification of Love in the Postmodern Age', *Sociological Perspectives*, 43:4, 549–80.

Dubino, Jeanne (1993), 'The Cinderella Complex: Romance Fiction, Patriarchy, and Capitalism', Journal *of Popular Culture*, 27:3, 103–18.

DuCille, Ann (1993), *The Coupling Convention: Sex, Text, and Tradition in Black Women's Fiction*, New York: Oxford University Press.

Dunn, Francis M. (1996), *Tragedy's End: Closure and Innovation in Euripedean Drama*, Oxford: Oxford University Press.

Durgnat, Raymond (1969), *The Crazy Mirror: Hollywood Comedy and the American Image*, London: Faber and Faber.

Dyer, Richard (2007), *Pastiche*, London: Routledge.

Earley, Annie (2007), *What Was I Thinking? How Not to Date*, Eynon: Tribute Books.

Eliot, George [1871] (2003), *Middlemarch: A Study of Provincial Life*, London: Signet.

Eliot, George (2005), *George Eliot's Life as Related in Her Letters and Journals*, Vol. 2, John Walter Cross (ed.), London: Elibron Classics.

Elsaesser, Thomas (1987), 'Tales of Sound and Fury: Observations on the Family Melodrama', in Christine Gledhill (ed.), *Home is Where the Heart is: Studies in Melodrama and the Woman's Film*, London: BFI, 43–69.

Feuer, Jane (1993), *The Hollywood Musical*, Bloomington: Indiana University Press.

Forster, Edward Morgan (1962), *Aspects of the Novel*, Harmondsworth: Penguin Books.

Forster, Edward Morgan (1971), *Maurice*, Toronto: Macmillan.

Foucault, Michel (1979), *The Will to Knowledge: History of Sexuality*, trans. by Robert Hurley, London: Allen Lane.

Freud, Sigmund (1961); 'Humor', *The Future of an Illusion: Civilization and Its Discontents and Other Works*, London: The Hogarth Press, 159–66.

Frye, Northrop (1948), 'The Argument of Comedy', in D. A. Robertson, (ed.), *English Institute Essays, 1948*, New York: Columbia University Press, 58–74.

Frye, Northrop (1963), *Fables of Identity: Studies in Poetic Mythology*, New York: Harcourt.

Frye, Northrop (1969), 'Old and New Comedy', in Kenneth Muir (ed.), *Shakespeare Survey: Aspects of Shakespearian Comedy*, Cambridge: Cambridge University Press, 1–6.

Frye, Northrop (2002), *Northrop Frye on Literature and Society, 1936–1989: Unpublished Papers*, Robert B. Denham (ed.), London: University of Toronto Press.

Galcian, Mary-Lou (2004), *Sex, Love & Romance in the Mass Media: Analysis and Criticism of Unrealistic Portrayals and their Influence*, Mahwah: Lawrence Erlbaum Associates.

Gallop, Jane (1982), *The Daughter's Seduction: Feminism and Psychoanalysis*, Ithaca: Cornell University Press.

Garrett, Peter K. (1980), *The Multiplot Novel: Studies in Dialogic Form*, New Haven: Yale University Press.

Garrett, Roberta (2007), *Postmodern Chick Flicks: the Return of the Woman's Film*, New York: Palgrave Macmillan.

Garrett Cooper, Mark (2003), *Love Rules: Silent Hollywood and the Rise of the Managerial Class*, Minneapolis: University of Minnesota Press.

Geertz, Clifford (1973), *The Interpretation of Cultures*, New York: Basic Books.

Geraghty, Christine (2009), 'Foregrounding the Media: *Atonement* (2007) as an Adaptation, *Adaptation*, 2:2, 91–109.

Gerber, David A. (2000), *Disabled Veterans in History*, Ann Arbor: University of Michigan Press.

Gerhard, Jane (2001), *Desiring Revolution: Second-Wave Feminism and the Rewriting of American Sexual Thought, 1920 to 1982*, New York: Columbia University Press.

Gianos, Phillip L. (1998), *Politics and Politicians in American Film*, Westport: Praeger Publishers.

Gibson, Pamela Church (2006), 'New Stars, New Fashions and the Female

Audience', in Christopher Breward and David Gilbert (eds), *Fashion's World Cities*, Oxford: Berg.

Giddens, Anthony (1992), *The Transformation of Intimacy: Sexuality, Love & Eroticism in Modern Societies*, Stanford: Stanford University Press.

Gilbert, Sandra M. and Susan Gubar (1979), *The Madwoman in the Attic: The Woman Writer and the Nineteenth-Century Literary Imagination*, New Haven: Yale University Press.

Gledhill, Christine (ed.) (1987), *Home is Where the Heart Is*, London: BFI.

Glitre, Kathrina (2006), *Hollywood Romantic Comedy: States of the Union, 1934–65*, Manchester: Manchester University Press.

Gotta, Gabrielle, Robert-Jay Green, Esther Rothblum, Sondra Solomon, Kimberly Balsam and Pepper Schwartz (2011), 'Heterosexual, Lesbian and Gay Male Relationships: A Comparison of Couples in 1975 and 2000,' *Family Process*, 50:3, 353–376.

Grant, Barry Keith (2007), *Film Genre: From Iconography to Ideology*, London: Wallflower.

Greer, Germaine (1971), *The Female Eunuch*, London: Paladin.

Haberer, Adolphe (2005), 'A Defence of the Cliché', *Journal of English Studies* 5.6, 139–53.

Hall, Mordaunt (1931), 'The Skin Game', *The New York Times*, available at <http://movies.nytimes.com/movie/review?_r=2&res=9D01E0DD123B E433A25753C2A9609C946094D6CF> (last accessed 25 November 2010).

Hall, Stuart (1980), 'Encoding/Decoding', in Stuart Hall, Dorothy Hobson, Andrew Lowe, Paul Willis (eds), *Culture, Media, Language*, London: Hutchinson, 128–38.

Hallam, Julia and Margaret Marshment (2000), *Realism and Popular Cinema*, Manchester: Manchester University Press.

Halliday, John (1997), *Sirk on Sirk*, London: Faber and Faber.

Haralovich, Mary Beth (1990), '*All That Heaven Allows*: Color, Narrative Space, and Melodrama', in Peter Lehman (ed.), *Close Viewings*, Gainesville: Florida University Press, 57–72.

Harbidge, Lesley (2009), 'A New Direction in Comedian Comedy? *Eternal Sunshine of the Spotless Mind*, *Punch-Drunk Love* and the Post-Comedian Rom-Com', in Stacey Abbott, Deborah Jermyn (eds), *Falling in Love Again: Romantic Comedy in Contemporary Cinema*, London: I. B. Tauris, 176–189.

Harvey, James (2002), *Movie Love in the Fifties*, New York: Da Capo Press.

Haskell, Molly (1962), *From Reverence to Rape: The Treatment of Women in the Movies*, New York: Holt.

Hayward, Susan (2006), *Cinema Studies: The Key Concepts*, third edition, London: Routledge.

Heath, Stephen (1975), 'Film and System: Terms of Analysis, Part 1', *Screen*, 16:1, 7–77.

Henderson, Brian (1982), 'Harvard Film Studies: A Review', *Film Quarterly* 35:4, 22–34.

Henderson, Lisa (2007), 'Simple Pleasures: Lesbian Community and GoFish', in Suzanne Ferris and Mallory Young (eds), *Chick Flicks: Contemporary Women at the Movies*, New York: Routledge, 132–57.

Henke, Richard (1994), '*Imitation of Life*: Imitation in a World of Vaudeville', *Jump Cut* 39, 31–9.

Hess Wright, Judith (1995), 'Genre Films and the Status Quo', in Barry Keith Grant (ed.), Film *Genre Reader II*, Austin: University of Texas Press, 41–9.

Holmes, Bjarne M. and Kimberly R. Johnson (2009), 'Contradictory Messages: A Content Analysis of Hollywood-Produced Romantic Comedy Feature Films', *Communication Quarterly*, 57:3, 352–73.

Hume, David (1998), 'Of Tragedy', in Stephen Copley, Andrew Edgar (eds), *Selected Essays*, Oxford: Oxford University Press.

Hunter, Tim (1968), '*The Graduate*', *The Harvard Crimson*, available at http://www.thecrimson.com/article/1968/1/19/the-graduate-pmike-nichols-ithe-graduatei (last accessed 18 January 2009).

Ingraham, Chrys (2008), *White Weddings: Romancing Heterosexuality in Popular Culture*, New York: Routledge.

Jacobs, Lea (1991), *The Wages of Sin: Censorship and the Fallen Woman Film 1928–1942*, Madison: University of Wisconsin Press.

Jagendorf, Zvi (1984), *The Happy End of Comedy: Jonson, Molière and Shakespeare*, London: Associated University Press.

James, Henry (1956), *The Future of the Novel*, Leon Edel (ed.), New York: Vintage Press.

James, Henry (1957), *The House of Fiction*, Leon Edel (ed.), London: Hart-Davis.

Jameson, Fredric (1981), *The Political Unconscious*, London: Methuen & Co.

Jameson, Fredric (1991), *Postmodernism, or The Cultural Logic of Late Capitalism*, London: Duke University Press.

Jerslev, Anne (2002), *Realism and 'Reality' in Film and Media*, Copenhagen: Museum Tusculanum Press.

Jollimore, Troy (2009), 'Miserably Ever After: Forgetting, Repeating and Affirming Love in *Eternal Sunshine of the Spotless Mind*', in Christopher Grau (ed.), *Eternal Sunshine of Spotless Mind*, New York: Routledge, 31–61.

Jones, Dorothy B. (1942), 'Quantitative Analysis of Motion Picture Content', *Public Opinion Quarterly*, 6:3, 411–28.

Kaplan, Ann E. (1983), 'Theories of Melodrama: A Feminist Perspective', *Women and Performance*, 1:1, 40–8.

Kapsis, Robert E. (1990), *Hitchcock: the Making of a Reputation*, Chicago: University of Chicago Press.

Keating, Patrick (2006), 'Emotional Curves and Linear Narratives', *Velvet Light Trap*, 58:1, 4–15.

Kellner, Douglas M. and Michael Ryan (1990), *Camera Politica: The Politics and Ideology of Contemporary Hollywood Film*, London: Midland Books.

Kermode, Frank (1967), *The Sense of an Ending: Studies in the Theory of Fiction*, Oxford: Oxford University Press.

Kerr, Walter (2006), *Silent Clowns*, London: Alfred A. Knopf.

King, Geoff (2002a), *Film Comedy*, London: Wallflower.

King, Geoff (2002b), *New Hollywood Cinema: an Introduction*, London: I. B. Tauris.

King, Geoff (2009), *Indiewood, USA: Where Hollywood Meets Independent Cinema*, London: I. B. Tauris.

Kipnis, Laura (2003), *Against Love: A Polemic*, New York: Pantheon Books.

Kirkland, Ewan (2007), 'Romantic Comedy and the Construction of Heterosexuality'. *Scope*, Issue 9, available at <http://www.scope.nottingham.ac.uk/article.php?issue=9&id=957> (last accessed 13 December 2007).

Klevan, Andrew (2005), *Film Performance: From Achievement to Appreciation*, London: Wallflower.

Klinger, Barbara (1984a), *Melodrama and Meaning: History, Culture and the films of Douglas Sirk*, Bloomington: Indiana University Press.

Klinger, Barbara (1984b), '"Cinema/Ideology/Criticism" Revisited: The Progressive Text, *Screen*, 25:1, 30–44.

Knight, Deborah (1997), 'Aristotelians on *Speed*: Paradoxes of Genre in the Context of Cinema', in Richard Allen, Murray Smith (eds), *Film Theory and Philosophy*, Oxford: Oxford University Press, 343–63.

Kolker, Robert (2006), *Film, Form & Culture*, third edition, New York: McGraw-Hill.

Kotsopoulos, Aspasia (2001), '"Reading Against the Grain" Revisited', *Jump Cut* 44, available at <http://www.ejumpcut.org/archive/jc44.2001/asp asia/againstgrain1.html> (last accessed 16 January 2010).

Kracauer, Siegfried (1960), *Theory of Film*, Oxford: Oxford University Press.

Krämer, Peter (2005), *The New Hollywood: From Bonnie and Clyde to Star Wars*, London: Wallflower.

Krentz, Jayne Ann (ed.) (1992), *Dangerous Men & Adventurous Women: Romance Writers on the Appeal of the Romance*, Philadelphia: University of Pennsylvania Press.

Kristeva, Julia (1980), *Desire in Language: a Semiotic Approach to Literature and Art*, Oxford: Basil Blackwell.

Krutnik, Frank (1998), 'Love Lies: Romantic Fabrication in Contemporary Romantic Comedy', in Celestino Deleyto and Peter Williams Evans (eds),

Terms of Endearment: Hollywood Romantic Comedies of the 80s and 90s, Edinburgh: Edinburgh University Press, 15–36.

Kuhn, Annette (1994), *Women's Pictures: Feminism and Cinema*, second edition, London: Verso.

Lamb, Charles (1818), 'On the Tragedies of Shakespeare', *The Works of Charles Lamb*, Vol. II, London: C. & J. Ollier.

Lang, Fritz (1948), 'Happily Ever After', in Roger Manvell (ed.), *Penguin Film Review 5*, 22–9.

Lang, Robert (1989), *The American Film Melodrama*, Guildford: Princeton University Press.

Lapsley, Robert and Michael Westlake (1992), 'From *Casablanca* to *Pretty Woman*: the Politics of Romance', *Screen*, 33:1, 27–49.

Larkin, Philip (1988), *Collected Poems*, Anthony Thwaite (ed.), London: Marvell Press.

Leitch, Thomas (2002) 'Twice-Told Tales: Disavowal and the Rhetoric of the Remake'. *Dead Ringers: The Remake in Theory and Practice*, (eds) Jennifer Forrest and Leonard R. Koos, Albany: State University of New York Press.

Leonard, Suzanne (2007), '"I Hate My Job, I Hate Everybody Here": Adultery, Boredom, and the "Working Girl" in Twenty-First-Century American Cinema', in Yvonne Tasker and Diane Negra (eds), *Interrogating Postfeminism: Gender and the Politics of Popular Culture*, London: Duke University Press, 110–31.

Lévi-Strauss, Claude (1955), 'The Structural Study of Myth', *Journal of American Folklore*, 68.270, 428–44.

Levin, Harry (1966), *The Gate of Horn: A Study of Five French Realists*, Oxford: Oxford University Press.

Lippert, Leopold (2010), 'Negotiating Postmodernity and Queer Utopianism in *Shortbus*', in Petra Eckhard, Michael Fuchs and Walter Höbling (eds), *Landscapes of Postmodernity: Concepts and Paradigms of Critical Theory*, London: Transaction Publishers, 195–205.

Lodge, David (1982), *Working with Structuralism*, London: Routledge.

Lodge, David (1990), *After Bakhtin: Essays on Fiction and Criticism*, London: Routledge.

Ludot-Vlazak, Ronan (2010), 'Woody Allen's Impossible Tragedy: Tragic Expectations and Happy Ending in *Match Point*', in Armelle Parey, Isabelle Roblin and Dominique Sipière (eds), *Happy Endings and Films*, Paris: Michel Houdiard, 64–76.

Macarthur, Elizabeth J. (1990), *Extravagant Narratives: Closure and Dynamics in the Epistolary Form*, Princeton: Princeton University Press.

MacCabe, Colin (1974), 'Realism and the Cinema: Notes on Some Brechtian Theses', *Screen*, 15:2, 7–27.

MacDowell, James (2005), 'Happy Endings and True Love: Part 3', *Alternate Takes*, available at <http://www.alternatetakes.co.uk/?2005,10,32> (last accessed 17 April 2012).

MacDowell, James (2010), 'Does the Hollywood Happy Ending Exist?', in Armelle Parey, Isabelle Roblin and Dominique Sipière (eds), *Happy Endings and Films*, Paris: Michel Houdiard, 15–27.

MacDowell, James (2013), 'Romantic Comedy and the "Unsuitable" Partner: Macaulay Connor in *The Philadelphia Story*', *The Lesser Feat*, available at <http://thelesserfeat.blogspot.co.uk/2013/01/romantic-comedy-and-unsuitable-partner.html> (last accessed 1 January 2013).

McCabe, Janet (2009), 'Lost in Transition: Problems of Modern (Heterosexual) Romance and the Catatonic Male Hero in the Post-Feminist Age', in Stacey Abbott and Deborah Jermyn, *Falling in Love Again: Romantic Comedy in Contemporary Cinema*, London: I. B. Tauris, 160–75.

McDonald, Tamar Jeffers (2007), *Romantic Comedy: Boy Meets Girl Meets Genre*, London: Wallflower.

McNiven, Roger D. (1985), 'The Middle-Class American Home of the Fifties: the use of Architecture in Nicholas Ray's *Bigger Than Life* and Douglas Sirk's *All That Heaven Allows*', *Cinema Journal*, 22:4, 38–57.

Maltby, Richard (2003), *Hollywood Cinema*, second edition, Oxford: Blackwell Publishing.

Massie, Brenda (1980), 'Stylistic Melodrama: The Medium is the Message in Douglas Sirk's *All that Heaven Allows*', *Psychology Review*, 4:2, 267–82.

Mayer, John and Brian Rowan (1977), 'Institutionalized Organizations: Formal Structure as Myth and Ceremony', *American Journal of Sociology* 83:2, 340–63.

Mayne, Judith (1990), 'Fassbinder's *Ali: Fear Eats the Soul* and Spectatorship', in Peter Lehman (ed.), *Close Viewings: An Anthology of New Film Criticism*, Gainesville: Florida University Press, 353–69.

Mayne, Judith (2002), in Graeme Turner (ed.), 'Paradoxes of Spectatorship', *The Film Cultures Reader*, London: Routledge, 28–45.

Mellencamp, Patricia (1995), *A Fine Romance: Five Ages of Feminism*, Philadelphia: Temple University Press.

Mercer, John and Martin Shingler (2004), *Melodrama: Genre, Style, Sensibility*, London: Wallflower.

Mernit, Billy (2000), *Writing the Romantic Comedy*, New York: HarperCollins.

Metz, Christian (1968), *Film Language: A Semiotics of Cinema*, New York: Oxford University Press.

Meyer, Michael J. (2008), 'Reflections on Comic Reconciliations: Ethics, Memory, and Anxious Happy Endings', *Journal of Aesthetics and Art Criticism*, 66:1, 77–87.

Miller, D. A. (1981), *Narrative and its Discontents*, Princeton: Princeton University Press.

Moddelmog, Debra A. (2009), 'Can Romantic Comedy Be Gay? Hollywood, Citizenship, and Same-Sex Marriage Panic', *The Journal of Popular Film and Television*, 36: 4, 162–73.

Modleski, Tania (1979), 'Notes on a Feminine Narrative Form: The Search for Tomorrow in Today's Soap Operas', *Film Quarterly*, 33:1, 12–21.

Modleski, Tania (1982), *Loving With a Vengeance: Mass-produced Fantasies for Women*, Hamden: Archon Books.

Modleski, Tania (1988), *The Women Who Knew Too Much: Hitchcock and Feminist Theory*, London: Methuen.

Modleski, Tania (1989), 'Some Functions of Feminist Criticism, or The Scandal of the Mute Body', *October* 49, 3–24.

Morley, David (1980), 'Texts, Readers, Subjects', in Stuart Hall, Dorothy Hobson, Andrew Lowe and Paul Willis (eds), *Culture, Media, Language*, London: Hutchinson.

Mortimer, Armine Kotin (1985), *La Clôture Narrative*, Paris: José Corti.

Mortimer, Claire (2010), *Romantic Comedy*, London: Routledge.

Mulvey, Laura (1975), 'Visual Pleasure and Narrative Cinema', *Screen*, 16:3, 6–18.

Mulvey, Laura (1977), 'Notes on Sirk and Melodrama', *Movie* 25, 53–6.

Mulvey, Laura (1989), 'Afterthoughts on "Visual Pleasure and Narrative Cinema" Inspired by King Vidor's *Duel in the Sun* [1946]', *Visual and Other Pleasures*, London: Palgrave Macmillan, 31–40.

Murdoch, Iris (1977), 'Against Dryness', *The Novel Today*, Malcolm Bradbury (ed.), London: Fontana/Collins.

Myers, Jack Elliott and Don C. Wukasch (1985), *The Dictionary of Poetic Terms*, Denton: University of North Texas Press.

Nash, Cristopher (2001), *The Unravelling of the Postmodern Mind*, Edinburgh: Edinburgh University Press.

Neale, Steve (1986), 'Melodrama and Tears', *Screen*, 27:6, 6–23.

Neale, Steve (1992), 'The Big Romance or Something Wild? Romantic Comedy Today', *Screen* 33:3, 284–99.

Neale, Steve and Frank Krutnik (1990), *Popular Film and Television Comedy*, London: Routledge.

Neupert, Richard (1995), *The End: Narration and Closure in the Cinema*, Detroit: Wayne State University Press.

Nochimson, Martha P. (1992), *No End to Her: Soap Opera and the Female Subject*, Los Angeles: University of California Press.

Nochimson, Martha P. (2002), *Screen Couple Chemistry: The Power of 2*, Austin: University of Texas Press.

Nowell-Smith, Geoffrey (1977), 'Minnelli and Melodrama', *Screen*, 18:2, 113–118.

Orr, Christopher (1991), 'Closure and Containment: Marylee Hadley in *Written on the Wind*', in Marcia Landy (ed.), *Imitations of Life: a Reader on Film & Television Melodrama*, Detroit: Wayne State University Press, 380–7.

Oudart, Jean-Pierre (1971), 'L'idéologie moderniste dans quelques films récents: Un Discours en Défaut', *Cahiers du Cinéma* 232, 4–12.

Parey, Armelle, Isabelle Roblin and Dominique Sipière (eds) (2010), *Happy Endings and Films*, Paris: Michel Houdiard.

Pascoe, Peggy (2009), *What Comes Naturally: Miscegenation Law and the Making of Race in America*, Oxford: Oxford University Press.

Pearce, Lynne (2004), 'Popular Romance and its Readers', in Corrine Saunders (ed.), *A Companion to Romance: From Classical to Contemporary*, Oxford: Blackwell Publishing, 521–38.

Perez, Gilberto (1998), *The Material Ghost: Films and Their Medium*, London: Johns Hopkins University Press.

Perkins, Victor F. (1990), 'Must We Say What They Mean? Film Criticism and Interpretation', *Movie* 34, 1–6.

Perkins, Victor F. (1993), *Film as Film: Understanding and Judging Movies*, second edition, New York: Da Capo Press.

Perkins, Victor F. (1999), *The Magnificent Ambersons*, London: BFI.

Permyakov, G. L. (1979), *From Proverb to Folk-Tale: Notes on the General Theory of Cliché*, Moscow: Nauka.

Pillai, Nicolas (2012) 'The Happy Couple: American marriages in Hollywood Films 1934–1948', PhD thesis, University of Warwick.

Pinedo, Isabel Cristina (1997), *Recreational Terror: Women and the Pleasures of Horror Film Viewing*, Albany: State University of New York Press.

Plantinga, Carl (1994), 'Movie Pleasures and the Spectator's Experience: Toward a Cognitive Approach, *Film and Philosophy* 2, 3–19.

Plantinga, Carl (2009), *Moving Viewers: American Film and the Spectator's Experience*, Los Angeles: University of California Press.

Poe, Edgar Allan [1842] (1994), 'Review of Twice-Told Tales', in Charles E. May (ed.), *The New Short Story Theories*, Athens: Ohio State University Press, 59–72.

Polan, Dana (1985), 'The Felicity of Ideology: Speech-acts and the Happy Ending in American Films of the 1940s', *Iris*, 3:1, 35–45.

Polan, Dana (1991), 'The Light Side of Genius: Hitchcock's *Mr. & Mrs. Smith* in the Screwball Tradition', in Andrew S. Horton (ed.), *Comedy/Cinema/Theory*, Oxford: University of California Press, 131–52.

Pollock, Griselda (1977), 'Dossier on Melodrama: Report on the Weekend School', *Screen*, 18:2, 105–13.

Preis, Eran (1990), 'Not Such a Happy Ending: the Ideology of the Open Ending', *Journal of Film and Video*, 42:3, 18–23.

Preston, Catherine L. (2000), 'Hanging on a Star: the Resurrection of the Romance Film in the 1990s', in Wheeler W. Dixon (ed.), *Film Genre 2000: New Critical Essays*, 227–44.

Pye, Douglas (1975), 'Genre and Movies', *Movie* 20, 29–43.

Pye, Douglas (2000), 'Movies and Point of View', *Movie* 36, 2–34.

Pye, Douglas (2007), 'Movies and Tone', in John Gibbs, Douglas Pye, *Close-Up 02*, London: Wallflower, 1–80.

Quart, Alissa (2005), 'Networked', *Film Comment*, 41:4, 48–5.

Radway, Janice (1991), *Reading the Romance: Women, Patriarchy and Popular Literature*, London: University of North Carolina Press.

Ray, Robert B. (1985), *A Certain Tendency of the Hollywood Cinema, 1930–1980*, Princeton: Princeton University Press.

Redman, Jessica H. E. (2003), 'The American Happy Family That Never Was: Ambivalence in the Hollywood Family Melodrama', *European Journal of American Culture*, 22:1, 49–69.

Reising, Russell (1996), *Loose Ends: Closure and Crisis in the American Social Text*, London: Duke University Press.

Retter, Yolanda and Walter L. Williams (2003), *Gay and Lesbian Rights in the United States: A Documentary History*, Westport: Greenwood Publishing.

Rich, Adrienne (1980), 'Compulsory Heterosexuality and Lesbian Existence', *Signs* 5:4, 631–60.

Richardson, Brian (2002), *Narrative Dynamics: Essays on Time, Plot, Closure, and Frame*, Athens: Ohio State University Press.

Richardson, Niall (2006), 'Poison in the Sirkian System: The Political Agenda of Todd Haynes's *Far From Heaven*', *Scope* 6, available at <http://www.scope.nottingham.ac.uk/article.php?id=183&issue=6> (last accessed 8 November 2012).

Ricoeur, Paul (1984), *Time and Narrative* Vol. 2, trans. by Kathleen MacLaughlin and David Pellauer, Chicago: University of Chicago Press.

Ridley, Jim (2006), 'The Harder They Come', *The Village Voice*, available at <http://www.villagevoice.com/2006-09-26/film/the-harder-they-come/> (last accessed 20 January 2011).

Rios, Diana I. and Xae Alicia Reyes (2007), 'Jennifer Lopez and a Hollywood Latina Romance Film: Mythic Motifs in *Maid in Manhattan*', in Mary-Lou Galcian and Debra L. Merskin (eds.), *Critical Thinking About Sex, Love & Romance in the Mass Media*, Mahwah: Lawrence Erlbaum Associates, 107–20.

Rodowick, D. N. (1987), 'Madness, Authority and Ideology in the Domestic Melodrama of the 1950s, in Christine Gledhill (ed.), *Home is Where the Heart is: Studies in Melodrama and the Woman's Film*, London: BFI, 237–47.

Rodowick, D. N. (1994), *The Crisis of Political Modernism: Criticism and Ideology in Contemporary Film Theory*, Los Angeles: University of California Press.

Rohdie, Sam (1971), 'Editorial', *Screen* 12:2, 4–6.

Roiphe, Katie (2001), 'Why We All Want a Happy Ending', *The Guardian*, available at <http://www.guardian.co.uk/world/2001/mar/27/gender.uk> (last accessed 24 January 2010).

Roof, Judith (1996), *Come as You Are: Sexuality and Narrative*, New York: Columbia University Press.

Rowe, Allen and Paul Wells (2003), 'Film Form & Narrative', in Jill Nelmes (ed.), *An Introduction to Film Studies*, third edition, London: Routledge, 54–90.

Rowe, Kathleen (1995a), 'Comedy, Melodrama and Gender: Theorizing the Genres of Laughter', in Kristine Brunovska Karnick and Henry Jenkins (eds), *Classical Hollywood Comedy*, New York: Routledge, 39–59.

Rowe, Kathleen (1995b), *The Unruly Woman: Gender and the Genres of Laughter*, Austin: University of Texas Press.

Ruiz Pardos, Manuela (2010), '"Not Quite the End": The Boundaries of Narrative Closure in Hollywood Romantic Comedy', in Armelle Parey, Isabelle Roblin and Dominique Sipière (eds), *Happy Endings and Films*, Paris: Michel Houdiard, 113–23.

Rushton, Richard (2011), *The Reality of Film: Theories of Filmic Reality*, Manchester: Manchester University Press.

Russell, Catherine (1995), *Narrative Mortality: Death, Closure, and New Wave Cinemas*, Minneapolis: University of Minnesota Press.

Ryan, Christopher and Cacilda Jetha (2010), *Sex at Dawn: The Prehistoric Origins of Modern Sexuality*, New York: Harper Publishing.

Sargent, Epes Winthrop (1911), 'Technique of the Photoplay: Chapter VII,' *Motion Picture World*, 9:8 (Sept. 2), 613.

Schatz, Thomas (1981), *Hollywood Genres: Formulas, Filmmaking, and the Studio System*, New York: Random House.

Schatz, Thomas (1988), *The Genius of the System*, New York: Pantheon Books.

Schatz, Thomas (1991), 'The Family Melodrama', in Marcia Landy (ed.), *Imitations of Life: A Reader on Film and Television Melodrama*, Detroit: Wayne State University Press, 148–67.

Schneider, Steven Jay (2003), 'Suck . . . don't suck': Framing Ideology in Kathryn Bigelow's *Near Dark*', in Deborah Jermyn, Sean Redmond (eds), *The Cinema of Kathryn Bigelow: Hollywood Transgressor*, London: Wallflower, 72–91.

Seiter, Ellen (1991), 'Men, Sex, and Money in Recent Family Melodramas', in Marcia Landy (ed.), *Imitations of Life: A Reader on Film and Television Melodrama*, Detroit: Wayne State University Press, 525–38.

Shakespeare, William (2005), *The Oxford Shakespeare, the Complete Works*, second edition, Stanley W. Wells, Gary Taylor (eds), Oxford: Clarendon Press.

Sharrett, Christopher (2007), '*Home from the Hill*, Minnelli and the Crisis of Post-War Patriarchy,' *Film International*, 5:5, 54–62.

Sharrett, Christopher (2010), 'Douglas Sirk's *There's Always Tomorrow*', *Cineaste*, available at <http://www.cineaste.com/articles/douglas-sirks-emtheres-always-tomorrowem-web-eclusive> (last accessed 24 December 2010).

Shumway, David R. (1991), 'Screwball Comedies: Constructing Romance, Mystifying Marriage', *Cinema Journal*, 30:4, 7–23.

Shumway, David R. (2003), *Modern Love: Romance, Intimacy and the Marriage Crisis*, London: New York University Press.

Silbergleid, Robin (1997), 'Women, Utopia, and Narrative: Toward a Postmodern Feminist Citizenship', *Hypatia*, 12:4, 156–77.

Singer, Irving (1987), *The Nature of Love, Volume 3: The Modern World*, Chicago: University of Chicago Press.

Sipière, Dominique (2010), 'Defining Happy Endings in Classical Films', in Armelle Parey, Isabelle Roblin and Dominique Sipière (eds), *Happy Endings and Films*, Paris: Michel Houdiard, 28–39.

Slocum, J. David (2005), 'Cinema and the Civilizing Process: Rethinking Violence in the World War II Combat Film', *Cinema Journal*, 44:3, 35–63.

Smith, Barbara Herrnstein (1968), *Poetic Closure*, Chicago: University of Chicago Press.

Smith, Murray (1995), *Engaging Characters*, Oxford: Clarendon Press.

Smith, Robert E. (1977), 'Love Affairs That Always Fade', *Bright Lights*, available at http://www.brightlightsfilm.com/48/sirkloveaffairs.htm> (last accessed 12 December, 2009).

Sontag, Susan (1969), 'Notes on Camp', *Against Interpretation*, second edition, New York: Dell Publishing, 277–93.

Spencer, Amy (2011), 'Regain Your Dating Optimism', *Afro Toronto*, available at <http://www.afrotoronto.com/site/index.php/lifestyle-health> (last accessed 1 December 2011).

Springer, Claudia (1984), 'Black Female Filmmakers', *Jump Cut*, available at <http://www.ejumpcut.org/archive/onlinessays/JC29folder/BlackWomenFilmkrs.html> (last accessed 17 March, 2008).

Stacey, Jackie (1995), '"If You Don't Play You Can't Win": *Desert Hearts* and the Lesbian Romance Film', in Tamsin Wilton (ed.), *Immortal, Invisible: Lesbians and the Moving Image*, London: Routledge, 92–114.

Staiger, Janet (1992), *Interpreting Films: Studies in the Historical Reception of American Cinema*, Princeton: Princeton University Press.

Stern, Michael (1977), 'Two Weeks in Another Town: An Interview with Douglas Sirk'. *Bright Lights Film Journal*, available at <http://www.bright-lightsfilm.com/48/sirkinterview.php> (last accessed 10 August 2009).

Stern, Michael (1979), *Douglas Sirk*, Boston: Twayne Publishers.

Sterrit, David (1993), *The Films of Alfred Hitchcock*, New York: Cambridge University Press.

Straumann, Barbara (2008), *Figurations of Exile in Hitchcock and Nabokov*, Edinburgh: Edinburgh University Press.

Strinati, Dominic (2000), *An Introduction to Studying Popular Culture*, London: Routledge.

Sutton, Paul (2009), 'Après le Coup de Foudre: Narrative, Love and Spectatorship in *Groundhog Day*', in Stacey Abbott and Deborah Jermyn (eds), *Falling in Love Again: Romantic Comedy in Contemporary Cinema*, London: I. B. Tauris, 38–51.

Swidler, Anne (2003), *Talk of Love: How Culture Matters*, London: University of Chicago Press.

Tallis, Raymond (1988), *In Defence of Realism*, Nebraska: University of Nebraska Press.

Tally, Margaret (2007), 'Something's Gotta Give: Hollywood, Female Sexuality and the "Older Bird" Chick Flick', in Suzanne Ferriss and Mallory Young (eds), *Chick Flicks: Contemporary Women at the Movies*, London: Routledge, 119–131.

Tasker, Yvonne (1991), 'Having it all: Feminism and the Pleasures of the Popular', in Sarah Franklin, Celia Lury and Jackie Stacey (eds), *Off-Centre: Feminism and Cultural Studies*, London: HarperCollins, 85–96.

Taylor, Helen (1989), *Scarlett's Women: Gone With the Wind and its Female Fans*, New York: Rutgers University Press.

Taylor, Kate (2006), 'More sentimental than erotic', *The Globe and Mail*, available at <http://www.theglobeandmail.com/arts/more-sentimental-than-erotic-shortbus-cant-take-us-all-the-way/article732245/> (last accessed 23 October 2011).

Thickstun, William R. (1988), *Visionary Closure in the Modern Novel*, Basingstoke: Macmillan.

Thomas, Deborah (2000), *Beyond Genre: Melodrama, Comedy and Romance in Hollywood Films*, Dumfriesshire: Cameron and Hollis.

Thompson, Kristin (1988), *Breaking the Glass Armor: Neoformalist Film Analysis*, New Jersey: Princeton University Press.

Toles, George (2001), *A House Made of Light: Essays on the Art of Film*, Detroit: Wayne State University Press.

Tookey, Chris (2006), 'Don't Fancy Yours Much', *The Daily Mail*, available at http://www.dailymail.co.uk/tvshowbiz/reviews/article-419758/Dont-fancy-much.html> (last accessed 6 February 2011).

Torgovnick, Mariana (1980), *Closure in the Novel*, Princeton: Princeton University Press.

Trollope, Anthony (1879), 'The Genius of Nathaniel Hawthorne', *The North American Review* 129:274, 203–22.

Tudor, Andrew (1972), 'The Many Mythologies of Realism', *Screen*, 13:1, 27–36.

Tuhkunen, Taina (2010), 'The Pursuit of Happiness in Contemporary American RomComs', in Armelle Parey, Isabelle Roblin and Dominique Sipière (eds), *Happy Endings and Films*, Paris: Michel Houdiard, 124–35.

Twain, Mark (1980), *The Works of Mark Twain*, Vol. 4, Berkley: University of California Press.

Twomey, Rebecca (2008), 'Are You Really Ready For Marriage?' *Cosmopolitan*, available at <http://www.cosmopolitan.co.uk/love-&-sex/love-and-relationship-advice-are-you-really-ready-for-marriage/v1> (last accessed 9 June 2010).

Tyler, Parker (1970), *The Hollywood Hallucination*, New York: Simon and Schuster.

Umphlett, Wiley Lee (2006), *From Television to the Internet: Postmodern Visions of American Media Culture in the Twentieth Century*, Cranbury: Rosemont Publishing.

Vaughn, Stephen (1990), 'Morality and Entertainment: The Origins of the Motion Picture Production Code, *Journal of American History*, 77:1, 39–65.

Veronesi, Micaela (2005), *La Soglie del Film: Inizio e Fine nel Cinema*, Torino: Kaplan.

Vidal, Gore (2002), 'Remembering Orson Welles', in Mark W. Estrin (ed.) *Orson Welles: Interviews*, Jackson: University Press of Mississippi, 210–22.

Walker, Michael (2008), 'The Rhetoric of an Ending: the Example of Steven Spielberg', conference paper delivered at *Beginnings and Endings in Films, Film and Film Studies*, University of Warwick, 13 June 2008.

Walsh, Andrea S. (1984), *Women's Film and Female Experience, 1940–1950*, New York: Praeger.

Walters, James (2008), *Alternative Worlds in Hollywood Cinema: Resonance Between Realms*, Bristol: Intellect.

Warhol, Robyn R. (2003), *Having a Good Cry: Effeminate Feelings and Pop-Culture Forms*, Athens: Ohio State University Press.

Wartenberg, Thomas E. (1999), *Unlikely Couples: Movie Romance as Social Criticism*, Oxford: Westview.

Wells-Lassagne, Shannon (2010), 'Heritage and Happy Endings: Adapting to Audience Expectations', in Armelle Parey, Isabelle Roblin and Dominque Sipière (eds), *Happy Endings and Films*, Paris: Michel Houdiard, 89–100.

Wexman, Virgina Wright (1993), *Creating the Couple: Love, Marriage and Hollywood Performance*, Princeton: Princeton University Press.

White, Hayden (1981), 'The Value of Narrativity', in W. J. T. Mitchell (ed.), *On Narrative*, London: University of Chicago Press, 1–23.

White, Patricia (1999), *Uninvited: Classical Hollywood Cinema and Lesbian Representability*, Bloomington: Indiana University Press.

White, R. S. (1981), *Shakespeare and the Romance Ending*, Newcastle: Tyneside Free Press.

Wilde, Oscar [1895] (1990), *The Importance of Being Ernest*, Alexandria: Orchises Press.

Willemen, Paul (1971), 'Distanciation and Douglas Sirk', *Screen* 12.2: 63–7.

Williams, Christopher (1994), 'After the Classic, the Classical and Ideology: The Differences of Realism', *Screen*, 35:3, 275–92.

Williams, Linda (1984), '"Something Else Besides a Mother": *Stella Dallas* and the Maternal Melodrama', *Cinema Journal*, 24:1, 2–27.

Williams, Linda (1998), 'Melodrama Revised', in Nick Browne (ed.), *Refiguring American Film Genres: Theory and History*, Berkeley: University of California Press, 42–88.

Williams, Linda (2008), *Screening Sex*, London: Duke University Press.

Williams, Raymond (1977), 'A Lecture on Realism', *Screen*, 18:1, 61–74.

Wilson, George M. (1986), *Narration in Light: Studies in Cinematic Point of View*, London: Johns Hopkins University Press.

Wollen, Peter (1985), 'Godard and Counter-Cinema: *Vent D'Est*', in Bill Nichols (ed.), *Movies and Methods Volume II*, London: University of California Press.

Wollen, Peter (1998), *Signs and Meaning in the Cinema, Expanded Edition*, London: BFI.

Wolosky, Shira (2001), *The Art of Poetry: How to Read a Poem*, Oxford: Oxford University Press.

Wood, Robin (1986), *Hollywood From Vietnam to Reagan*, New York: Columbia University Press.

Wood, Robin (1988/89), 'Symmetry, Closure, Disruption: The Ambiguity of *Blackmail*', *Cineaction* 15, 13–25.

Wood, Robin (1989), *Hitchcock's Films Revisited*, New York: Columbia University Press.

Wood, Robin (1998), *Sexual Politics and Narrative Film, Hollywood and Beyond*, New York: Columbia University Press.

Wood, Robin (2003), 'Ideology, Genre, Auteur', in Barry Keith Grant (ed.), *Film Genre Reader III*, Austin: University of Texas Press, 60–74.

Woods, Frank (1910), 'Spectator's Comments', *New York Dramatic Mirror*, 63 (29 January), 16.

Yeatman, Bevin (2008), 'Who Laughs? A Moment of Laughter in *Shortbus*', *P.O.V: A Danish Journal of Film Studies* 26, available at <http://pov.imv.au.dk/Issue_26/section_1/artc7A.html> (last accessed 15 December 2012).

Zijderveld, C. (1979), *On Clichés: The Supersedure of Meaning by Function in Modernity*, London: Routledge.

Zipes, Jack (2006), *Fairy Tales and the Art of Subversion: The Classical Genre for Children and the Process of Civilization*, London: Routledge.

Žižek, Slavoj (1991), 'Alfred Hitchcock, or the Form and its Historical Mediation', in Slavoj Žižek (ed.), *Everything You Always Wanted to Know About Lacan but Were Afraid to Ask Hitchcock*, New York: Verso, 1–14.

Žižek, Slavoj (2001), *Enjoy Your Symptom! Jacques Lacan in Hollywood and out*, second edition, London: Routledge.

Index